I0879696

Sheva's Promise

Religion, Theology, and the Holocaust

Other titles in Religion, Theology, and the Holocaust

Disenchantment: George Steiner and the Meaning of Western Civilization after Auschwitz
Catherine D. Chatterley

Fiorello's Sister: Gemma La Guardia Gluck's Story
Gemma La Guardia; Rochelle G. Saidel, ed.

Four Letters to the Witnesses of My Childhood
Helena Ganor

Harry Haft: Survivor of Auschwitz, Challenger of Rocky Marciano
Alan Scott Haft

The Life and Thought of Louis Lowy: Social Work Through the Holocaust
Lorrie Greenhouse Gardella

Life in the Ghettos: During the Holocaust
Eric J. Sterling, ed.

Murder Without Hatred: Estonians and the Holocaust
Anton Weiss-Wendt

Nitzotz: The Spark of Resistance in Kovno Ghetto and Dachau-Kaufering Concentration Camp
Laura M. Weinrib, ed., Estee Weinrib, tran.

A Portrait of Pacifists: Le Chambon, the Holocaust, and the Lives of André and Magda Trocmé
Richard P. Unsworth

When the Danube Ran Red
Zsuzsanna Ozsváth

Sheva's Promise

Chronicle of Escape from a Nazi Ghetto

SYLVIA LEDERMAN

SYRACUSE UNIVERSITY PRESS

Copyright © 2013 by Syracuse University Press
Syracuse, New York 13244-5290

All Rights Reserved

First Edition 2013
13 14 15 16 17 18 6 5 4 3 2 1

∞ The paper used in this publication meets the minimum requirements of the American National Standard for Information Sciences—Permanence of Paper for Printed Library Materials, ANSI Z39.48-1992.

For a listing of books published and distributed by Syracuse University Press, visit our website at SyracuseUniversityPress.syr.edu.

ISBN: 978-0-8156-1018-2

Library of Congress Cataloging-in-Publication Data

Lederman, Sylvia, author.
Sheva's promise : chronicle of escape from a Nazi ghetto / Sylvia Lederman. — First Edition 2013.
pages cm. — (Religion, theology, and the Holocaust)
ISBN 978-0-8156-1018-2 (cloth : alk. paper) 1. Lederman, Sylvia. 2. Jews—Poland—Biography. 3. Holocaust, Jewish (1939–1945)—Poland—Personal narratives. 4. Poland—Biography. I. Title.
DS134.72.L44A3 2013
940.53'18092—dc23
[B] 2013003948

Manufactured in the United States of America

Dedicated in memory of my beloved mother Gitel Weiler and my beloved sister Rose Weiler. They were burned alive in Rohatyn Ghetto, Poland, with many more Jews when the Ghetto was liquidated June 6, 1943. I'll never forget them. They will remain in my heart and I will love them forever, until I die.

Sheva

Sylvia Lederman immigrated to New York, where she and her husband worked in the garment industry, and spent the rest of their lives in Queens, New York. She was known for being a caring and compassionate person who kept ties to her roots in her native Poland by becoming a member of two expatriate societies, the Rohatyn Society and the Lodzier Society, both fellowships of people from Poland. Her life's work was to publish this memoir so the story told within would never be forgotten.

Contents

Illustrations

Sheva's Promise

1

The Gathering Storm

IT WAS A WARM, SUMMER DAY—July 6, 1941. The town of Rohatyn was suffused with bright sunlight. At this time of year nature could fill human hearts with happiness; people could be out in the fresh air, taking advantage of those lovely days and feeling full of courage and hope for a good tomorrow. The streets were alive with people. Some appeared to be in a holiday mood, expecting something, anticipating a coming change. But there were others for whom the same sun and the same bright day held no joy, and for whom the beauty of this town—all this natural beauty—meant little or nothing. They felt like strangers on these streets, as though they no longer belonged there.

This was the feeling of the Jews in Rohatyn. We were all withdrawn, lost in our own thoughts, concerned for our futures. Several days earlier, the Russians had abandoned the town to the advancing Germans. The Russians had occupied Rohatyn, together with all that part of southeastern Poland, since September 1939. For almost two years we had lived under Russian rule, not knowing exactly what was permitted and what was forbidden. Everything was nationalized; the wealthy citizens—at least, those the Russians considered wealthy—were deported at once to Siberia. Those of us who remained, and who were employed by the Russians, had no right to change our jobs, and we constantly lived in fear; any little thing we did could condemn us to five years in a Russian prison or to deportation to the dreaded Siberian wastelands. Every able-bodied person was expected to work, and any unemployed man was branded a "capitalist." There was a general shortage of food and a lack of clothing.

Everything was rationed. The Russians grabbed whatever they could lay their hands on and took it out of the country. We lived as though standing on one leg—everything uncertain, out of balance.

During the Russian occupation I was employed in a bookstore called the Knigokultur. It was one of several government-operated stores under Soviet control, and the only bookstore in Rohatyn. While I worked there I was always in fear of a five-year prison sentence for even the slightest infraction of the rules.

Only a week previously I had returned from a vacation in Yaremcze, a mountain resort, glad in spite of everything to be home again in my native town. I had had to cut my vacation short after just one week because of the outbreak of the war. When I returned to the bookstore I found the woman manager already packing, getting ready to flee back to Russia. Knowing the Germans' hatred for Jews, the manager begged me to leave with her; she realized that we could expect nothing good from them. I thanked her, but said that I had done nothing to the Germans to make them punish me. I told her that my family and I had been born in Rohatyn, that we had lived here all our lives, and that I did not see why I should run.

In town chaos reigned. Some men and young fellows were mobilized for the war, and a few willingly made preparations to leave with the Russians. When they began to leave, my manager went with them, but promised hopefully that she would be back again in a short time. I was left with the keys to the store, not knowing whether to keep the store open or to lock it up and stay home. Rohatyn was now without any civil or military authorities. It seems best to stay home and wait.

The next few days seemed like eternity. Everyone was eager to get these first moments of the new occupation over with, to face the reality that, come what may, we would be under Hitler's domination from now on. Even we were aware of the Germans' hate campaign against Jews in other parts of occupied Poland since the 1939 invasion. So, although we waited patiently, we greatly feared their coming.

Then—on July 6, 1941—the silence was shattered by a violent bombardment somewhere outside the town. As if moved by one impulse, all the tenants of our building rushed to the cellar and stood in a corner, clinging to each other in terror. One bomb fell on a house very close to ours and there was a wild commotion. I fainted from the shock. Later, after they revived me, I sat up and rested my head on my mother's shoulder. The shelling had stopped and all was quiet. We went upstairs and reassembled in one room and sat there in silence, staring at one another. Our hearts were pounding. The faces around me were pallid with fear, and from time to time I heard muffled sighs and groans and whispered prayers.

One of our neighbors lifted up his voice. "Listen," he said, "our God is a great God. We must believe in Him firmly." *Shema Yisra'el,* the ancient prayer echoed: "Hear, O Israel! The Lord our God is one Lord. Blessed is He . . . We are now in his hands, and He will protect us against our enemies."

The night that followed was long. When the pale light of dawn at last filtered through the curtains, we began to look out of the windows, trying to catch new signs of the coming of the Germans. Now again we heard shots—at closer range, this time—and it was not long before someone shouted from the street, "The Germans are here!"

After a while we saw from the window two Jewish boys going from house to house. Finally they approached and told us to close our windows and doors and to stay inside. They needn't have bothered; none of us wanted to go out looking for trouble—or to greet the Germans. Yet there were other people who were waiting with flowers . . .

Trembling, we heard the clatter of their horses' hoofs and the thunder of their motorized equipment as it rolled through the cobbled streets of our town. The evening was approaching, and not knowing what the next hour might bring, we started to put on as much clothing as we could. In case of evacuation or deportation, we had to be prepared and a little protected. We all looked like clowns in our layers of apparel—clowns with sad faces.

Now everyone has the same thought: Would we be allowed to remain in our apartments? Would they let us keep our jobs? Would they let us have a chance to lead normal lives? As yet no one imagined that we would be tortured and murdered; that such crimes could be perpetrated en masse by a people who called themselves civilized and cultured was simply unthinkable. Our neighbors told us that my mother and sister and I had nothing to fear, because the Germans would not do anything to women and girls. The men, yes—they would be pressed into hard labor—but women would be left alone. And children—what could they ask from children? Our neighbors told us we were lucky that there were no men in our immediate family.

What irony! For many years past we had felt keenly the lack of our father, and we felt sorry for Mamma, who had only her memories to live with. She never wanted to remarry, and she still grieved over the loss of her beloved and ideal husband, Laizor. Now a time had come when we were lucky for having no father, or no brother, for the Germans to take away.

By the next day, Thursday, July 7, the Germans were in complete control of Rohatyn. They did not have to waste time in enforcing new regulations against the Jews; in the carrying out of their master plan they already had the help of many Gentile people, who had arranged everything in advance. All the Jews were released from their places of employment, while most Gentiles remained at their jobs in the nationalized stores. Thus, even the Gentiles whom we had known for so many years assisted in the destruction of the Rohatyn Jewry. Three days later, on Saturday morning, we awoke to shouts and lamentations. Jewish women and children were running along the streets in panic, trying to warn the men and to find them places to hide. Some prayed aloud, raising their hands and eyes to heaven. We soon learned that the elders of the Jewish community assembly, from the Rabbis to the leader of the Jews, had been rounded up and taken to the synagogue. There they had been locked up, beaten, and tortured. The Germans began to move from house to house, hunting down whatever Jews they could find, searching attics and dragging their victims away. Whoever tried to oppose them was beaten to the raw and pulled by the arms through the streets over the rough cobblestones. The gutters ran with blood. Rabbi Leizer was dragged out from his house and thrown into the public latrines, alive, where he sank in the sewage.

When they had collected all the male Jews inside the synagogue, the Germans took away their money, watches, and whatever else they had of value on their persons. This operation lasted almost the entire day, and in the sadistic beatings and tortures that attended it even young boys of the local Ukrainian community took part. Meanwhile the distraught women came to the synagogue, bringing food and parcels for their men inside, but were turned away. They tried to petition the Germans to release the prisoners, but were told that the synagogue would be burned down—with all the Jews in it.

Later that day, with a great deal of ransom money, much haranguing, and the help of God, the synagogue and the Jews were spared. Although some of the men were shot on their way home, most of them returned to their families. Beaten, broken, bitterly humiliated, and resigned . . . What a beginning! We now had a clear vision of our future under the Germans.

While this was going on in the town, my mother and sister Rose and I stayed at home, like frightened mice. Suddenly, the door of our apartment was flung open and a Gentile militiaman entered. Brusquely, he asked my mother, "Where is your husband? Where is your son?" As he looked around the room, his eyes rested on me and I saw in them a flash of recognition: he had come by the bookstore when he was still in the Soviet militia to buy office supplies. I returned his stare with cold defiance, and after a moment of uncertainty he turned and left our apartment. I thought, *They are like straws in the wind—only yesterday with Russia, today with the Nazis!* Our only consolation was that we indeed had no men at home.

But we did have male relatives in town, including my favorite uncle, Hirsch Wiener. Although mother and Rose did not want to let me go, when things quieted down, I ran to the Wieners' house. They lived not far from the synagogue, and I expected that Uncle Hirsch would have been among the first to be involved in the manhunt. I loved my uncle; he was like a father to me.

Alas, when I found him at his home, Uncle Hirsch was a mass of wounds. They had pulled out hair from his head and his beard. He had been a very tall, strong man, but now I could hardly recognize him as he sat in a chair, his head bent forward, moaning. He gathered me to his breast and wept bitter tears, and I also sobbed as though my heart would break, and I looked at his misery and touched his head sticky with congealed blood.

"See, little Shevele," he said, "you are very young, you are smart and full of courage. Maybe you will live through these times. But I cannot endure any more . . . I was so proud and happy. I saw my daughter married well. I have two grandsons. Alas, what does the future hold for them, for my son Chaimek—for all of us?"

Uncle Hirsch's baby grandson Yehuda, scarcely a year old, stopped crawling on all fours and looked up at us with his great, blue eyes, as if understanding that something was terribly wrong. Uncle Hirsch sighed at the sight of this innocent child. "This child is fortunate now," Uncle Hirsch said, "for he doesn't know what awaits him. But *we* know there is nothing good in the future—nothing."

Chaimek stood beside his father, tears in his eyes. During the raid his mother had hidden him in a wardrobe. Now, sad and frightened, he said to me: "Sheva, you often pass for a Christian because you do not look Jewish. You have so many Christian friends. Tell me, what do they—the people you know—think will happen to us?"

Gently I stroked the boy's face. I told him that I wanted to take him home with me because I thought that he would be safer there. But he refused to leave: "What will become of my father and mother, my sister Glickel—the whole family? No, I'll stay here. I don't want to live without them." I kissed the boy, and with tears in my eyes, I said goodbye. Even on the street, walking slowly homeward, I could not control my weeping.

On Monday morning, July 11, two Ukrainian men of the town came by our house. They told us they had been chosen by the Germans to manage the Knigokultur bookshop and that they had come for the keys. I was asked to go to the store with them, take an inventory, and give them all the prices of the books and stationery supplies. Naturally I went, though with a sad heart, for I realized that I would not have the right to work there anymore after I completed these final tasks. I worked at the store for the next several days, but each time we saw a German about to enter they asked me to hide in the storeroom back of the shelves.

Soon we had the inventory completed and I was told not to come anymore. I felt unnecessary and unwanted; it was hard for me to accept the fact that I was unemployed. There was nothing I could do but stay home and listen to rumors. Our food supplies were beginning to disappear, and we had no right to purchase anything in the shops. We did not even have the courage to enter a store to buy what we needed. Before long we saw signs in almost all the store windows: IT IS FORBIDDEN FOR DOGS AND JEWS

TO ENTER! Because I was well-known and liked in Rohatyn, I occasionally managed to get inside some friendly shop to purchase some food—a loaf of bread, a little sugar, just enough to fill our daily needs. My mother sometimes ventured to go to the marketplace to try to buy eggs or a hen, or potatoes. She also did not look Jewish, but quite often she returned pale and terrified, having almost fallen into a German trap.

These harsh conditions grew even more severe, however, when all Jews were ordered to live within a circumscribed locality—a single quarter, a ghetto. As long as the Jews remained scattered throughout the town, the Nazis could not exercise sufficient control over us. They attempted to further isolate us from the rest of the population by proclaiming that it was degrading to Gentiles to dwell in the same building with a Jewish family, or even to walk on the same street with Jews. In this oppression, the Nazis received most help from the Ukrainians.

For a time, we did not know where the ghetto would be established—the problem was to find a place that would be able to accommodate such a large number of Jewish families. It was understood that the central marketplace and all the chief streets of the town would have to be free of Jews. It was also quite obvious that we would not be allotted the same living space we had had before. My family would have been fortunate, indeed, to get one room for the three of us. As it turned out, we had to leave many surplus belongings behind—some of them costly and beautiful—when we moved to our tiny quarters in the ghetto.

Everything was done in a hurry. The room we were allotted was in a two-family house not far from a church that stood on the borderline of the newly organized ghetto, and so, though our quarters were hardly comfortable, we found ourselves at the very center of rumors and activity. After these orders were issued, the Germans formed a Jewish police and a Jewish council (the Judenrat), at the head of which stood the former leader of the Jewish community. A young fellow was elected chief of the Jewish police. He was energetic, bold, and somewhat callous—qualities that were indispensable in his position, for no one who was sensitive or had any qualms whatsoever could have carried out the orders that were given him. The Jewish communal police and the council were quartered in a large building, from which they were to govern the ghetto. The Judenrat had to see to it that the ghetto was kept clean, that the people should not walk on streets forbidden to them, that people were delivered to work—in a word, they had to do everything to please the authorities. Otherwise, we would be punished, even for the smallest and most insignificant transgression of German orders. And the Ukrainians were worse than the Germans.

Now we were confronted with the problem of getting work to supply us with the necessities of life. The Jewish militia began to recruit men and women for compulsory labor. The women were assigned to clean offices, schools, and other public buildings. Each job had its supervisor—often Ukrainian—and each supervisor had the right to beat, kick, or abuse anyone he disliked. We received our food supplies from the Judenrat. We no longer had any dreams of getting sugar or butter—these were unattainable luxuries; we were happy with a loaf of bread. Everyone tried on his own to obtain some small extras by begging or buying them from friendly Poles or Ukrainians. Besides our usual population of around ten thousand Rohatyn Jews, the ghetto was soon further swelled by a large number of so-called refugees who had come in from various other towns. These newcomers found living conditions here even worse than we did, for they had few friends among the townspeople and they were already exhausted and impoverished because of their wanderings since the beginning of the war. Consequently, they became the first victims of the hunt for compulsory laborers, as they had no people to shield them; they were strangers in our midst. In other times the sight of their emaciated faces and their despair would have filled us with pity, but we could now think only of our own survival.

Officially, no Jew could leave the ghetto, except those who were sent to work outside. To distinguish us from what the Germans—and soon we too—called the "Aryan" population, every Jew had to wear a wide sleeve band of white cloth emblazoned with a blue Star of David. These bands were worn on the left arm above the elbow. We grown-ups understood why, but it was difficult to explain to the children why they had to be decorated in this manner—they could not understand why they were any different from other human beings.

My personal problem was to discover how to walk out of the ghetto and into the Aryan section. With a Jewish armband on my sleeve, it would have been impossible. Though the ghetto was not yet completely sealed off, one had to have a foolhardy kind of courage in order to venture beyond the gates. But when hunger twisted our entrails, I found the strength and the daring to try it. I could no longer bear the sight of my mother's and sister's pale, wasted faces. Once having successfully stepped out of the confines of the ghetto, I began to go almost every day to visit people I knew outside—mostly Ukrainians. Very often I would return home, discouraged and sad, with no results from my dangerous venture; but from time to time I succeeded in bringing home a whole loaf of bread, or even some butter or cheese! On such occasions my mother, seeing from the window the happy expression on my face as I returned, ran to open the door. "Shevele, what would we ever do without you!" she exclaimed tearfully. "God grant you, my darling Shevele, such courage that you may continue to make your way in life!"

There was a little boy, Izio Horn, whom I used to tutor when I was a student before the war. His father had a bakery, which now supplied bread to the Judenrat. Izio remembered and appreciated the help I had given him in school, and on several occasions he brought loaves of freshly baked bread to our house. It touched me deeply, and one day I went to thank his mother. With tears in her eyes, she said, "No one had to tell him to do this. He stands by the oven and as soon as the bread is baked he grabs a loaf, saying 'This is for my former teacher.'" "I am proud of your son," I said. "And I am proud of my pupil." I loved Izio for his thoughtfulness.

Occasionally my mother wanted to go out of the ghetto, but we forbade her doing so. In spite of her Aryan features, she might have been caught—and she would not have been able to squirm out of a bad situation as well as I, who was young, quick-witted, and always had everything planned in advance and would know what to say if the authorities caught me.

Even in this miserable ghetto, where each day seemed like a week and each night was like a year, Rose, my shy, easy-going, and unassuming sister, used to say to Mamma, "I don't care if they give us just a little food, or if they send us to hard labor, if only they will let us stay together—if only they will not torture us . . ." My sister Rose had blonde hair and blue eyes. We did our best to comfort and reassure her. Thus our days and nights passed in gray monotony. Mother tried to keep busy, cleaning the place just as in normal times. "Always," she used to say, "we must sleep in a clean bed, and the food we eat must be served on clean plates. We cannot give in to despair. Every war brings changes. Each one of us has a role to perform."

We keenly felt our tragic situation—we saw very well what we could expect—but we had to go on living and hoping. What else could we do? And so, in order to be able to go on, we tried to help each other. My job was to get food supplies and to obtain news from the town. My mother's was to keep our little family together. And my sister—it was my sister's job to cry over every beggar who knocked at our door and pleaded for a bit of warm food. Actually, these were not real beggars; mostly they were refugees who came to Rohatyn in 1939, displaced persons who could not take much with them when they fled. Now, in rags, after two years of poverty, they took on the appearance of professional beggars, worn out with hunger. Some of them were highly educated people who, before the war, had occupied high positions—but now they were broken, homeless, and impoverished. My sister had a heart full of pity for them. If one of the beggars had the luck to come to our house just before dinner, Rose would always say right away that she was not hungry and would give her share to him! She would say, "Mamma, look how awfully thin he is! He must have been without food for several days. I have had my breakfast this morning, I'm not hungry." And thus the beggar would get her plate of hot soup, or whatever we were having. Not only did Rose do without food to aid those less fortunate, but she often went without sleep, trying to find an explanation for why God allowed us to suffer as we did; after all, she reasoned, we did not harm anyone. Yet she could not find a satisfactory answer. Rose could not reconcile herself to this injustice. In time, it became apparent that she was terribly afraid. She grew thinner from day to day; her dresses just hung upon her bony frame. And her guileless blue eyes became larger and deeper with the fear that lurked within them—it was as though fear was devouring her physically as well as morally.

Whenever I could, I went out of the ghetto to sell something or to barter for food from the Christian population. Among the Gentiles, I knew a few Ukrainian people, and in particular a family named Krupka. I frequently went to visit them with the idea of exchanging some item in our possession for bread. I liked these fine people and they received me very hospitably, always offering me some refreshment or a meal depending on the time of day I called. (Through a false sense of pride I usually thanked them and did not accept the food, though it made my mouth water just to see it on the table.) If I sold something to them, they paid me fairly to the last zloty of its value, or if they could not pay immediately they would pay me a few days later. They never let me feel that I had no rights now, or that by being Jewish I was to be despised, and in this they belonged to a tiny minority.

Outside the ghetto lived another family I knew, that of the lawyer Babink. During the Russian occupation Mr. Babink, an attorney, was not allowed to practice law, but taught school in a village nearby. I remembered that I had once been able to procure an anode battery for his radio, not an easy task in those days. It had been good to see the gratitude in his eyes when I gave it to him, and he assured me, "Miss Sheva, I'll never forget your great kindness. Whenever you need anything, come to me."

Well, why not visit the Babink family now? Surely, they would not throw me out, and maybe they would like to barter with me for food? And indeed, when I called on the family one afternoon, they were very kind to me, and gave me some bread and potatoes.

Difficult as life had become for us, we had to go on living. When the Judenrat summoned us to work, we girls did not let our mother go but went, by turns, in her place. Frequently there were alarming rumors about an impending *akcja*[1]—a purge of the ghetto by the Germans. Then we hastily put on as much clothing as we could, ready to run at any moment. But the akcjas didn't occur. And, as the days went on, more and more refugees flowed into our town from various villages and smaller towns. The ghetto was filled to overflowing, and there was now no place where

1. *Akcja*, from German *Aktion*, refers to the roundup of Jews, followed by their extermination on sight, in ghettos, or in a concentration or death camp.

we could get food. Perhaps once every few weeks, the Judenrat issued a loaf of bread per person. Problems mounted on problems.

Eventually, after what seemed like years, the holy days approached—Rosh Hashana and Yom Kippur. The rainy season began, the cold rains of autumn, bringing the discomfort of deeply mired streets. There wasn't enough wood to heat our apartment. The days were gray and dismal. Mother once remarked sadly that the supply of potatoes was dwindling rapidly—and there was no flour left at all. We had no alternative but to organize our energies and do something once again.

I finally decided to go again to the marketplace outside the ghetto. On the way I summoned sufficient courage to remove my armband. There were usually many Germans and Ukrainians at the market, and as a Jewess, I had no right to be there. Going from one village vendor to the other, I looked into the women's faces, wondering if I might meet someone who knew me. Many people from the villages used to come to the Knigokultur bookshop I used to work in, and they all knew me. Perhaps I could exchange something for food? It was no longer a matter of some small household item; I thought of bartering a piece of furniture, or linens, or pillows—anything. We needed wood for fuel most urgently; it was impossible to remain through the winter in an unheated house, and mother had to have fire to cook something. Finally I met a few villagers whom I recognized. Some talked to me, but others dared not show they knew me for fear of the Germans. Suddenly I noticed a farmer whom I knew, standing by his wagon. I approached him confidently, for I was not bashful by nature, yet I would have to weigh each word in talking with him. I would have to be brief, and yet I would have to explain our desperate situation to him in hopes that he would take pity. He heard me out and nodded his head; he knew of our plight. And yet he said that he could sell us nothing. As I turned sadly away, however, he called me back and asked if I wanted to come out to the village and work a few days in the fields. When he added that I could earn a hundred-kilo sack of potatoes, I couldn't believe my ears. Naturally, I was overjoyed. Only those who had to live in a ghetto would appreciate what a treasure that was, to be able to obtain an entire sack of potatoes . . . I accepted his offer gratefully, and he explained how I could get to his farm on the following day.

As I walked home, I dreamed of the wonderful things that my clever mother would make from this anticipated bounty—potato dumplings, latki, potato soup, baked potatoes. And, of course, we would give a few to our neighbors as a treat! And I couldn't forget our aunts and cousins! I rushed into the house, my face beaming with joy, and rattled off my good news. My mother, however, was not favorably impressed. Even Rose said that I should not be allowed to go dig potatoes on a farm. "Mamma, don't let Sheva take that job," she exclaimed. "They will turn her over to the Germans and they'll kill her. I'd rather starve than see her go there!" But I explained to Rose that it was useless to sit at home, doing nothing but moaning. We had to have food to keep alive, and we had to fight for it, if necessary.

I could hardly wait for morning to come. I arose very early, put on a full-skirted peasant-style dress, tied a kerchief on my head, pulled on a coarse jacket—and when I looked in a mirror I hardly recognized myself. Poor Mother sighed and prayed incessantly. I tried to turn the adventure into a joke, saying, "Mamma, I must be your husband now, and it's my responsibility as head of this family to provide for you and Rose!" Feeling like the brave heroine of a melodrama, I left the house in high spirits. When I turned around in the street to wave to her, I saw my mother standing in the window, sadly shaking her head.

I had to go a long way to reach the farm, which lay outside the village of Zaluze. I had to cross the small bridge over a river from the side where, nearby, the Rohatyn ghetto ended. My best friend, Liba Teichman, lived near this bridge and I had to pass her house. It was still dark; the sun had not yet come up. I thought, *If I were to knock on her door, perhaps Liba would accompany me to the village,* but I did not want to wake her family and alarm them needlessly. Passing her house, I could not help but reminisce about the many times that I visited with her; how we spent happy hours in her garden, laughing with our school friends, and how often we used to meet boys on the bridge, flirting and taking snapshots of each other.

Beyond the bridge I removed my armband and went ahead, quietly, calmly, seeing no one. My feet slipped in the miry road and the walking became more difficult; my shoes were soon coated thickly with mud. As I neared the village, I began to meet people, and they greeted me with the traditional words, "May Jesus Christ be praised!" I answered them with a smile and continued on my way.

Again my thoughts turned to breakfast at the farmhouse, for I was growing hungry. Would I get something to eat? I had not let my mother prepare anything for me before I left home, as it was so early. I hoped I'd get pierogi—a kind of small pie filled with potatoes or other delicious things.

The farmer and his wife were already waiting for me. They gave me hot coffee and as much bread as I wanted to eat. It was wonderful! They asked me not to talk to the other workers and to keep my kerchief drawn down about my face so that no one would recognize me. I promised to be careful.

We went out to the fields together. Now I was thinking only of food; that I must work quickly, earn the potatoes, and bring them home as soon as possible. I knew that my mother was worried about me, but it was now too late to turn back. I must work through the whole day, and perhaps even several days, if all went well. The holy days were coming and we had to eat decently.

Bent over the clods of earth, I gathered the potatoes. A strong, cold wind was blowing. My back began to ache, but I did not complain aloud. I gritted my teeth and kept on digging. From time to time, some of the other workers, Ukrainians, would say something—about the war, about the Jews. Their words cut me sharper than the wind. My face was burning, my knees hurt, but their remarks hurt more, and they added to my physical misery.

I could hardly wait for the noonday pause. I felt that if I did not get some rest, I would faint. My strength was already depleted by my recent experiences. It seemed I could lie down in the mud and sleep for several hours—or maybe forever. Such a life was not worth living. Why was it a curse to have been born a Jew? Was it my fault? What was my crime? Why did these people think themselves better than Jews? I felt like crying, crying loud and long; perhaps somewhere in this world someone would hear me and help.

I recalled the words of the Russian woman who had worked with me in the Knigokultur bookshop. "Sheva," she had said, "come with me, away from here. The Germans are like animals; they hate the Jews." Now, it occurred to me that maybe I should have run away. But again, why should I? After all, I wasn't a Communist. Neither I, nor my mother, nor Rose, had done anything against the Germans—so what could they hold against us?

At last, a moment's respite! I saw the farmer's daughter coming toward us, carrying a large basin from which a tantalizing vapor rose. *Umm,* I thought, *maybe it will be my favorite, pierogi—anyway, it will be something warm and I'll be strengthened and refreshed. Maybe the afternoon's work will go more easily.*

It wasn't pierogi, but rather rice with hot milk, bread, and coffee. Each one of us received a large bowl of rice, as much as we wanted, and a piece of bread. I wished I could immediately share my meal with my loved ones at home, but it was a futile thought. I swallowed the food voraciously, even though the rice burned my tongue and lips; I was afraid that someone would find it strange to see me eating so rapidly, but I could not control my eagerness for food. At last, having satisfied my hunger, I rested a bit and went back to work. Many thoughts came to my mind as I bent over the field. Oh, God—what changes have occurred in my life! There was a time, not so long ago, when we lived like human beings, went wherever we wished, freely. Now we were slaves . . .

The afternoon dragged slowly. Would the evening ever come? As the sun sank lower over the horizon, I felt the cold creeping into my bones, but I consoled myself with the thought that soon I'd be going home. The farmer must have seen the weariness in my face, for, with a pitying smile, he whispered, "It won't be long now and you will be going home. I don't want to have you stay until it's dark, for it is dangerous to walk alone at night."

I thanked him, and soon afterward I left the potato field, promising I'd return the next morning—though I was not really sure that I would. But how could I return home empty-handed? Gathering up the courage, I asked the farmer if he'd give me a small basket of potatoes so that we would have something to eat for supper. He agreed. We went to the farm buildings, and there he told me to take two basketfuls out of the silo—adding, on a generous impulse, a small loaf of bread. Blessing him, I turned homeward.

Happiness filled my heart, so that I even forgot for a while who I was, and forgot the dangers on the road. The cold wind had whipped my cheeks to a burning redness, but that made me look all the more like a peasant girl, so that I did not attract attention from the passersby. When I approached the bridge that led to our ghetto, I saw in the distance a familiar silhouette. As I neared it, I recognized in the dusky light my mother, bent with cold and fear, waiting for me. When at last she saw me coming, she began to weep for joy. How relieved she was to see me safe—and not only that, but to see me carrying the fruits of my labors.

"Give me one of the baskets, Shevele darling," she insisted. When she realized how heavy it was, she wondered how I could have carried so much, so far.

"Oh, I didn't carry it," I replied jokingly. "My arms did." Mamma gave me a look. My gay mood must have seemed strange to her, I suppose.

When we entered the ghetto, we walked more slowly and sighed with a feeling of relaxation, even as I put on my armband. Oddly, we thought ourselves safe, even in this danger-ridden ghetto, simply because our home was here. From a distance we could already see Rose looking out of the window, frightened and uneasy. When she saw us, she ran to open the door wide. Joy radiated from her blue eyes and her lips parted in a welcoming smile as she embraced us.

"Oh, what a day this was!" Rose exclaimed over and over. "I did not know what to think could have happened to you. Look at your dirty hands, Sheva! They're red and cracked from the cold. You're not going back tomorrow; tomorrow you will find the work even harder."

Mother and Rosie joined in begging me not to go back to the potato field tomorrow, but I was tempted to earn a whole sack of potatoes—even though we already had enough for supper and for breakfast. The loaf of bread was a surprise for my mother; I had covered it with newspapers under the potatoes in the basket. When she emptied it, there was the bread! Mamma said, "Only Shevele knows how to provide for us," and again her face was wet with happy tears. "We love you."

As the next few days passed, I began to find the work a bit easier. After three days in the fields, I had earned a sack of potatoes weighing one hundred kilos. This was a fortune for us! In normal times one could have bought such a sack for 1 zloty, but not now. My problem now was how to get these potatoes back into the ghetto. To carry them in baskets would take much too long—and we never knew what the next day would bring.

Struck by an idea, I told the farmer that we owned a good Singer sewing machine that Mamma would willingly trade, and maybe also offer some bed linens or a piece of furniture, if he would come with me and talk to her and at the same time deliver the potatoes to our house. It was truly dangerous to venture with a farm wagon onto the streets of the ghetto, but the farmer agreed to deliver the sack of potatoes. Also, he told me that at a later date, he would bring us other food products in exchange for the sewing machine. And so it was that in a few days he came with a wagonload of corn, flour, some butter—and took the sewing machine away! Everything had to be arranged on schedule and was done quickly, for he would have been fined heavily if caught delivering foodstuffs to us—and we would have certainly been punished.

With a grieving heart my poor mother gave away her prized possession. She always used to sew for us—negligees, pajamas, all sorts of things—but it was more important now to have something to eat. For a machine that once cost fifty dollars, we received food products worth about one dollar. However, this was not the time for sentimental feelings about one's household treasures.

The holy days came and went. There was always distressing news circulating in the ghetto. Now we heard that the Nazis were taking all Jewish men to labor in another city—and that these men never returned. Again, we heard that the Germans were demanding a contribution from the Jews in the ghetto—actually, a money ransom that we had to deposit in the Judenrat for the SS troops.

Meanwhile, streams of Jews recently expelled from other towns and villages continued to flow into Rohatyn, having been ordered to live here. These people arrived hungry and in rags. No one knew where they could be housed; the Judenrat as well as the Jewish militia had to find a solution. We were now terribly overcrowded in the ghetto and we wondered what the reason could be for bringing us all together in such a way. We did not know the answer to this riddle—not yet.

I spent my days knitting sweaters from skeins of wool that I still had from before the war. This is my favorite hobby—and for Christmas I knitted a sweater for Mrs. Krupka's little son, Janko, who was then only about two and a half years old. The last time I had been to see Mrs. Krupka she had asked my advice on what to give her husband and their little boy for a Christmas present, and I had volunteered to knit sweaters for them. There was little time, so my sister and Mamma helped me with the knitting. By Christmas Eve, the two sweaters were finished and I ran over to deliver them, though it was night and I risked my life to keep my word. But Mrs. Krupka truly appreciated my efforts to please her. Out of the goodness of her heart, she packed a large bag of food for me to take home, for she knew how much we needed it. She was marvelous and I loved her.

Whenever we could spare some food, we would take it over to my aunt's house to share it with her son and grandchildren. My favorite cousin was Chaimek—whom I had loved from his infancy. When he was still only a baby, I used to stop on my way from school to play with him. My mother was always sewing or knitting things for him; the child practically grew up in our house, staying with us frequently, and was like our very own. Now, since my grandmother had come recently to live with us, he came even more often. He was a tall, thin lad of almost twelve, with a delicate and intelligent face.

Winter had come and the earth was frozen hard under the deep drifts of snow. People came down with the grippe; from time to time we heard of one or another of the ghetto's population dying from it. The older inhabitants of the ghetto had less resistance to hunger and cold, and they succumbed. Our grandmother became very ill and was confined to bed for over two months. We did whatever we could to help her and she lived with us. With considerable difficulty we summoned a doctor, but he said that in such circumstances he could not promise much. She developed pneumonia and on March 10, 1942, she died.

At such moments one always recalls the good deeds of the deceased, and I, too, remembered how good Grandma had always been to us. Grandmother never could rest until she had checked to see that her grandchildren were safely home and in bed before her. When we were small she used to live only a few streets away, and whenever she came to our house she always brought us chocolates. For each good report card I used to get a present from Grandma; once it was a real watch, once a lovely bookcase, and most often a gift of money.

Now, on this cold March morning, we followed Grandma to her last resting place in the cemetery. Mother and her two sisters sat at home for seven days, the traditional Shivah mourning period. Our house was filled with a great sadness.

The loss of our dear Grandma, our family's first victim in the ghetto, was only the beginning. Little did we know what different kinds of death the future held in store; all we could feel was sorrow because of our loss. Our only diversion was to visit relatives, and have them come see us. I remember as though it were yesterday how my mother asked Chaimek to come eat with us, after our period of mourning was over; she even wanted him to sleep in Grandma's bed. I remember it was March 19, and Mamma made pierogi especially for Chaimek because he liked them so much, though she had only potatoes to fill them with. We all sat down to eat, and then Chaimek took a nap. Although it was still early, he was exhausted from his lack of sleep the preceding night. Fear of the Germans, constant listening for their sudden raids, made us all nervous and afraid.

When evening approached, we wanted to keep him with us overnight, but Chaimek, fresh from his nap, refused to stay. The boy insisted he must be with his parents at night, so he started to get dressed. I gave him my pullover sweater and warm woolen socks. He kissed my mother goodbye, and Rose and I went out to see him home safely. At the door he turned back to thank Mamma. "Auntie Gitel," he said, "those were delicious pierogi. I would like to come back tomorrow to eat the rest of them. You are a better cook than my mother!"

Laughing at his childish remark, Mamma packed up a few of the pierogi so that he could take them home and share them with his family; his sister's children particularly would be glad to have something nice for supper.

Chaimek had no foreboding that there would be no tomorrow for him; that he was kissing his aunt and cousins for the last time; that this was to be his last meal. None of us had the slightest premonition. On the way back, Rose and I stopped to see my friend Liba Teichman who lived nearby, but we stayed only a few minutes because it was late and we were not allowed to be out at night. Taking leave of Liba, we hastened home. We did not know that it would be our last visit to her; that the next morning her house would stand empty, without a living soul, and that Liba, my childhood companion, along with her whole family and thousands of other Jews from Rohatyn would be laying in the bottom of a mass grave.

2

The First Akcja

THE MORNING OF MARCH 20, 1942, dawned cold and icy. The people in the ghetto were still abed when, at about six o'clock, we were awakened by loud shouting. At first the voices seemed quite distant, but soon they came nearer; we could hear the crying of children amid the noise of pistol shots. Mamma, Rosie, and I jumped out of bed and ran to the windows. I saw a helmeted German soldier with a gun in his hand, leading one of our neighbors by the beard. My sister, looking out of the other window, cried out, "They're shooting the people!"

Nervous spasms shook my body. Quickly, I threw a coat over my pajamas, and in house slippers I ran to the outhouse in the rear yard, calling them, "Run, hide yourselves!"

My sister, seeing me flee, ran after me. She rapped on the door of the privy, thinking that I meant to hide there, but it was too late to explain. The shouts and shots were heard on all sides. We shook as in a fever. It was too crowded in the privy and too dangerous for both of us to remain. I told Rose that I would leave. "Don't lock the door after me," I said.

"Where are you going?"

But there was no time to answer. In any case, I didn't know where I would go, except that I would try to leave the ghetto. Rose still tried to detain me. "I'm sorry for you," she said, "they will kill you." She caught hold of my hand, but I pulled it away and ran.

I heard shots close behind me, but I didn't look back. I ran and ran, until I felt the cold bite into my bones and my legs felt stiff, but I kept on running. I was afraid to stop. When I found myself outside the ghetto, I turned in the direction of the Krupka's house. Maybe they would take me in . . . I burst into their house like a bomb. There was no one in sight except their servant woman, who was scrubbing the kitchen floor. Realizing that there was not a moment to lose, I snatched the brush out of her hands, tore the kerchief from her head and tied it around my own, telling her to busy herself with something else while I started to wash the floor on my knees. If the Gestapo happened to be looking in all the houses for escaped Jews, they would not recognize me . . .

The servant thought that I had gone mad. She waved her arms, utterly confused, but I had no time to waste on explanations. "Just do as I say!" I repeated, sternly.

Before long, another Jew, an acquaintance of the Krupkas, also came in, seeking a hiding place. He started to tell the servant what was going on in the ghetto, but at that moment Mr. Krupka entered, pale with fear. Standing on the threshold, he took in the situation with a glance. Here I was, in pajamas under my coat, scouring the floor; there was this other Jew, obviously seeking refuge. He looked inquiringly at the servant, but she only shook her head from side to side, as if trying to justify herself.

"For God's sake!" Mr. Krupka exclaimed. "Do you want to bring misfortune to this house? The Germans are searching everywhere. If they find us sheltering escaped Jews, they will punish us or kill us most likely. Go, hide yourself in the yard, in the latrine, or in the barn. I don't have to be responsible for what goes on outside my house, but if you stay in my house the Germans will kill me along with you."

The other Jew went out—I don't know where. I also left, and kept on running straight ahead, still wearing the kerchief over my head. Behind the Krupkas' home was a school that I had to pass if I was to continue. I heard someone shouting, "There's a girl wearing a coat over her pajamas, running away!" But I kept on, without looking back. I passed the suburb of Babince and neared the village of Kutce. I felt that my forehead was burning like fire; I could scarcely catch my breath. In the distance I saw a small hut and decided to try to reach it before my legs gave way. With each moment I felt weaker and weaker, but now I was near the house. Suddenly, I slipped on the icy ground, fell, and blacked out.

I don't know how long I lay there unconscious. When I opened my eyes I saw a peasant woman standing over me. She spoke in Ukrainian, which I understood perfectly.

"You are sent from God, and I will help you."

I stared at her, uncomprehending. What had happened?

She helped me get up and took me to her home. As soon as we were inside, she began to prepare warm food for me, saying, "I had a dream last night that a great calamity befell the entire country. Then I saw a young girl, like an angel, in a white kerchief, who asked me to help her. Just now I was looking out of the window because I heard shooting in the distance. And I saw you, just like the angel in my dream, only you were lying on the icy ground in front of my house. God must have wanted me to aid you. I will save you, because you are sent from Heaven."

I listened to all of this, hardly believing my own ears. There was a whirring noise in my head. Here I was, among strangers, a runaway from the akcja, and they—these strangers—wanted to help me! It surely must be a divine miracle!

The peasant woman stood near me, praying. Now I noticed a little child creeping along the floor of the hut, from one end of the room to the other. A baby girl, maybe a year old; unable to talk, but constantly smiling at me.

The man of the house came in. He stood in the doorway, looking at his wife and then at me through narrowed eyes, as if unable to take in what he saw. At last his wife broke the heavy silence.

"See, here she is. I told you about my dream last night—and it came true! She's wearing the same white kerchief . . ."

Again, the farmer observed me thoughtfully. Then he nodded his head. "Yes, we must save her because she was sent by God, and she is holy."

These events left me so shaken that I too began to believe in the dream and to call it a miracle from God. Seated by the table, waiting for the food to be heated, I saw through the window two uniformed Ukrainian policemen with rifles slung over their shoulders, and two Gestapo men in helmets—and a small boy who was indicating to them the house in which I had taken refuge. My heart began to pound, and without much thought I jumped to the ledge above the kitchen stove and hid myself behind some burlap bags that were piled there. In peasant cottages, kitchen stoves have vent-hoods with a pipe that leads to the chimney, and this is where I crouched. It all happened so quickly that my hosts, their backs turned to where I was seated, did not notice.

Almost immediately, I heard a knocking at the door, growing louder and louder. The peasant's wife opened the door and I heard a man's voice: "This boy told us that there is a Jewess hiding here. We know she was wearing pajamas and a green coat."

The woman looked around and, not seeing me at the table, thought that I had run away and disappeared again. "What? There is no one here," she finally said. "Look for yourselves. We're not hiding anyone."

The policemen translated this to the Germans, brokenly, but they began to search the house anyway. They looked under the bed, in the closet, even inside the bedclothes. The woman insisted they were not hiding anyone, and her husband, too, swore that there was no one here.

Meanwhile, I was beginning to feel the heat of the stove, and the burlap bags were suffocating me. To make matters worse, the woman nervously kept throwing more wood into the stove. I thought, if they don't go away soon, I'll be burned alive here in these rags . . . The baby continued to crawl upon the floor. Then it began to cry, so one of the policemen picked it up and sat down with the child on his lap. Talking and amusing themselves with the baby, the men stayed on for something like half an hour. The peasants offered coffee and bread with butter, but they refused; perhaps they thought that they had already wasted enough time that could have been used to hunt down and kill escaped Jews. Anyway, they apologized to the peasants and left. I still feared to leave my hiding place, for I could not be certain whether they would return. The voices of the peasant couple drifted up to me.

The woman said, "I told you it was a divine apparition. How could she disappear so suddenly?"

The man replied, "You must have a talk with the priest and say a prayer in church on Sunday."

Finally, after a long time, I crawled out of the vent-hood, unable to bear the heat of the stove any longer. They looked at me, incredulously, and then at each other, making the sign of the cross.

My face and hands—my whole body—were burning like fire. Indeed, it was a marvel that I had held still in that hole so long. I tried to explain to them how I managed to hide myself, but they could not understand how I could have done it so quickly.

Then the man said to me, "Since you have been saved here and they did not find you when they searched the house, you must remain with us. Our house will be blessed." His wife gave me something to eat in a bowl, but I could not even swallow the food. I was much too upset by the experience, and I fell into a state of semiconsciousness.

We could hear shots outside, not far away, though we were so far from the ghetto. I wondered why the sounds carried so far . . . The man said, "Perhaps I should not tell you this, but for the past several weeks the Germans have ordered trenches to be dug nearby, behind a brick factory. The Jews themselves had to dig these trenches, never guessing it would be for their graves. All the Jews had been taken there from the ghetto, and they are now being shot and thrown into the trenches."

What could I say to this? In silence I lowered my head and tears began to course down my cheeks. I had no strength to cry aloud.

Now I recalled that for the past several weeks they had rounded up the men from the ghetto to do forced labor, to dig trenches. No one knew for what purpose, but no one thought that it would be for themselves. There were many rumors; some said that it was to make foundations for a new brick factory; others supposed that the trenches would serve to offset attacks if the Russians returned. Sometimes one would indulge in a morbid jest and say, "Maybe they are for us!"—never thinking that the jest would become a fact. In our flat, we kept silent. Once in a while we heard the cry of a neighbor's child, but otherwise there was only a fearful quiet.

I sat thus for a long while. I imagined that I had not heard right, that my confusion was due to a humming noise in my head—could it be a fever? Maybe I had suffered a mental shock, a brain concussion, a temporary paralysis—I no longer knew what was happening to me. At last, I sprang from the chair and said, "Please, give me a skirt and boots! I must go see what is going on out there. My family and all my friends are there—I must go! If they perish, my life isn't worth anything anyway. I cannot sit here and do nothing. I must go."

But they did not let me go, saying that it was too dangerous. At the moment, however, I did not care if I would be shot and killed. I wanted to be with my people . . .

Exhausted, broken, I crouched in the peasant hut until nightfall without a drop of water to moisten my burning lips. When it got dark outside, the shooting ceased. Now, I thought, I can go—it is all over. But "No," they said, "you cannot go out there in the dark. Where, to whom, would you go? Stay here, you can return in the morning."

Because they were afraid that some of their friends or relatives might come to their house in the evening, they told me to go out to the stable and spend the night there. If there was a search, they could safely say that I hid myself there without their knowing.

Stealthily, I ran through the darkness to the stable. I fell upon some straw near the cow stalls and lay there in the darkness, trying to sleep, to forget everything. But, unable to sleep, I huddled, frozen, through a night that seemed to have no ending. I envied the dumb cattle—they had more rights and freedom than we humans at the moment. It seemed to me that I'd rather be an animal, anything, than what I was myself. Can anyone sink lower than that in his own estimation? I could not believe that I could think this way . . .

Eventually, the night waned and I heard someone opening the door to the stable. After a moment of fright, I made out the figure of the farmer's wife. She whispered, "Don't panic, it's only me!"

She looked outside, and then came back in again. "There is yet very little daylight, so when I leave you follow me to the house. I'll cook some hot food for you."

I must have presented a haggard appearance when I entered their house, for she looked at me pityingly and said, "You look like a walking ghost. Here, drink something hot."

I took the cup of coffee she gave me and a piece of bread, but I could hardly swallow. She told me that last night some neighbors had come by and had told them that nearly three thousand people had been shot in the hours from morning until about four in the afternoon. They had heard moans and cries from the pits. The people were first stripped naked and then thrown into the pits, dead or still half-alive.

While she narrated this, I tried with all my will to conceal my emotions, but finally I buried my face in my hands and burst out with loud weeping.

"So I had dreamed," she said, wringing her hands like a figure in a tragedy, "and so it came to pass."

Her husband came out of the corner near the bed and said, "You will stay here, and I will go to the town to see what is happening and whether the Gestapo have left. I heard there were about a hundred Gestapo there. After I return, we'll decide what you should do. But I must wait until it is full daylight."

Needless to say, the hours of waiting seemed to never end, but there was nothing else that I could do but sit. About ten that morning, the farmer returned and assured us that the Gestapo had left the town. The ghetto, he said, looked like a battlefield; the streets were filled with corpses and the road leading to the village was strewn with bodies. He doubted if anyone was left alive. He said that in the pits nearby there were nearly three thousand dead bodies, left where they had been shot yesterday. The Gestapo had done its work and had not even bothered to cover the pits.

I said very little, for words were useless. I put on the peasant skirt and the pair of worn-out boots that they had given me, thanked them, and went out, promising that I would return and repay them for their kindness. I took the road to the ghetto. There was no need to hurry now, for there was no one to run to, and besides, I had no strength left. Passersby took no notice of me, for I was dressed like any peasant girl. I was sure that no one recognized me. Then, in the distance, I saw the figure of a girl, also wearing a shawl, with a package under her arm. Something about her walk was very familiar, and I hurried to get close enough to recognize her. To my surprise, I saw Tyla Nemeth, who lived in the same house as I. I called out her name.

She replied in astonishment, "Sheva! Are you alive? Go home quickly. Let your mother and sister see you are alive!"

It was such a blessed relief to know that they too were saved that I began to cry. "How did they escape? Tell me!"

Tyla was obviously nervous and impatient to be on her way. In a few words she told me that her father had been rounded up with the others in the marketplace, brought to the pits, stripped naked, shot, and thrown into the mass grave. During the night, when all was quiet, he had summoned the last remnants of his strength and had thrown off the corpses that had fallen on top of him in the pit. Then, naked as he was, he had run to the nearest house for shelter. The Gentile owner of that house had taken pity on him. In the morning, he had gone to the ghetto to let the Nemeth family know that he was alive and that they should bring him some clothes. That is all that she told me before we parted, because—she said—I would hear the rest from my mother and sister directly.

Now, as I hastened to the ghetto, I beheld scenes of incredible horror. The city was deadly still. The streets were empty. When I reached the ghetto I saw corpses lying on all sides. I'll never forget! Near the old courthouse lay the body of a teenage boy whom I recognized—he was Margulies' son. He had been shot, his head frozen to the icy ground. The boots had been pulled off his legs by some ghoul . . . A little further on lay the body of a big man, stretched out on the pavement. I knew him very well; it was Mr. Huter. His son was a very good friend of mine. His body was frozen to the ground. My heart contracted with grief, remembering how much he loved his only son and how proud he was of him, and now his son was gone and so was he.

But the most horrible scene of all met my eyes as I finally neared my home: There in the street lay a woman's head, its gray hair frozen to the pavement. The forehead was bashed in. To my great surprise and shock, my cousin Anka was standing before the skull, her own head bowed, lamenting, "Mother, Mother!" When she saw me, she began to scream, "Sheva, Sheva, look what they did to my mother!" I joined in her lamentations, almost hysterical in our sorrow, for it was the head of my father's sister that I saw before me on the ground. Shaking like a leaf, I walked into the hallway of the building, and there, to one side, lay the body of an old woman. I recognized it as the mother of a Mrs. Felker. My heart throbbing wildly, I put my hand on our door handle, feeling that my head could not contain all these horrors around me, and that I could expect yet more to come.

When I opened our door a heavy, excremental odor hit me. Rose was sitting in a chair, her hair matted with filth from the outhouse. As soon as she saw me, she started crying, "Mamma, Mamma, Sheva is here, she is alive!" Then, turning to me, she asked, "Where were you? Where were you?"

Her body showed bruises, and the stench was so unbearable that I became nauseated. Mother was helping her clean up, and to my surprise she did not show much emotion. This wasn't like our mother. The whole scene suddenly made me cry, cry as loud as I could, and I threw myself on Mamma's shoulder. "Mamma, Mamma, what is going to happen to us? We are alive, but what is next?" I wailed.

Seeing her unnatural apathy, her face so distorted and despairing, pained me deeply. Mother's face was always so gentle, so delicate, and so beautiful. But not now. Now it was changed, hard. I realized that the akcja had affected her. She could adjust to almost any situation in life, but it seemed that this was too much. I could, despite my efforts, evoke no sign of responsive emotion from her; there was no expression on her face, and she seemed turned to stone. And no wonder: she had been outside and had seen everything with her own eyes.

In an attempt to divert her thoughts, I tried to explain how I managed to save myself. Then Rose said that as soon as I had left the outhouse she had locked herself inside and when she saw the Gestapo searching in the storehouse near the latrine, had quickly unlatched the door to make it appear that there was no one there—and had jumped into the opening of the cesspool, holding on to the rim of the toilet seat and to the protruding stones in the wall. Even so, she had been immersed in the excreta up to her chin.

There Rose had stayed through the night. Around dawn, she recognized the voices of some of our neighbors in the yard—and then she heard Mother crying for us. She realized that the akcja was over at last! But her strength was used up, and she felt that she would soon sink completely in the filth. She began to scream for help. In a little while Mother and the neighbors pulled her out—and here she was now, trying to clean herself of the unspeakable dirt . . . My sister, who was always so fastidious and neat!

Mother was saved by a quick-thinking neighbor who had pulled her into the cellar while she had been looking for Rose and me. The neighbor's foresight proved to have been their salvation, for the Germans seldom dared to enter a cellar for fear they might be attacked by someone hidden in the darkness below. They only came as far as the door, looked inside and yelled, *"Juden heraus!"* They fired some shots at random; one woman who stood near my mother had been hit, but Mamma and the kind neighbor were hidden behind a heavy door and had escaped unharmed.

After I had heard this story, my mother sighed deeply and seemed about to say something, collecting all her strength to form the words. "Yes, we are safe," she said slowly, "but I am far from happy, for this is only the beginning of a greater tragedy . . ." Her voice trailed off weakly, but after a while she continued: "Happy are those who have already been taken and killed. Nothing good awaits us here. Our death will be even worse." She became lost in her thoughts, finally breaking out into violent sobs. We let her cry. Rose and I looked at each other, and at her, and we knew how she felt, knew it as sincerely as if we had looked straight into her soul. We were her life, and now she had to stand by and watch us being brutally destroyed. I could read her thoughts as though in a mirror. People used to say to our mother, "You have lost a husband, but you still have two brilliant jewels." And now? Her plans, her years of sacrifice and devotion—everything lost! And worst of all was the great fear of what tomorrow might bring. These thoughts, these unspoken words, were clearly etched in my mother's sorrowful face.

Weeping piteously, I rested my head on her shoulder and spoke to her as gently as I knew how. "Mamma, you'll see. We will get rid of the Germans yet. We won't give in. This blow was unexpected. But you'll see, Mamma, something will have to be done. The world wouldn't let this happen. There are Jews everywhere; there are Jews in America. If news of what is happening to us reaches them, they will do something . . . And Mamma, where is your faith in God? You always used to say that He was with you. And, you see, he has saved us, after all!"

Changing the subject abruptly, I asked, "Have you heard anything from Uncle Hirsch?" My sister immediately added, "And Chaimek and Glickel, and the children? Or have you heard from our father's brothers and their families?" Again I could not believe my ears when Mother said, dispassionately, "The less we know, the better. There is no difference either way. You saw your aunt, your father's sister—so you can imagine the others." I could not understand how my mother did not seem to care what happened to Chaimek, our precious favorite!

Without even taking time to have something to eat, I said, "I must go and see what happened to them. I promise I'll be back soon."

So I left the house, hoping to return with good news. I walked with a slow and fearful step. Occasionally a wagon laden with corpses rumbled by. The Germans apparently had given orders to remove the dead from the streets of the ghetto. This was accomplished through the Jewish militia with the help of conscripted Jews, who transported the corpses to the Jewish cemetery. Some bodies were frozen to the ground so solidly that they had to be dug out with shovels along with the earth.

The little houses in the ghetto stood as if in a desert, forsaken, icicles hanging from their eaves. Many doors were shut tight, enclosing the panic-stricken inhabitants within an illusory feeling of security. Some doors were wide open—the people who once had lived in those houses were no longer there; they had been taken away to the mass graves. From time to time I saw somebody stealing along the walls, like a thief.

Now, as I neared my goal, I walked through narrow, twisting lanes to the Wieners' home, on a small hill near the powerhouse. My heart beat more rapidly the closer I came. At last I stood in front of the house. The door was closed. I hesitated on the threshold, looking in at the windows, wondering whether I should enter. Everything was turned upside down, some of the pillows ripped open, goose feathers on the floor. I called and called, thinking that perhaps they were hiding, but there was no answer. It puzzled me that someone had closed and locked the door—who could have done that unless there was a survivor? I called again with growing apprehension, but receiving no answer, I slowly descended the hill.

Tears bedimmed my eyes. I could not believe that of the entire family—five adults and three children—not one was left, that all had been murdered within one day.

But then I felt a flicker of hope, for at that moment I recalled that my uncle and Aunt Wiener were on very friendly terms with a Polish woman who lived on the Aryan side near the ghetto and who helped them occasionally with gifts of food. I knew her, too, and it occurred to me that perhaps they had found a hiding place in her home. I tried to remember exactly where she lived as I crossed the boundary of the ghetto to go in the direction of her house. Ah, it was there! I knocked timidly upon the door and after a while a frightened voice asked, "Who is it?"

Bending over and placing my lips close to the keyhole, I whispered, "I am a relative of the Wieners."

The door opened and I saw the pale, very sad face of the woman. From her expression I could read all I needed to know. "They are dead, aren't they?" I managed to say. "Can you tell me anything more?"

She began to cry, and our tears mingled in mutual sorrow. She took me by the hand and led me toward the barn. There, close by, lay two bodies—my uncle Hirsch and Chaimek his son . . .

"Chaim!" I cried. "Chaim, why didn't you stay with us!" Now, in death, he had attained the stature of a martyr—no longer did I call him by his childhood name. But my words were futile, my tears useless now. He looked so innocent, lying there; he was still wearing the sweater and hose I had given him two days ago.

The Polish woman was lamenting, "Such good people! Such decent people! And they perished so miserably . . . From my window I saw how the Gestapo ran after them. Little Chaimek was crying, and his father tried to hold him close. Then they started to shoot. First, they killed the father, your uncle. Then Chaimek cried out, 'Daddy!' so they hit him with the butts of their rifles. He fell across his father's body and was shot to death. What a terrible thing!"

"And what of the others?" I asked. "Do you know anything about the rest of the family?"

"Yes," the woman replied. "They took Mrs. Wiener and her daughter to the market square. The others, I believe, were saved—thank Heaven! But I don't know where they are now. Their son-in-law, Shloma Handschau, was here with his older boy, and he mentioned that Mrs. Wiener's sister—who now shared the apartment with them—and his little boy had gone into hiding and survived. Oh, God, help us in these terrible times!"

"God help us!" I echoed, and as there was nothing else to do I thanked the good woman for her efforts and sympathy. Once again I looked upon these two innocent victims of terror, and in numb grief, turned to leave the tragic scene.

I hastened home, without stopping to see my father's family, to tell my mother and Rose what I had seen and heard. It might be some small consolation to Mamma to know that one of her sisters was still alive, and that Handschau and his children were saved.

But how could I break the news to her that Uncle Hirsch and Chaimek, and the entire Wiener family were murdered? We loved Chaimek so dearly! It was hard even for me to realize that my Aunt Ryfka and Uncle Hirsch and their children were dead. All the way home I seemed to see them before my eyes . . . Uncle Hirsch, who was like a father to me: When I was a little girl he used to take me on his knee and let me sip a small glass of vodka with sugar. I'd dip the cubes of sugar in the spirits and crunch on them; every time I swallowed a morsel, he threw another sugar cube into the glass. As I grew older, he'd let me write the addresses on the cases of butter that he had to ship out; and for this "work" he'd give me spending money—two, or three, or even five zlotys. And whenever I had a bad cold and had to stay in bed, Uncle Hirsch would come immediately and bring me chocolate, halvah, candy—and Aunt Ryfka, such a good soul! And Glickel, their daughter . . . all gone now! My heart remembered and nearly broke with grief. All of them, my dear ones, all gone—in one day!

Just before I entered our house I heard loud noises coming from within, and when I opened the door to our apartment there was the Wieners' son-in-law, Shloma Handschau, with his five-year-old son, Nuchem.

"We know everything already," Mother said, tears rolling down her face, as she broke into Shloma's torrent of talk. I saw Rose had also been crying. I caught up little Nuchem in my arms; his lovely blond hair fell in ringlets upon his forehead. Handschau went on talking, ignoring the interruption, telling us that he and little Nuchem had taken refuge with some Catholic people he knew and had hidden in a barn until the akcja was over. And it wrung our hearts to hear little Nuchem say, "I have no Mamma, no Grandma, no Grandpa anymore; even Chaimek is dead. They all got shot, with guns. Why did they shoot them? Why?"

I watched my mother's sad, brown eyes fill with pain and resignation; I saw her suffering for us, for everyone. She said, "Now we have a picture of our future. Now we see what some people had feared. The fear had not been unfounded. They were wiser than we; they foresaw what would happen. But in one thing they were wrong, for they thought that the women would be spared. But here they kill not only women but children, little children who don't even know who or what they are, children who might someday grow into useful citizens—whom even they could train to be whatever they wanted. They murder these children."

Soon afterward my aunt Sara came to our house with Handschau's younger son in her arms. She was pale, exhausted, with the tragedy of the akcja written in her face. At the sight of her, none of us could say a word. She was glad, of course, that we were alive and safe, but she also could find no words to express it. And the child's big, blue eyes stared out of the tiny, frightened face as though, somehow, he understood everything.

At last, Aunt Sara opened her mouth to speak. "What will happen now?" She echoed the question everyone had in mind. Looking at the two little children, she said, "And what will happen to those kids?" We could not answer.

After Handschau's family left, we received news that my father's brothers and their families had survived the akcja. But my best friend Liba, along with her family, had been shot and thrown into the mass grave. Our neighbor, Yoyne Nemeth, gave us a clear picture of how the people had been gathered in the marketplace, loaded on trucks, and taken to the common graves to be shot. They had been packed so tightly that many had panicked, lost their senses, and began to laugh hysterically, screaming and tearing their hair. Many perished before they got to the place of execution. Many young girls had first been stripped and tortured and beaten before they died, while their parents had had to look on while the Nazi soldiers made fun of them. Though Nemeth told us so much, we felt that there were things we would never know fully. They were impossible to describe, too horrible to tell.

People outside of the ghetto, Nemeth said, looked on while all this was going on, but no one raised a voice of protest. And he had also witnessed many of the local Gentiles assisting the Nazis in their action against the Jews.

We sat silently. Who knew what was still waiting for us? Perhaps we should have envied those who were already dead: they were finished with all this brutality and terror. My mother sat and listened, sadly shaking her head. Having two young daughters, she feared for us.

3

The Face of Hate

WITH THIS TERRIBLE EXPERIENCE still fresh in their minds, those who were left alive in the ghetto—there were over two thousand—had sufficient reason to dwell in mortal fear of repercussions. Most of the people did not undress to go to bed and were afraid to fall asleep, sitting instead in readiness for any emergency, all night, night after night. How long could one go on like this? We had to devise some plan of mutual assistance.

At last the neighbors got together and decided to take turns keeping watch outside our homes. A member from each family would be assigned a time to stand guard and in case of any suspicious noise or movement, they would alarm the entire neighborhood. These "sentries" were changed every few hours.

The second step was to find a hiding place in which to build a shelter in the event of another akcja, which could take place any day. This was quite a serious problem. Meanwhile, of course, our stomachs demanded food, and we needed wood to cook by and to heat our homes with.

Though more than three thousand men, women, and children had been killed, the Germans brought in other Jews from surrounding towns and thrust them into our ghetto. These people had been forbidden to take anything with them, save what they had on their persons—which usually amounted to only a few rags of clothing, and perhaps diseases or lice. As if we hadn't enough misery, enough mouths to feed up until this time, our situation was worsened by the arrival of these newcomers. But these horrible sights and all our forebodings were nothing before the imperious demands of our empty stomachs. Generally, the people on the Aryan side of town were growing more and more reluctant to exchange food for other articles of value. And the reason was obvious: Why should they barter with us when they could wait for another akcja to take whatever they pleased? All they had to do was wait. The next akcja seemed to be hanging in the air, ready to strike at us any day.

I could remain not disillusioned only in my friends, the Babinks and the Krupkas. Whenever I went to see them, they always helped me with whatever they could. And each time I brought something home, my mother would bless them. Truly, this was the only source from which the fountain of mercy flowed for us. From time to time I went to the marketplace without my armband and tried to barter an angora sweater or other woolen things that I had made, or possibly my sister Rose's beautiful handiwork, for a few potatoes, beets, or carrots. And this was at the risk of my life—not only for the attempt to barter, but for removing my armband. I could not make many such trips, especially when I began to see large signs in store windows: IT IS FORBIDDEN FOR JEWS AND DOGS TO ENTER HERE.

Besides this fear for our lives and our constant hunger, there was not a day that the German storm troopers did not make some demands of us. For example, they ordered the Judenrat to form a hospital in the ghetto immediately. The hospital had to be filled with patients and fully staffed. As for patients, those were not hard to find; but who would want to go to such a hospital? At the moment, however, it was easier to find patients than beds and bedding.

And where were we to find such supplies if not from the poor, oppressed people of the ghetto? I was chosen, among others, by the Judenrat to assist in this collection, since they claimed that people liked and had confidence in me and that I had the ability to work effectively on such a project. There were several of us engaged in this work: Yoyne Nemeth, who lived in the same house as us, his daughter Tyla; Mrs. Kleinwaks and her daughters; and my sister and I. Our task was to collect the needed pillows, sheets, and towels; Nemeth, with someone else's help, carried the metal beds. The people gave, because they knew that if the order was not carried out they would get, instead of the hospital, an akcja.

When furnished, the hospital rapidly filled up with patients. Some did not have to be asked to come; they were carried in, no longer able to walk. Then the Germans came, and not a soul stirred in the streets for fear of being shot. While the Germans had plans to exterminate all the sick, they would not spurn killing off any healthy Jews who might get in their way. When they did away with all the sick people in the hospital, their vacant places were immediately filled with new victims and the process began all over again. The Germans had it all calculated mathematically. If even one patient succeeded in hiding or escaping, he had to be returned—or the Germans, with the help of the Ukrainian police, would shoot tens or hundreds in his place.

While going around collecting bed linens, I met a young man named Hugo Goldberg, from the city of Bielsko, near the Polish-German border. He came to Rohatyn in 1939, when the Germans occupied Bielsko, and had resided here ever since. Hugo was tall and handsome. When we met at some friends' home, he was astonished that I should be collecting for the Jewish hospital—for he took me to be Polish, a Gentile, and of course it was forbidden for them to enter the ghetto. But then he noticed the band on my sleeve and said, "With a face like yours, there's no need for you to stay in the ghetto!"

I explained that I was not alone. I had my mother and sister, thank God! I could not leave them, and it was useless for me to plan an escape; they needed me and I could not visualize them living without me—or me without them. He understood my reasons perfectly, but again he said, "What an opportunity for you to go away from here—anywhere! You simply do not look Jewish. If you could just get out of the ghetto! Here, you only wait for a horrible death. That seems to be our inexorable lot; there is no hope for any of us."

This was the substance of our first conversation; somehow his words sank deeply into my consciousness and gave me no rest. *Perhaps he is right,* I could not help thinking; perhaps I should get away, and then try to help Mamma and Rose escape from the ghetto, too. I said nothing about this to anyone, but I thought of it often. I wished I had talked to Hugo Goldberg longer; he might have known of someone who could fabricate the necessary document for my departure. After all, I could not travel under my real name, Sheva Weiler; I would have to assume a fictitious name and pose as a Gentile. I was consumed by the idea of leaving the ghetto and going out into the world—there was nothing here for us but death . . . yet how could I safely accomplish my escape to freedom?

Meanwhile, I was called upon to assist in a new project—to help operate a kitchen for the hungry. Getting the food was the most difficult part; the Judenrat was able to provide some potatoes, vegetables, and bread, but in very limited quantities. Who came to the kitchen? Mostly the displaced, homeless people, refugees, they were always hungry and swollen from starvation. Some of the newcomers from surrounding towns and villages came also. My heart was sorrowful at the sight of them; they were a picture of misery and despair as they stood in humble queues for a bowl of soup. And if someone happened to walk or run quickly, they would panic, thinking that it was the start of the akcja, and like frightened mice, they would throw down their bowls and scurry away to safety.

The soup kitchen did not last long. People stopped coming, fearing they would be picked up there and taken to the hospital. And the food they received was not worth the risk; besides, the portions grew smaller each day.

My mother and Tyla Nemeth's mother were proud of our work, but they were just as well pleased that we did not have to go there anymore. This did not mean, however, that I ceased going out of the ghetto. I continued to visit the Aryan section for as long as I could. My acquaintances there could not have been delighted with my visits, but as long as they allowed me to come in and showed me even a little heart, I persisted in being their uninvited guest. Through them I learned what was going on in the world outside, though the news did not give me much comfort.

Suddenly, summer came. It was warm and beyond the river the trees and gardens were green, but there we could not go. I could only stare at the river and remember how, when I was a little girl, we used to live near it, and how I spent many happy hours there, in the shade of orchard trees, or sitting on its banks and dangling my legs in the water. Now that world of my childhood seemed strange, and forgotten . . .

I was not alone in my nostalgic fascination with the river. Among those of my contemporaries who were left alive was Klara Altman, Mayer

Altman's daughter. Her father had gone to America before the war with the intention of sending for his wife, daughter, and two sons; before he could realize his plan, however, the war broke out. Klara was young, intelligent, and refined, always dreaming and hoping that the war would end soon so that she could rejoin her father beyond the ocean. Almost every day she would come to the tea room, where I worked after the soup kitchen closed, and we became the best of friends. Poor girl! She still believed that any day now her father would get them out of the ghetto. Listening to her, I thought—and sometimes even tried to explain to her—how little it depended on her father's willingness or ability to save them. Had it been possible for our people in America to do anything, there would not have been a soul left in the ghetto—everyone would try to save his kin from such a fate. But Klara could not believe that they would let the Germans effect a complete destruction of our people. Her hopes, of course, were in vain . . .

On the other hand, I seemed to be guided by a sure instinct. Though I was very active and tried to fill my days with work, I could not forget the lesson the first akcja taught me. I still remember the suffering, the dreadful sights, the various raids and manhunts that followed, and the excesses that the Germans committed. I heard the various rumors coming from my Gentile acquaintances; I knew the Germans would sit in judgment upon us. I kept remembering the words of Hugo Goldberg: "Escape from the ghetto!" I could not forget, and slowly plans were forming in my mind.

As time went on, I never ceased to go whenever I could barter something for food. Returning from one of my foraging expeditions, I found our apartment empty. It frightened me, for always either Mamma or Rose would wait until I came home. A neighbor looked in at the opened door and told me that my mother had gone to the Judenrat. Trembling, I inquired what had happened.

"They called your sister to report to the Judenrat office," she explained. "When she did not return after several hours, your mother became very worried and decided to go there and see what had become of Rose. We heard the Germans were rounding up girls to send to concentration camps, and not for the usual work duty . . ."

Tired and hungry though I was, I ran immediately to the Judenrat. When I entered the vestibule, I saw a Jewish policeman standing on guard in front of a door that led to a cell. Through the iron grating I could see several girls, among them my sister Rose, her face swollen from crying. Indescribable panic was reflected in her eyes.

"Sheva!" she called out shrilly, as soon as she perceived me in the dim hallway. Her face instantly radiated joy at my coming. "Look, they told me to report here, and they put me in this cell! Tomorrow morning they are going to send us to a 'camp'—to our death. I know they will kill us!"

"Quiet, quiet!" I said, trying to comfort her. "Don't cry. Try to be calm. Tell me, where is Mamma?"

"She went upstairs somewhere, I think," Rose replied, "to see the chief of police."

I ran upstairs and met Mamma coming out of the office. She was greatly agitated and had been weeping. "Mamma, I know everything already," I said. "I was talking to Rose."

Mother told me that she had been to see the Obman and the chief of police, but they could do nothing. The Sonderdienst (the Nazi Special Services) demanded girls to be sent to work in a camp beyond Rohatyn, and the girls had to be delivered, or else the Jewish community would face another akcja. That was the answer they gave her.

I had heard about that camp—Belzec; it was the place where they burned our people in gas ovens. Mother went on to say, "And as for us, the Judenrat decided that since you and Rose both have escaped alive from the last akcja, one of you must go. Rose is so terribly miserable about this, that I am afraid she will not reach the camp; she will die on the way." We knew that to be sent to Belzec meant death, though as yet no one from Rohatyn or the vicinity had been taken to any camp.

"I realize that," I said. "If Rose has to go, she won't survive." I told Mamma to turn around—we would both try to talk to the chief of police. And so we went back upstairs. It was not easy to gain entrance to his office, but somehow we did. I gave my name to the policeman at the door, and he told us to wait. We stood there for a rather long time, but at last we were admitted inside. Though I tried to speak calmly and convincingly, it was all for nothing. Finally, I decided to offer myself in place of Rose; hearing that, my mother began to weep again.

"What difference will that make?" she protested. "Whether you or Rose have to go, it will be the same to me." I pressed my mother's hand to make her understand that I had something in mind.

The police chief gave his consent, and we were led downstairs. When the cell door was opened, Rose smiled hopefully, guessing she was going to be released. But when I entered the cell and told her to go, she hesitated. "Please, go home!" I repeated firmly.

"Mamma," Rose wailed, turning her puzzled eyes from me to Mother. "Where is she going? Why are you looking so pale?"

I pushed Rose through the door, and the policeman locked it behind her. Now the iron gratings separated us, and I realized that I was in prison. I still did not know whether I had made a wise decision, but the desperate idea was born of the conviction that Rose would have collapsed under the trial. I was made of tougher stuff; I could endure. Mother and Rose took a sad farewell, standing before the iron gate as long as they were permitted. At last, they had to leave.

For some time I remained motionless at that forbidding door, wondering what to do next. Whom should I notify of my predicament? I knew a few members of the Judenrat. They always treated me with great respect. How could I get in touch with them? I could have asked Mamma to go to them, but I did not want to involve her further. Better she and Rose should go home and eat and rest.

The policeman who stood guard at the door of the cell was a young, nice fellow, whom I knew quite well. I whispered to him through the grating: "Listen, I must get out of here! They can't send me to hard labor. Help me!"

Barely turning around to look at me, he muttered, "I'd gladly let you go, Sheva, but there aren't many girls left. You know that nearly all were killed in the akcja. They don't want older women, so there's no alternative. Anyway, it doesn't depend on me; I only carry out orders."

I assured him that I only wanted to get a message to one of the members of the Judenrat who knew me very well. If Max, the guard, couldn't take it himself, he could summon another friend, Sal Kreisler, to send the message. Max consented to do this.

When Kreisler came to the cell and saw me, he exclaimed, "Sheva, what are you doing here behind these bars?"

"They are sending me to hard labor," I said bluntly. "That is why I asked to see you, sir. I know what you will say: They need girls for the work, and there aren't enough in supply. It is an order. Right? But please let Attorney Freiwald know that I am here. I hope he will remember how I used to supply him illegally with stationery when I worked at the bookstore under Russian occupation."

He bit his lip and thought a while. Then, without a word, he turned and ran upstairs. He returned with Dr. Freiwald, the attorney who knew me so well. From the expression on their faces I understood that my situation was really serious.

I tried to explain to them that if I were taken away, my mother and sister would be left helpless, that they would die of starvation. Besides, I argued, did they forget how I helped to organize the hospital and the kitchen? Didn't they remember how one night they sent someone to wake me from sleep so that I could help collect the tea and coffee that was demanded by the SS, and how once I and three others went the rounds of the ghetto, reminding people to bring their emergency contributions—thousands of zlotys—to the Gestapo?

The two men left, promising to return. In the meanwhile, relatives of the other girls who were in the jail with me also came and tried to do something for them. The prison corridor swarmed with people. Among them I noticed Mendel Weiler, my father's brother. He lived across the street from the Judenrat office, and my mother, instead of going home as I had begged her, had gone there to ask him to help me. Not satisfied with that, Mamma herself also came from time to time to inquire what was being done. Again I begged her to go home.

The hours dragged by slowly. The girls talked among themselves, each one contributing some new bit of information, and all their conjectures were dismal. At last one of the men returned and told me, in a low whisper, that there was a chance . . . He said that they wanted a ransom for me! Three kilograms of sausage and three bottles of vodka. I did not ask who "they" were, but told him to get in touch with my cousin Chaim Weiler, who knew a sausage maker. I was stunned; I could not believe that the life of a human being should be valued at the price of sausage and vodka.

Knowing that several people in the Judenrat were trying to help my cause made me feel sure that I would be freed. And indeed, after a time, one of the policemen opened the door and called out: "Sheva Weiler, report upstairs!"

When I stood before the chief of police, he said, "You are lucky. We managed to buy one off of them, but now you must go away quickly. Go home and don't show your face on the street until things quiet down again!"

I thanked him and left. As I came out of the Judenrat building, I saw Mamma, overjoyed, looking out of the window in my uncle's house directly across the street. She told me later that she had to part with some of her household belongings in exchange for three bottles of vodka, which she obtained with the help of one of my uncles.

With every passing day, more people came to the ghetto from other places. Rumors of akcjas in surrounding towns became more frequent. There were some who even began to talk about suicide. When the Judenrat distributed bread—a quarter of a loaf, or sometimes a half, for each person—people would start a rush for it. Whoever was able to push his way forward to the head of the queue received his allotment, but the weaker ones and those who were not aggressive often stood in line for a long time, half-frozen and exhausted, and then went away without receiving any bread. Life under such conditions made us self-centered; everyone thought only of himself, and the only goal was to survive.

Whenever we heard that food supplies were delivered to the Aryan population, we hoped to be able to barter some of our possessions for something to eat. That was my role in the family: to beg from my Gentile acquaintances. Whenever I went to the Aryan section, I dressed as well as I could, for I did not want to draw attention to myself or to evoke pity as "that poor girl from the ghetto." And I removed my armband when I went to visit my Christian acquaintances, not wishing to endanger them.

But most of my visits were futile, only a strain on my nerves and a needless peril. As I would return homeward, often empty-handed, brooding and pensive in the chilly drizzle that wet me to the skin, I would wonder what happened to all the prayers that were said in the synagogues . . . At least to His faithful, God should have shown that the days and years they worshipped Him in these places were not lost and in vain. But alas, facts seemed to point to the opposite.

Once, I recalled how Chief Rabbi Tumin was put to death: Because he was a rabbi, the Germans wanted to make his death more painful and humiliating. They placed him on the ground between the legs of a horse and forced the animal to stamp on him with his hoofs until Rabbi Tumin was trodden to death. How could I find an answer to such a crime?

While I was crossing a narrow street one day, engrossed in such dismal thoughts as these, our acquaintance Hugo Goldberg suddenly appeared before me. Smiling and bowing politely, he said: "You are still here! I thought you would have escaped from the ghetto by now!"

As I started to explain why I remained, he took my umbrella and we walked in the direction of my home. We were so engrossed in our conversation that we almost walked past the house; we sat down on a bench in front of the building. Hugo was telling me that he had an uncle in Warsaw who passed as a Catholic, using a fictitious name and a forged identification card. Hugo said that he would try to get in touch with his uncle to see what could be done for himself and me. As he talked, I listened with intense pleasure to his voice. Hugo Goldberg was very charming, intelligent, and highly educated; a chemist, he had studied in foreign countries and had a fluent command of several languages. He was dark-haired, but his eyes were greenish-gray, and when he talked they were full of sincere emotion and warmth. I hardly knew him—this was only our second meeting—but I felt a complete confidence and trust in relation to him. It was a good feeling to know that a total stranger was so interested in my life.

Hugo was older than I, and this I liked, too; it deepened my trust in him, for I regarded him as I would a guardian. It was so good to be able to sit here and talk that for the moment I forgot that we were like people living atop a volcano; I had the illusion that there were normal times again, that here in the company of another intelligent and sympathetic human being I could sit and talk and laugh and be happy as I had used to be before all our troubles began. But the moments flew by too rapidly. Dusk was falling and the air was cold. Not wishing to terminate our conversation, I asked him to come inside and meet my mother and sister. Mamma took a great liking to Hugo at once, and upon learning that he came from Bielsko, she began to reminisce about her girlhood days when she used to make trips to that city.

After this first visit, Hugo became a frequent guest in our house. We hailed his coming with joy, for he was a wonderful person, well-mannered and always ready to cheer us up, lifting clouds of despair from our shoulders and giving us courage to go on living. Oddly, we always knew he was coming even before he knocked on our door, because we could hear him scraping his shoes on the mat outside. Mamma used to say that it was a waste of time; with the way things were nowadays a little more dirt in the house would hardly be noticeable. But he claimed that habits of a lifetime could not be forgotten.

Hugo was very helpful in many ways. Being a chemist, he soon found a way to cure the rash that I had had on my legs since the akcja of March 20. We could get neither doctors nor medicines then, and if I had made a big tragedy of the rash they might have sent me to the dreaded hospital—which was the equivalent of a death sentence. But it had kept getting worse, until I had eruptions from the soles of my feet to my knees. Mamma had tried all sorts of poultices, but my condition did not improve. When we got to know him better, we asked Hugo's advice, and fortunately he was able to help.

Whenever it was our turn to stand on guard outside the house, Hugo did not let my mother or sister perform this duty. Instead, he and I would substitute for them. We often sat on the courtyard outside the house and talked in whispers, while we listened and watched for the approach of the Gestapo. During these vigils we planned how to escape the bleak tomorrows that threatened us with death. Whenever Hugo Goldberg talked with Mamma or Rose, he tried to console them and, seeing their spirits falter, tried to give them courage to live. Yet when he talked with me alone he did not try to disguise the fact that we Jews could be exterminated totally. That was Hitler's goal, he said, and the only hope was to escape.

Day after day I thought about leaving under an assumed name. I trembled when I thought of what could happen if I fell into the clutches of the Germans—and the punishment I would receive. I was not so much afraid of getting shot—a bullet through the head would be a quick finish—but I dreaded the tortures and sufferings that might be inflicted upon me before I died. Yet staying in the ghetto seemed no better. All around me I saw things happening. Every day someone would be hunted down on the street and taken to the compulsory labor. If anyone ventured out to a neighboring village, or to the Aryan quarter to obtain food through barter, it was certain death. We heard that some adults were hanged and that some children were held by the feet and dashed against the trees until they died while their mothers had to stand by and witness the horror. No matter which way one looked at our situation, there seemed to be only one answer: Death!

Because of these rumors, I began to fear going out alone from the ghetto. So now, whenever I went to see the Krupka or the Babink families, it was in the evenings—and with Hugo Goldberg. I usually went ahead, as a scout—without my Jewish armband, of course. He followed at a little distance, and if I noticed anything alarming I would wave to him from behind as a signal to hide. It was a dangerous thing to do, but we had to eat.

There was also the problem of constructing a shelter, a hiding place where we could go in case of another akcja. The Germans already knew the usual hiding places: closets, attics, cellars, and storerooms. We had to devise something that they would not immediately discover. And where, if not underground? Deep in the earth. Many meetings were held by our neighbors, and the several families planned together how much space they needed to dig their "graves." Everyone had some suggestion to make and as each plan had some drawback, they could not decide. And the threat of another akcja hung in the air—it could descend upon us like a thunderbolt out of the sky, suddenly.

As our situation became more ominous, I began to come around by degrees to Hugo Goldberg's way of reasoning. I had to admit that there was but one possibility of surviving: to escape. Even my mother perceived that this was the only hope.

Through Goldberg I made the acquaintance of his friend from Warsaw, Simon Srebrnik, who now lived in Rohatyn. Srebrnik, a tall, blond, and blue-eyed man, did not look Jewish at all. He spoke Polish faultlessly, and he too dreamed of escaping from the ghetto. The three of us used to discuss various plans; we saw that an escape had to be made soon, before it became too late. The first step was to obtain documents. The latest passports we had were issued by the Russian authorities, and they were marked "Yevrey"—Russian for "Jew"—a damning brand that rendered the document useless. Besides, we would have to change our names. Here was where Goldberg's profession as chemist would be of help in forging the documents.

At last I decided to speak of our plans openly to my mother and sister. I told Rose that I would take her passport and have it changed, and that she should be prepared to escape. I realized that our mother would be satisfied if we could leave and survive; as for herself, she did not care if she could only see us saved . . . Rose was frightened, but she wanted to live; she gave Hugo her passport and so did I. He managed to concoct an ink eradicator that would leave no trace on the paper, and the blank spaces were to be filled in with different names. He also, with considerable effort, succeeded in finding a Pole who counterfeited documents and who was able to imitate the original handwriting perfectly. All this was done in the greatest secrecy; if we had been caught, it would have meant death for all. After a couple of days we received our passports back, and no one could have told that they had been tampered with. I had a new name, Maria Bandera, and I was now a Ukrainian.

But it was not enough to have forged passports. We had yet to solve another problem: Where to go? Where to escape? Who could help us in this escape? The only ones who might be able and willing to help were the Gentiles, but in helping us, they would be placing their own lives in danger. Discovery meant death for them and for us. And even if we succeeded in escaping, we still had to worry about how we would live, where we could locate. We thought about all this constantly, day and night, taxing our brains to the utmost. But, while we planned, the daily life in the ghetto continued to go on all around us. The Germans kept thinking up ways of complicating our existence, leaving us no peace. And still I would have to make trips to the Aryan side occasionally to barter for food and to listen for news. The people in town seemed to know more about what was going on than we in the ghetto; in fact, many of them worked for the Germans.

One day, while outside the ghetto at the Krupkas, Mrs. Krupka happened to mention that her husband was being transferred to a new and higher position in the town of Brody and that the whole family would move there. She said that she would try to give me something for the things I had brought to barter, and that she felt sorry that she would not be able to help me or my family any longer. The news came as a big shock to me, and tears sprang to my eyes. For a while I stood still, not being able to utter a word, but after a couple of minutes an idea came to my mind. Without hesitation, I asked if it would be possible for them to take me along. I was willing to do any kind of work; I could be a governess to their child, Janko, or even a simple servant. "You wouldn't need another servant," I said, "and you know me well enough to know you can trust me. I just want to get away and save my life."

Mrs. Krupka listened to me with tears in her eyes. Knowing how good-hearted she was, I realized that she was deeply moved, but she said that she would have to discuss this with her husband. And, she added, did I fully understand what danger this would mean to their family? Yes, indeed, I knew . . . and I also realized what danger threatened me if I went with them.

Meanwhile, Jews in the ghetto were called with greater frequency for compulsory labor—usually menial jobs calculated to humiliate us—cleaning offices, classrooms, toilets. Sometimes, when one brutal guard—Ukrainian—wanted to debase us further, he would tell us to clean the toilets with our hands, without a brush. We had to endure this in silence.

In addition to our worries about obtaining food supplies, fuel, and water, a new and important problem obsessed the inhabitants of the ghetto: where to hide from the threat of extermination? It seemed impossible to continue existing without a shelter of some kind, and all the other problems now appeared of lesser urgency. We finally gathered in the living room of a neighbor's apartment and began exchanging plans and suggestions. After a lengthy discussion, we decided to make the entrance to a shelter for the tenants of the building under a sofa in our bedroom. We took out a few planks of wood from the floor, nailed them together, and made a sort of handle on the underside, to permit grasping and locking of the cover from within the shelter. When the sofa was replaced over the opening, no one would be wiser—but, of course, this meant that we would have to engage the assistance of someone on the outside, someone we could trust implicitly. Most of the shelters in the ghetto were constructed in complete secrecy, because people were afraid to entrust their plans to anyone outside their most intimate circle. We thought about the problem for a long time, until we found someone who was satisfactory in this respect to all concerned. He was the son of Schachter, the butcher, and he lived in the house next to where we lived. All he would have to do would be to get across the broken-down fence to reach our house. We took him into our confidence, and he promised to help us.

All our neighbors pitched in to dig the hole under our house. The earth had to be carried at night to some spot far away, because traces of freshly excavated soil would have betrayed our secret to the Germans. All day long the digging went on behind locked doors, and when dusk fell the earth was carried out in pails or whatever utensils were at hand. We estimated the number of persons and the amount of space needed to accommodate them in our shelter—adding a little extra space for a small barrel of water and a place to store food.

After a fortnight the shelter was finished; it could give refuge, though in cramped quarters, to about fifteen people. We made a test drill and found out that not only did our shelter work, but that it would be difficult to discern the entrance to it under our sofa. We also decided that in the event of a real emergency, we would scatter everything in the room in great disorder to make it seem as if we had fled in haste, or had been taken away already by another party of bloodthirsty Germans.

Having this shelter, however flimsy, gave us at least some sense of security amidst the chaos.

4

The Second Akcja

WITH ALL OUR TROUBLES, we did not even realize that the holy days were approaching, and before we knew it Rosh Hashana, the Jewish New Year, was only a few days away. Several families in our house decided to gather in the home of a neighbor to say their prayers. We had no right to pray in public, and the synagogues were on the Aryan side of the city, besides being burned and in ruins.

All of us had but one prayer that day: that the New Year would bring a change for the better in our lives; that we could be delivered from our persecutors and murderers; that the war would end. When the prayers were finished, we exchanged personal wishes among our friends and relatives, but without the customary wine and refreshments. That did not matter now, as long as our wishes came true.

After Rosh Hashana, the weather became worse; the rainy days turned the streets into seas of mud. In our houses dampness penetrated everything. I had to go to the market square once again to barter some more of our dwindling possessions. Our greatest need was for wood, for we had to have a fire to cook our food and to heat our room. Fortunately, we could count on Hugo Goldberg to help. When I traded two tablecloths for some wood, he helped me to carry it home; he also gave Mamma some useful hints on how to use the wood most economically and how to get the most good out of our dwindling food supplies. It was delightfully amusing for me to watch these two master "cooks"—Mamma and Goldberg—concocting some mysterious potions in our kitchen.

After a week of enjoying some comparative relaxation, it was time to prepare for the great fast—Yom Kippur. On the eve of this holy day we again gathered for prayers at the neighbor's home. I am sure that these people prayed from the depths of their souls—but the time had not come for God to hear them.

Yom Kippur that year fell on September 21. The ghetto was quiet in the early morning. At about five o'clock, half asleep, we heard someone knocking on our window. Mamma was the first to jump out of bed to see who it was; to her surprise, she saw Hugo Goldberg's face through the window pane. As soon as he came in—wearing house slippers and a robe over his pajamas—we knew that something had happened. He said that the neighbors in his building had gone into hiding, hearing that the Gestapo had surrounded the city and that a new akcja was expected. No one else knew about it yet, but as soon as he learned of the rumor he had come to warn us.

We ran to alert our next-door neighbors, the Nemeths. Opening the door, Mrs. Nemeth heard me out, then began to cry woefully. She said that she had dreamed last night that her deceased father had come to tell them to hide because there would be an akcja. Cutting her remarks short, we urged her to get all the other neighbors together into our bedroom and to notify the butcher's son. We moved the sofa aside and uncovered the little door leading to our hiding place. There were fifteen of us by the time the last person squeezed in, packed together as tightly as herrings in a barrel. As soon as we were packed into this hole, the helpful neighbor moved the sofa back against the wall and left, leaving the door open so that the Germans would think that we had fled from the house into the street. After that, he went to his own house to hide. Because Hugo Goldberg lived at the other end of the ghetto, we feared that he would not have time to go back, and so he remained with us.

We lay there in the crowded darkness, not knowing whether this was a false alarm or the real thing. Several times already we had sought shelter, only to learn later that the rumors were untrue. Even now, we hoped against hope—but in a short while we began to hear cries and shooting, and the shouts of the Germans. The Gestapo had arrived! They yelled, "*Juden, heraus!*" We could hear their heavy booted footsteps. We tried to hold our breath, though we shook with fear, half-dead in our tomblike refuge.

Then, with a crash that came from the house next door to ours, we heard terrible lamentations from the people who were being dragged out of the neighboring shelter. There was only a thin wall of bricks between them and us. They were discovered, and now it might be our turn. We heard the tramp of soldiers' boots coming very close. In our panic, we covered our mouths so as not to cry out, not to breathe heavily. Some dogs were growling nearby—those dreaded police dogs! And then, more shouts: *"Juden, heraus! Verfluchte Juden!"*

No one in our shelter dared to move, knowing that the end was coming closer. We could hear more people speaking Ukrainian in the room above us—they were moving things around in the kitchen—and it sounded as if they were removing the floor boards. Soon they would find the entrance to our hiding place . . .

Then a young voice cried out, "We've found a shelter full of Jews—there are about seventy of them inside. We need help to drag them out in the open."

A miracle! The Germans left. We heard the dogs, their growling sounding always further away, until all was quiet again. But we were still afraid to move. We didn't know whether we had managed to escape the hunt for long. No one said a word yet, but with a squeeze of the hand we tried to convey the feeling of relief. And there we remained, lying in the cellar side by side, the whole day and night of Yom Kippur, and even past dusk the following day, without light, without a morsel of food, without a drop of water.

The morning of the next day, the neighbor who had locked us in—and who had managed to escape himself—came and spoke to us in Yiddish. "Come out! It's all over!" We did not answer at once, fearing a trap, but when our neighbor started calling each one of us by name, we recognized his voice and called back to him to remove the sofa and let us out.

One by one we emerged from the shelter. Our appearance cannot be described, but can be imagined. The apartment looked as though a revolution had turned it upside down. Some floorboards in the kitchen had been ripped up. Only one item of food was in sight: a jar of pickles left on a stool. We flung ourselves on those pickles like wild animals and ate until there was nothing left in the jar. What a sight we must have been: dirty, emaciated, unkempt, wet from urine and excrement!

An ominous silence reigned in the ghetto. This time, the Germans did not do much shooting—bullets were too valuable—and they did not throw their Jewish victims into the pits outside the city. The Jews were loaded into freight cars and taken to Belzec where the infamous gas ovens were. The ghetto had been decimated, but at least we—thanks to Hugo Goldberg's coming in time to let us know—had survived.

And again, our first thought was to find out whether any of our relatives were still alive. I ran to Shloma Handschau's house; he had taken refuge in a village with his older son, Nuchem. My mother's younger sister, my aunt Sara, had been looking after his younger boy, Yudah. God help her! She was taken, along with the eighteen-month-old baby, in the transport to Belzec. I learned later that most of the people from the ghetto were packed so tightly into the box cars that many did not arrive alive at their destination.

We—Mamma, Rose and I—were saved again . . . but for how long? There were only several hundred Jews left in the ghetto. Now we knew that any day could bring a complete liquidation. We had no illusions about the 100 percent probability—indeed the certainty—of our death. I had to take the only chance possible: escape from the ghetto.

And so we got together one day, Goldberg, Srebrnik, and I, to discuss our plans of escape very seriously and to make a final decision. Srebrnik had formed a new acquaintance with a young Polish fellow, Kowalski, the son of a Polish official, who promised to get him out of the ghetto to Lvov, from where he could include him in a transport to Dnepropetrovsk in Russia in the guise of a laborer. The idea seemed good. They agreed, and in a few days Kowalski was to meet Srebrnik in the ghetto. He kept his promise and came to pick him up. Srebrnik took leave of us sadly, but promised to let us know if and when he arrived safely. Before their departure, Kowalski promised Hugo Goldberg that he would help him escape to the same place, and if I wished it, he would help me too. At Dnepropetrovsk was a Gentile work camp for craftsmen and workers of various trades. Obviously, I could not go there, but Kowalski said that he would try to locate me someplace in Lvov, and he gave me his address there.

Goldberg arranged for the payment of a rather large sum—he would have paid any price asked. I still had hopes that Mr. Krupka would take me along with his family to the town of Brody when he relocated there, but if not I would leave with the help of Kowalski. I would sell my mother's jewelry that was left, everything I could turn into cash, to raise the necessary amount. Slowly I began to put aside the things that I would take with me when I escaped.

In the meantime, we heard that in many small towns the ghettos were being liquidated and made *Judenfrei*—free of Jews. The ghetto in Rohatyn could expect the same fate. I called on the attorney Babink frequently; he promised me that when Mr. Krupka came to remove his furniture to Brody, he would let me know and would try to induce Mr. Krupka to take me, too. But the main thing was for me to have a passport showing that I was a Catholic.

True, I had a forged passport, but I didn't like the name of Maria Bandera, which had been entered on the passport without consulting me. Bandera was the leader of the Ukrainian Nationalists, who called themselves the Banderas; and I thought that if I got caught with a false passport that gave my name as Bandera, it might lead the Germans to think that I was in some way related to him. I spoke and could write Ukrainian perfectly, but there might be times when it would be safer to pass as a Pole. I began scheming how I could get still another forged passport, as a double precaution; if I got caught under one name, I might be able to escape under the other.

Fate took a hand in solving my problem. One day, returning with a couple of girls from work, I met a Polish woman who at one time had been a servant in the household of a family I knew very well. She recognized me at once and greeted me with a big smile, saying how glad she was that I was still alive. I let the other girls go on home and stopped to talk with her. She told me how sorry she was about the troubles the Jewish people had. She did not live in town now, but worked as a servant for a village priest in nearby Ruby. She only happened to be in Rohatyn that day on an errand. When I heard her express sympathy for my people, I immediately thought of an idea, and feeling confident that she would not betray me, I asked if she could possibly obtain for me a birth or baptismal certificate from the church archives. I would pay for it; it could be in my name, as long as the date and description fitted me. With such a document in my possession I could leave Rohatyn.

She pondered this a while and said, "If you wish, I can give you my own birth certificate. I don't have it with me, of course, but I'll tell the priest I need it and he will give it to me. So, after that your name will be Hanka Buczek—my name. Actually, I am much older than you, but that doesn't matter. You will put on a peasant skirt and shawl and no one will recognize you."

I wept for joy and gratitude, and the tender-hearted woman wept with me. We said goodbye and agreed to meet again in a few days; she promised to take care of everything. I went straight home from that chance meeting and burst into the house like dynamite. Hugo Goldberg was in our apartment, waiting. I blurted out my big news right away. Mother did not quite believe that the Buczek woman would keep her promise, but I remembered the honest expression on the peasant woman's face and believed that she would come back.

I hardly knew how I managed to live during the next few days—I didn't dare believe my luck! There were preparations to be made quickly; things to be packed, things to be sold. When I thought of having to part with my dearest ones, my heart was heavy. No one could say whether I would ever return, or whether we would ever meet again in this life. I could think of nothing else. I wanted so much to get away, and yet I feared I could collapse completely at the moment of parting.

I waited impatiently for the day when I would meet Hanka Buczek again, and when the time came I went to the appointed place with a beating heart. From a distance I saw her standing in a corner behind a house. "Hanka!" I called out, forgetting myself. She waved to me and grinned. I knew then that she must have had the certificate for me. In silence, like two thieves, we embraced. She handed me the birth certificate and I passed her the money. She wished me luck, but begged me not to reveal that it was she who gave me the certificate. If her complicity in the transaction were disclosed, she would pay for it with her life. I promised her the secret would be safe with me. Her good wishes echoed in my ears as I turned to go home.

I felt so rich now! To have two forged documents in those days was more than any fortune; one I would use as a passport, and the other I would sew into the lining of my coat to use in some emergency. But when I thought that I might get caught having two forged documents in my possession, shivers went up and down my spine. I tried not to dwell on the possibility, for if I did I wouldn't be able to make even one step. I prayed that God would give me strength and courage.

When I arrived home, I took out the birth certificate and kissed it before showing it to my mother and Rose. Now, Mamma and Rose, too, fully realized that I was not joking when I spoke of leaving Rohatyn. I could see the pain written in their faces, and I felt it too in my heart, but I tried to hide it from them, pretending that I was not doing anything unusual.

But my personal plans did not alter the circumstances in which we lived. With each day life in the ghetto became harder to endure. The Germans kept transferring the last remaining Jews from outlying villages and towns to Rohatyn. With lack of supplies and sanitary conditions, an epidemic of typhus broke out.

The following incident can serve as an example of life in the ghetto: One day a young Ukrainian woman came to our house. We knew her and admired her courage in entering the forbidden limits of the ghetto. She repeated rumors that we had been hearing from various people—that there would be another akcja soon and that everything, absolutely everything, would be taken away from the Jews. She said that she felt very sorry for us, for even if we managed to survive the akcja we would no longer have anything to exchange for food and other necessities. We looked at each other sadly, and at last Mamma ventured to ask her if she would be so kind as to keep some of our belongings; our clothes, table linens, the remainder of Rose's beautiful handmade nightgowns and slips from her dowry. Mamma naively complimented the girl, saying how smart she was and how worthy of confidence, and if she would agree to keep those things for us just until the danger passed, she would be rewarded for it. Her house, though of course it was in the Gentile quarter, was not too far from ours, and it would not be much trouble to carry the things over—everything was packed, in readiness for an emergency. The young woman agreed immediately and assured us that she would be more than glad to help us. She certainly did! We arranged that as soon as it got dark we would bring everything over to her house. My mother thanked her with tears in her eyes, and the girl went home.

Now we closed the door against possible intruders, and started choosing the best items that we still owned, the items we had been saving for barter. At last we had two large suitcases full, and when it grew dark Rose and I carried them over to her house. Going along the streets we felt a strange tenseness; surely, we thought, this night would bring on the expected raid. No one noticed us, thank God, and we didn't get caught. We left the suitcases, blessed and thanked the Ukrainian woman, and ran home, feeling quite satisfied with our accomplishment.

After a few quiet days, Mamma said that I should go to the house of that young woman and bring back some or all of our belongings. We should, she thought, be able to exchange some items for food before another storm came. When I went there and knocked on her door, however, her mother answered and stood blocking the entrance, her dog barking savagely. She denied knowing anything about our clothes, or her daughter hiding them, and claimed that her daughter was not home. I could hear her voice from somewhere in the rear of the house, but had no choice but to leave without saying a word. A couple of days later I tried again. This time I took Mamma with me, and we succeeded in seeing the young woman. She told us that they had been robbed and that our things had been stolen from the attic where she hid them. Everything was gone, she said, and we should not come back—for our visits might endanger their lives.

Mamma took this so hard she started to cry. At that moment the husband of the young woman entered the room, but my mother's tears had no effect upon either of them. The young woman persisted in her lies, and her husband and her parents backed her up in silence. We were even afraid to say too much, for she might call the police. We left brokenhearted and disillusioned. Sometime later, we saw the young woman wearing some of our clothes—I even saw her using my wallet, with my initials on it—yet there was nothing I could do, for we had no rights at all.

As decided, I resumed my preparations for departure with increased diligence and speed. Meanwhile, Mr. Kowalski kept his promise. After the departure of Simon Srebrnik was successful, Kowalski came to set the date with Hugo and to send him to the same place, to Dnepropetrovsk. The date was set for November 19. He also promised to find a place for me in Lvov until then and I would follow after Hugo. So far we were satisfied, and we looked forward to these promises. Everything had to be kept in the greatest secrecy, for if not, we would be dead before any move could be made.

A couple of days later, I came home with my friend Klara Altman. My mother told me that Babink, the attorney, had been to see me. He had taken a big risk to enter the ghetto, but he had come to let me know that if I wanted to leave I should not wait, because the ghetto would be enclosed with barbed wire and wooden walls at the beginning of December; escape would be impossible from then on. He said that the news about closing of the ghetto was still a big secret, and that if anything leaked out it would endanger his life; we must never mention his name to anyone. However, as he had promised me, he had persuaded Mr. Krupka to take me! Krupka would be in Rohatyn on November 20, and he had agreed to take me along with his furniture to Brody. Babink also said I should bring my valise to his house and that he would take care of it.

The news of being able to leave the ghetto made me glad, for it was what I wanted. But the other news—that the ghetto would be sealed off—was a big shock to all of us. This meant certain death for its inhabitants. We looked at each other in heavy silence. We dared not speak of what was in our minds. I realized now that I couldn't even be a help to my family; first of all, because when the Krupkas moved away from Rohatyn I had lost an important source of aid, and secondly, because I would no longer be able to go out of the ghetto to the Aryan side of town. If I stayed, I lost all my chances of helping Mamma and Rose. There might yet be a chance, a light of promise in the darkness, but that could only come from the Aryan side. There was no time to lose.

Klara soon left. Mamma and Rose were watching me gather up my last few belongings, only the most necessary things, and they helped me pack a valise. They were not able to hold back their tears, nor was I. We could not believe that at last the day would come when we had to say goodbye—maybe for forever. I looked over for the last time my albums, letters, photographs of my family and my young friends with whom I had spent so many happy and interesting years. I gave those treasures to Mamma for safekeeping, asking her to hide them well in case of robbery or raids. She said that she would put everything into a large metal box and hide it in the shelter. We did all this with the doors shut tight and locked; my escape was to be a deep secret.

The following evening I took my valise to the attorney's house, thanked them, and said goodbye. As for the feelings in my own house, I cannot attempt to describe them—one has to imagine. They might best be called our private Yom Kippur—a day of profound sorrow. It was a tragic parting, especially for my mother. Instead of living to see the day when both her daughters would be happily married, she saw one of them departing from home—without any certainty that she might not be killed during her escape—and the other, though she remained at home, certain to fall victim to the cruel persecutors of our people. Was it for this that our mother had raised us and sacrificed her life? All her plans, all her efforts, seemed only a waste.

By a bitter irony, the appointed day of my departure, November 20, was also my birthday. I so wanted to stay with my family on this day, but it was impossible. . . . I had to part from my dear ones on my birthday. Mother had not been able to sleep at all or eat for the last several days; she seemed to be losing all interest in life. Rose wept openly, begging me, "Please, don't go! Please. You will be caught. Who knows how they may punish you? Mamma will not live through this. It will be worse for her to have you go . . . worse than a bullet."

I joined her in sorrow, weeping bitter tears. I knew very well that what she said was true. I saw how our home would be empty without me—I had a vivid picture of it. It was I who had sustained their courage, their hope; it was I who helped them to go on. I had done whatever I could to protect them and to keep them safe from all dangers. Leaving meant taking away everything with me, almost their very lives. Though I would be physically away from home, however, my heart and soul would always remain with them. This too they knew very well.

And yet there was no power that could keep me from leaving. I said, "Rose, please, now listen to me. Get ready to leave, too. You have your passport, you have some money. It will be much easier for Mamma to know that we at least could be saved; much easier than to be forced to witness her daughters' deaths—or even worse, torture. Go, before it is too late!" But my sweet sister still refused to leave.

At last Mamma couldn't take any more of it and interrupted us. "Don't talk about it anymore, please. Do what you must, though I feel I'd rather die than part with you."

I felt that my heart was breaking, too. My only consolation was the thought that if only I could succeed in reaching my destination, I would perhaps be able to help my loved ones. I went once again to the Aryan section and attempted to sell some of our few remaining possessions for goods with which I could provide Mamma and Rose for some time, at least. I was especially anxious to leave them enough food to last for as long as possible, because I knew that after I was gone they would not be able to provide for themselves as I had done, all the more so after the ghetto was closed. As we already knew, this would take place very soon.

It was while returning to the ghetto one day that I found three children wandering around without anyone to look after them. They were lost from a transport of evacuees and had walked some twenty kilometers from the town of Bursztyn. There were two little boys, aged nine and four, and their sister, who was about seven—all ragged, dirty, cold, and hungry—going from door to door, begging. They told me that their parents had been killed and that they had no one left in the world. What could I do but bring them home with me? Knowing Rose's fondness for strays, and counting on Mamma's kind heart, I knew that they'd be welcome. They slept on an extra bed in the kitchen the first night. In the morning, we held a family council and decided that because I would be leaving in a few days, these children should stay and have my place. I realized, of course, that it would mean extra mouths to feed—but on the other hand, I felt that it would make the parting easier to some degree, if Mother and Rose had someone special to care for and to divert their thoughts from me. I never learned what became of them afterward . . .

On November 18, Mr. Kowalski arrived from Lvov. He came to the ghetto and told Hugo to be ready to leave the following day. We trusted him. Kowalski, the young son of a Polish treasury official, was considered quite smart; he had many contacts, which enabled him to smuggle people out of the town. The most important thing was for Hugo to reach Lvov without running into inspections on the way. It was dangerous, because the train from Rohatyn to Lvov made several stops, and at each station as well as in the train itself the authorities—Gestapo and Ukrainian police—made checks of personal documents. They were always looking for Jews.

As arranged, the next day Kowalski came to our house, and we three went in the direction of the railway station. It was not wise to be seen together lest someone suspect us of going away, and so I said goodbye to them in front of the courthouse. Hugo promised that as soon as he reached Lvov he would write to the Krupka family at Brody and that I'd find his letter waiting for me there. Saying goodbye, he added, "Happy birthday, Sheva, and many more which I want to share with you. Wait for me until I return after the war."

I did not have time to ponder his words, because things were happening so fast. The next day I too would leave.

All night long I cried, my pillow wet with tears. It was so hard to part from those with whom I lived all my life. It was hard to say farewell to the beautiful years of my youth. Not many people I had known were still alive, but at least the streets of the town were there to remind me of them or of something we had mutually known. I had happy moments to remember in my native town; joyful, dear moments. And how could I say farewell to my dear mother, whose whole life was devoted to her children? My sister, too, who had cared more for me than she had for herself. Oh, that I could fall asleep and wake up several days older, when that dreadful moment of parting would already be in the past!

Monday, November 20—my birthday! I was to leave at midnight. It was a long, dreary day. I'll never be able to erase it from my memory. Mamma made some pancakes for me from a coarse, dark flour, because she had no bread. She wanted me to have something to take along on my way. She stood by the kitchen stove, weeping. Sometimes a complaint escaped from her heart: "Why is God punishing me thus?" We put our arms around each other and wept together, we three. The little children, the waifs we had taken in, stood in a corner, watching us fearfully. They knew what tears meant.

Dusk was falling. Only a few more hours and I'd be gone. I went from corner to corner, trying to imprint everything on my memory—each piece of furniture, everything—in my mind forever. And when I turned around, I saw the pale, tear-stained face of Rose, and my mother's suffering eyes, and I could not say a word.

Mamma kept looking at me, repeating that she could not believe that such a great change could occur in our lives. She talked, we listened. She recounted how, as a young widow after our father was killed in World War I—I was three months old, my sister four years—she had managed to run our shoe store by herself. Later, we used to stop in on our way from school; she'd close the shop at noon to give us lunch. She told us how proud she was at the school conferences with our teachers, hearing that we had done well, and how she had always tried to give us everything. She wanted us not to feel too keenly the loss of our father. How happy she was to see us develop into lovely young ladies! Then, she began to dream of making good matches for us; when we'd be happily married, she could rest and take pleasure in the knowledge that she had brought us up properly, unaided. Life would be peaceful, and full of joy.

But then, breaking off her reverie and assuming a practical manner, Mamma gave me a package containing the pancakes. She also gave me another package, rather heavy, and said, "Take this, dear Shevele. This will be a souvenir from me and your father."

With shaking fingers I opened the second package. There was my father's gold watch, Mamma's gold necklace, a watch on a solid gold chain, and the rings and the necklace and earrings set with pear-shaped diamonds that she used to put on for the big holidays. Slowly, she removed from her hand the wedding ring and added it to the items in the package. I could not control my tears then. I thrust the valuables back into her hands; I did not want to deprive her of these costly things that held so many precious memories. But Mamma argued that the war was far from ended and that I would certainly need the gold to get me out of many a tight spot in my wanderings.

"You will be able to sell some of these things," she insisted. "We won't need anything here. Here it will fall into the hands of the Gestapo, and their wives will wear my jewelry. Why should we give them our jewelry in addition to all else?"

"But, Mamma—" I protested, still unconvinced. "You can sell these things and get some food. Or you can hide them away until after the war. You'll be able to enjoy them again yourself, someday."

Mamma shook her head. "I always thought you were so marvelously smart, Sheva, but you can't seem to understand that we won't need these things here. You have the world before you, if you attain your goal and survive the war. You will be able to make use of them. Just one thing I ask of you: do not forget what happened to us and to all our people." She began to cry again, softly. "Oh, why did I have to live to see this hour?" Then my mother lifted up her hands in blessing, and prayed: "Oh, God, protect and watch over my child. Let her survive. Let her be allowed to tell the world how we have been persecuted without just cause . . . And Laizor, my dear husband, please . . . I did as much as I could . . . Now, if you are close to God, help her, because it is not up to me or to any of us. You remember—this is the day she was born—and now this is the day I have to lose her!"

I felt that if I listened to Mamma any longer, I would waver—perhaps I would crack up and never be able to go. I could not hesitate any longer. I put on my high felt boots, a brown sport coat, and a heavy, woolen hood. It was time to leave. As solemn and as moving as this moment was—the most tragic moment in my life—I knew that everything had to be done quickly. There was so much more that I wanted to say, had to say, but the words choked up in my throat. I kissed my sister and reminded her to flee before it was too late. Then I kissed and hugged my mother. Weeping bitterly, she repeated, "Don't ever forget . . ." Those were her last words to me.

Very quietly, so that no one should hear me, I left the house to keep my midnight appointment. Once outside, I began to walk straight ahead, looking around more than once to see Mamma and Rose silhouetted against the window. They waved to me until at last we could see each other no longer.

Now I would begin a new life as a Gentile girl. Though the real Hanka Buczek, whose birth certificate was in my pocket, was very much alive in the nearby village of Ruby, for all official purposes I was—indeed, had to be—Hanka, a servant girl. Sheva Weiler had ceased to exist in Rohatyn.

There remained only her footprints in the snow . . .

5

A Counterfeit Life

NOW I BEGAN TO RUN FASTER AND FASTER. I had a long way to go. Already I had passed the ghetto and was near the post office. I looked around to see if anyone was near, but the street was empty and still. My heart began to pound wildly. I could hardly believe that I had actually taken this step . . . Now I was near the monastery, where we had agreed to meet. In the distance I saw a truck—it was waiting for me. A wave of relief flooded my heart and I hastened in that direction.

Mr. Krupka stood alongside the truck. In front, next to the driver, was Krupka's mother, and in the truck was a pile of furniture. He helped me onto the truck and told me to hide inside a wardrobe. That would be safer, in the event of an inspection on the road.

No one said much. I was unhappily thinking about the last moments before my departure. The Krupkas were filled with apprehension; they were risking their lives for me. The truck had to go slowly through the heavy snowdrifts that had frozen into an icy armor plate. Sometimes I could hear dogs barking. It made me shiver, remembering the growling dogs in our house, when we lay hidden in our underground shelter. I wondered if I should regard myself as a heroine or as a coward. Maybe I did a heroic thing when I dared to escape, not knowing what the next day, even the next moment, would bring. But because I feared death, I suppose I was a coward . . .

The long minutes passed. From time to time I looked out of my hiding place in the wardrobe. The bare outlines of trees cast shadows on the road.

The low huts were weighed down under their snowy coverlets. Nature seemed so deceptively clean and innocent.

It was a very long night. I wanted to sleep so badly, but could not. The cold kept me awake. I sat huddled and shivering in the wardrobe. Everything that happened seemed fantastic, unreal. I held on to one saving thought: the hope that someday I would be able to return and find someone here alive. I recalled the words of my aunt's little grandson, who had been only five: "Why did they take away my Mama and Granny and Grandpa and Chaimek? Why don't they let us live in peace? I'm hungry—why can't I eat?" Now I began to ask similarly childish questions: Why do I have to sit in this freezing weather, in a wardrobe on a truck, going to an unpredictable fate? I visualized my mother and Rosie lying awake in bed; or perhaps they were sitting huddled near the stove, brokenhearted, unable to accept the thought of losing me. But these questions that tormented me had only one answer: Because you are Jewish! Hitler hates the Jews.

This, then, was the start of my first journey as a homeless wanderer. Occasionally the truck was stopped by Gestapo guards who wanted to see the papers of the driver and the passengers. When I heard the guards I closed the door to the wardrobe, and my heart contracted with fear. But I can imagine how Mr. Krupka and his mother must have felt, nervous and tense at each such inspection. However, we kept on going. It was lucky for me that the guards did not inspect the furniture on the truck! All night long we rattled through Lvov and other, smaller towns. It was almost daybreak when we reached Brody.

The apartment assigned to the Krupka family was located upstairs in a house facing the marketplace; below it was a restaurant. They occupied three rooms and a kitchen. We were glad that we had made the trip without any serious incidents, but after a night spent in a cramped position on the truck I could hardly get down and walk. When I entered the cold and empty apartment, I was seized with a strange fear. I must have been running a temperature, for I was shaking with the chills. It was so quiet here, as in a graveyard. There was no furniture; the windows had some broken panes. It was cold and damp, not having been heated for a long time. No doubt a Jewish family had lived here once; now the place was filled with ghosts.

But this was no time for sentiment. We had to start getting the rooms in order. Soon after our arrival, Mrs. Krupka came with their little boy, Janko. She prepared breakfast for us and it warmed us, giving us the energy to tackle necessary chores. I ate but little. I felt sore all over and my head ached terribly, but I said nothing.

It all seemed like a strange dream. I had to get used to my new name, Hanka Buczek. They called me Hania. Yes, "Hania" was here and she mechanically responded, but Sheva remained in Rohatyn . . .

The first night I slept alone in the apartment; indeed, in the whole house. The Krupkas went to sleep at their friends' house. I'm not ashamed to admit I was afraid. In every corner I saw the unforgettable scenes projected by memory and imagination—the shootings, the beatings, the tortures. Though I desperately wanted to sleep, these visions gave me no rest. Lying there on a cot, fear gripping my heart, I covered my head with a shawl. Even though I nearly suffocated, I was afraid to remove it. I imagined I heard cries and weeping in the corners of the rooms. I could see the Gestapo herding the former unfortunate occupants of this house out of their quarters. Oh, how I wished I could find rest in my mother's arms. But Mamma was far away, and all I had was the small packet she had given me. This I pressed close, for I felt it was my hope to get Mamma and Rose out of the ghetto, too. Even in misfortune, a human being has to have hope to give him courage. My God, I thought, if You have not turned away Your face from us completely, if You have not forgotten us, help me—so I shall not die of fear! My body was on fire, yet chills shook me. I began to feel the pangs of hunger, but the idea of food repelled me. Though the broken windowpanes were stuffed with rags, an icy wind whistled through the rooms. My head hurt terribly. Vaguely, I remembered the pancakes that Mamma had given me—they must be here somewhere, for I hadn't touched them on the road. I thought I'd eat one now, if only because it had been the last meal prepared for me by my mother. But I was afraid to get out of the cot.

I could hardly wait for the dawn. I got up and dressed. The wood had to be brought in from the storeroom, and the coal from the cellar. Today, years later, I wonder where I got the courage to go down into the cellar in that empty house . . . But I knew that I had to start fires in all the stoves to heat the apartment. I had to heat water for washing the floors. I did all this and never knew I was running a high temperature, but I felt my knees giving way under me and there was a humming in my brain. When someone spoke to me I heard but faintly. I did not want to complain, but finally Mrs. Krupka realized that something was wrong with me.

She said, "Hania, I think you have a fever." But I wouldn't give in. I claimed that it was cold in the house and I was still under the shock of leaving my family. Although I felt I could hardly stand on my legs, I assured her that I would get over it, and tried to keep on working as best I could.

Meanwhile, the glazier came and installed windowpanes in the apartment, and it soon became warmer and more livable. At least now the heat from the stoves was not wasted. And in the evening a new acquaintance of the Krupkas came to visit, the woman from whom they rented a room temporarily. She was a tall, energetic Ukrainian woman. The superintendent helped move the furniture from place to place, while the woman stood by ready with her advice as to the arrangement of things.

Little Janko dashed from room to room, and we constantly had to remind him to keep out of everyone's way. There was so much commotion in the apartment that it hummed like a beehive. Throughout all this, I became aware that others were observing me—and apparently they were not pleased with what they saw. I must have looked as sick as I felt. But everyone was so busy that nothing was said, except once in a while Mrs. Krupka would ask, "Hania, what is the matter with you?"

Still I pretended not to hear her anxious voice. I kept thinking: What a helper they acquired when they took me along with them! Sometimes I felt like I would fall in a faint, and to avoid this I kept drinking water and splashing the cold water on my face in an effort to stay conscious. When evening came I went to bed after supper. My body shook with the fever and I did not close my eyes all night.

The following day I again tried to be a big hero, but when Mrs. Krupka found a thermometer among the things she was unpacking she came to me and said in a whisper, "Hania, I am certain that you have a fever." When she placed her hand on my forehead she screamed, "God help us! Your head is hot as fire!" She insisted on taking my temperature. At first she could not believe her eyes, so she let her mother-in-law look at the thermometer. She also exclaimed in alarm, "Dear God, what a high temperature!"

I felt near fainting. Now I realized the seriousness of my condition, yet I was not pleased when they insisted that I go to bed. Both women were wringing their hands, and as if in a dream I heard them saying, "What are we going to do?" The elder Mrs. Krupka went to the kitchen and returned with a glass of tea and some aspirin. By this time I was unable to hold the glass in my hands. I only groaned and moaned piteously, like a weak kitten. I heard the younger Mrs. Krupka weeping at my bedside, but I could see her only as through a fog. Then she sat on the edge of my sofa bed and gave me the tea by the spoonful, raising my pillow so that I could swallow the aspirin. But instead of tea I asked weakly, with a voice that was hardly audible, for water . . . water . . .

In the meantime someone else had entered the room and I heard furniture being moved around. Each movement, each noise seemed to drill holes in my head. From time to time Janko looked in, but they always chased him away. When Mr. Krupka came home and heard this latest piece of news, he came into my room and stood with his wife at my bedside, looking uncertain as to what to do with me. Hanka Buczek had become a real problem for the Krupka family right from the very beginning of her stay.

After they left me they must have discussed my illness at length, for afterwards whenever they passed my open door I could see their sad and worried faces. Of course, they had reason to be anxious. Neither the tea nor the aspirin helped me. I could hold no food or liquid in my stomach, and my temperature started rising higher and higher. I suffered agony, because I could not get even a little water to cool my burning lips.

In the morning when they came to my room I noticed that they were very upset. Instead of getting better, I became worse. After a few days without showing any change, Mr. Krupka held a long conference with his wife and mother in the adjoining room. I could not hear too much, even though the door was open, but I knew they were talking about my sickness. I saw everything as though through a fog, for my eyesight was weakening more and more, and I felt that without food or sleep my heart would give way—it would stop beating any minute.

Then Mrs. Krupka came into my room, sat down on the edge of my bed, and, crying, said, "Hania, Hania, only God knows what we should do! I pray constantly, but I see your health remains the same. We'd be willing to take you to the hospital, but sometimes you are delirious. When you are half-asleep you talk aloud in Yiddish and Polish, calling to your mother and Rose, and crying out to the Gestapo not to kill them. You even relive the akcjas. My husband would gladly call a physician, but he fears that you may babble something. That would be your—and our—end . . ." Mrs. Krupka fell on her knees at my bedside, and, weeping, prayed to God that He should help and give the right advice, because now it was up to Him. I understood and tears started welling up in my eyes, but I was too weak to cry. Thus days and nights went on, and there was no change.

The elder Mrs. Krupka suggested that cupping would be sure to help me. They would reduce my fever. But the problem was: who would set the cups? A barber, they thought, could do the cupping, but it would have to be someone who would not guess that I was Jewish. Finally, they decided to get the Jewish barber from the ghetto. Mr. Krupka already had made some acquaintances among the people in the Brody ghetto, though I don't know how he managed to do it, and the following day they engaged a barber who did cupping. As the ghetto in Brody was not sealed off, the man could leave—especially as his errand had to do with Mr. Krupka, who had contacts with the higher authorities and would be responsible for him. No doubt the barber was promised food supplies in return for his services.

When the Jewish barber came, I had to sit up in bed for the cupping operation, but I was so weak that Mrs. Krupka had to hold me up. The skin on my whole body was covered with a rash and was so rough and splotchy that I looked leprous. He set about forty cups, small cups of blown glass placed on the body to create a partial vacuum, thus drawing blood to the spot. There are two types: dry cupping, and cupping with incisions to make the blood run freely. Each time the barber hit the cups, I groaned aloud. He had to try a few times, for I was nothing but skin and bones.

After a while I felt him take the cups away. My back felt like a huge, red wound. I tried to let myself down on the bed, but I could only lie on my side. I heard Mrs. Krupka say to the barber that she would give him bread and other food if he'd follow her into the kitchen. He sounded very grateful. She paid him too, and he left.

My condition did not improve despite the cupping. In the evening Mr. Krupka talked a long time with his wife and mother in the other room. I heard Janko putting in his endless questions from time to time, until they sent him to bed with a last warning not to go near my room.

When Mr. Krupka came home for dinner the next day, I noticed that they ate hardly anything—for the food that they brought into the dining room went back to the kitchen. They were very upset and worried. Later, the same barber returned, this time to apply leeches. When he started to apply the leeches to my head behind my ears, both women looked on—even Janko watched, his eyes popping with curiosity, incessantly asking questions. The senior Mrs. Krupka said, "Now Hania will get well. She will be able soon to take Janko for a walk, or go sledding with him." Stroking the child's head, she tried to comfort him.

But after a couple of days it was evident that even the leeching did not help. I kept constantly talking in my delirium, both in Yiddish and in Polish, so they tried to prevent anybody from coming to see me. In my dreamy thoughts I prayed to God and to my mother. I asked my mother to help me get well. I recalled her last words, "If you survive, remember what has happened to us. Don't ever forget, Sheva!" So, I begged my mother to help me now. Mrs. Krupka tended me tenderly, as though I were her own sister. Many times she got up in the middle of the night; she prayed at my bedside and shed many tears. My illness was too protracted and until now nothing had helped. Three weeks passed by, and when they saw that I was dying, they decided to call two doctors in for a consultation. The two came—one was from Brody and the other originally from Berlin—they talked in German, not knowing that I understood the language. When Mr. Krupka asked the doctors, in German, what decision they had reached, they said, "She has typhus. If her fever does not drop during the night, she will surely die tomorrow. Already she is like a skeleton, and she wouldn't be able to resist any longer."

I heard their words as in a dream, but when the meaning penetrated my consciousness, I screamed in Ukrainian: "Help me! I don't want to die! I want to live!" And then I fainted.

I remained in that state for some time, but when I opened my eyes I saw them all standing around my bed, looking very worried. My whole body was wet with vinegar and water, with which they had tried to bring me around again. My mind was confused; I looked from one to the other, wondering what had happened, forgetting who these people were and why they were standing around me.

"You fainted," Mrs. Krupka said. "Maybe that was good—maybe a miracle will happen."

Something like a miracle did happen. My desire to live was so strong that after I regained consciousness my temperature dropped suddenly. And after a few days, it was completely normal. And so, after four long weeks of nearly hopeless illness, I began to believe that I would be well again. Though I had to remain in bed for still some time, there was a definite improvement. I was brought my meals, and waited on, so that I could hardly believe that such good people still existed in such an evil world, in such harrowing times. And now I was able to leave my bed, though I could not stand up for long. And slowly, weakness was replaced by a new strength, new hope.

As I regained my health more completely, I tried to be of service to the Krupka family, to show them my gratitude. We were now three "housekeepers" under the same roof, but for the really heavy work—laundering, washing of the windows and floors—a woman came in by the day. For the time being, Janko was mainly under his grandmother's care. I could tell from the elderly lady's expression that she admired her son and daughter-in-law for shielding me. Oftentimes, when they weren't at home, she would ask me, discreetly, whether—when I regained my complete health, and if the war continued—I would be satisfied with such a menial life. She'd also question me pointedly as to whether I fully realized what danger threatened her children.

"I know, I know," I assured her. "I can read the headlines, and I listen to the radio, so I know . . ." I sighed and did not want to say too much on this subject. Sometimes I felt like a parasite, utterly superfluous—in a word, expendable. With all my strength I tried to recover; I forced myself to eat, for it was most important to get well. In the event that I'd have to plan another escape, I must have health and energy. I told myself, *Sheva, don't give up! Don't lose courage! Hold on . . . Someday you will reach your life's goal, freedom!*

Though my morale was good, physically I had been weakened by the attack of typhus. It left me with running sores on my legs. The same sores that Hugo Goldberg had once helped to heal now returned and spread to my hands. At first, it was only a rash between the fingers, but day after day it got worse and the pus flowed freely from the open sores. One morning I awoke to find my legs were glued to the sheet because of the matter running from the loosened scabs—a green, watery fluid. My pajamas stuck to my body—I looked like a leper. I was afraid of what Mrs. Krupka would say when she saw me like this. I could cover my legs—but my hands? How could I do any work with my hands in such a state? My fingers stuck together and hurt terribly. But in my misery I had to stifle my lamentations, for it seemed even God did not want to hear them. The whole world had turned its back on us, outcasts and lepers . . .

While the others slept, I stole quietly out of bed and took an old sheet from the closet. This would do as a bandage for my legs. On top of that I put on heavy winter stockings and returned to bed. Now, at least, they would not see in what condition my legs were, but what could I do about my hands? Should I say I spilled boiling water over them? Perhaps they would not notice the rash that spread between my fingers? If my mother knew, she would immediately make a poultice, she would call a doctor—if this were in normal times. And not only my mother, but my grandmother, and Uncle Hirsch, and the whole family would be gathered at my bedside, trying to help in some way. But these were not normal times and I was far from home. I must help myself as best I could and just hope that I could keep it a secret.

When it grew light, I pulled the sheet off the bed and hid it, then I went to the kitchen. Mrs. Krupka was astonished to see me up early and already dressed. "It must be a holiday today," she said.

"Yes," I replied. "You know the old saying: God blesses the early riser and makes him wiser. I think it's time I got hold of myself and started being useful to you."

"But you've put on such warm stockings, Hania," she said. "Do you feel cold? You're not going out anywhere."

"No, but I still feel a chill. These stockings help keep my feet warm—and when the feet are warm, Mamma used to say, the whole body is warm." Thank heaven, she did not notice the rash on my hands. I helped prepare breakfast, and after we had eaten, I cleared the table. I dreaded putting my hands in the dishpan. Perhaps if I went out of the kitchen, the elder Mrs. Krupka would wash the dishes . . . So, when the head of the house went out, I asked if I could start cleaning the apartment.

"Do you feel strong enough to do that?"

"I'll try."

"Today you ate with a better appetite."

"Oh, I must . . . I must get back to health!"

"You see?" Mrs. Krupka beamed happily. "Now you're talking sensibly. I told you there's no use worrying. You must think positively and keep your eyes open if you want to survive."

Together with Mrs. Krupka I put the bedrooms in order, then we moved on to the other rooms—and when we returned to the kitchen, the dishes were already washed and dried. This time it had worked out all right. I helped pare the potatoes for dinner and set the table. I spent what free time was left playing with Janko. The child grew very attached to me; we spent almost every evening together, for his parents and grandmother often went to visit friends or to the cinema. They were always being invited to social gatherings.

Janko on such occasions soon went to sleep, and I sat alone until late. Every rustling noise outside made me shiver with fright. Back in the ghetto at Rohatyn they must know that I had escaped. Possibly even in the Aryan sector there might be rumors about me, for it was known that the Krupka family moved to Brody at about the same time—and people knew that I used to visit them often. My escape and their move were timed too closely to be merely coincidental. Anyone who could add two and two together could come up with the answer to my disappearance.

So here I was, with two sets of forged identification papers, in a Christian home, surrounded by plenty and enjoying their care and protection, yet with dreadful thoughts poisoning my mind. I was still afraid.

The Ukrainian Orthodox holidays, celebrated in early January, were looming ahead. The Krupkas were planning a big feast for Christmas

Eve. Mr. Krupka was a government employee and, as director-manager of several stores and warehouses, had many contacts among the municipal authorities: the German gendarmerie, the Gestapo, the Ukrainian police, and various high officials. He needed their friendship to obtain various passes to go to other towns for transport of materials of all kinds. In those days it was useful to have contacts and backing at every move, and hence Mr. Krupka fostered ties of friendship with those who could help him remain in his important post.

A few days before Christmas, we started to bake various cakes, babkas, and tortes. Mrs. Krupka was always a wonderful pastry chef. We were all busy with the preparations, blanching almonds, grinding nuts and poppy seeds, beating egg whites, creaming cocoa and sugar. Even Janko helped. He had his fingers in everything, literally.

In the meantime the letter carrier brought a letter from Mr. Krupka's sister Olga, who lived at Rohatyn, telling them that she would arrive for the holidays. That gave even more impetus to the preparations. For several days the cleaning woman came to set the house in order, polish the floors, and shake out the tapestries. I was still too weak to do this heavy work, but I helped as best I could.

There was now the problem of what to do about me during the holidays. Some of the Germans who were invited to come had also lived in Rohatyn prior to their transfer here, and we could not be sure that they would not recognize me. It would have seemed suspicious if the Krupkas sent me to stay with their friends. They would have wondered why I couldn't mix with the guests, or even help serve at the table. These friends who hailed from Brody knew only that I was a governess for Janko; why should it be necessary for me to be out of the house on Christmas Eve? It would seem strange.

One evening when Janko was already in bed and Mr. Krupka had gone to some meeting, we three sat down to talk things over. I suggested that I could stay in the storeroom during that time, but Mrs. Krupka objected to the idea.

"Have you forgotten already how sick you were? Do you want to freeze to death there? Or do you want the rats to chew you up?"

So, we decided that I'd stay in their bedroom—and if anyone happened to look in, they would say that I had a fever and that I couldn't get up. They hoped that this ruse would work. There was no alternative.

I was feeling better each day, except for the sores on my legs and hands. The bandages I made out of the old sheet still stuck to my legs and stockings, and every time I changed them I had to tear them away from the sores—they bled and hurt, but what could I do? When healing set in, my skin itched so that I wanted to scratch it raw. How long could I keep this condition a secret?

It was only when we met again after the war that Mrs. Krupka, the angel, told me that she had noticed the bandages on my legs, but had pretended not to notice so as not to add to my worries. "You had trouble enough without that," she said, "and you must have been made of iron to survive . . . But I always believed that God must have had some special reason for wanting you to live, and I tried to help you all I could."

From that time on, she relieved me of my work in the kitchen so as to spare my hands—and no doubt for hygienic reasons, too. Mrs. Krupka was meticulously clean about the house and rather particular. She joked about my being too elegant to be her servant, and that I ought to have a maid for myself!

One day she said to me, "Hania, my husband told me that it's time we should have you registered at city hall. It's the law that a person has to register after three days in a new location; otherwise there's a fine." And I had already been there a month!

I knew about that, of course, but tried to evade the duty of registering—I just didn't have the courage to go to the city hall or to the police to report my residence. "I—I think it's still too cold," I stammered. "Maybe after the holidays . . ."

She smiled knowingly. "Oh, you poor child. It's hard to let go, and hard to hold on, isn't it?"

In general we tried to avoid touching upon dangerous topics in our daily conversation, because Janko, who was a very bright child, quickly caught on to our words and plied us with constant questions. We feared that he might repeat what we had said when others were around. He was inquisitive about my origin, where I came from, whether I was related to them, why I didn't go with them to their church on Sunday, where my parents were, and so forth. Endless questions . . . The child was too smart!

I was eagerly counting the days to Christmas and to the arrival of Olga, Mr. Krupka's sister. When Mrs. Krupka wrote her the last time, I asked her to say, "If possible, bring greetings to Hania." Olga knew about my escape and she was intelligent, so she must have guessed that we meant for her to bring news about my mother and sister. I hadn't heard anything since leaving Rohatyn.

Olga arrived at last, fashionably dressed as always. She had graceful legs and her whole appearance was very chic.

"Hania!" she called out on seeing me. She knew from her sister-in-law's letters that this was my new name. It still sounded strangely in my ears—but I preferred to be called Hanka Buczek rather than Maria Bandera, the other name I could have assumed. Olga brought presents for everyone, especially toys for Janko.

The house was filled with a holiday atmosphere and gaiety. At the dinner table, Olga had to tell her brother all about their mutual friends in Rohatyn and the latest town news—who had what position now, who had been dismissed, who had been arrested, and so forth. Olga's pleasant voice filled the room and Mr. Krupka and his family listened avidly. Mrs. Krupka, sensing my impatience, gave me signs that she would get Olga to talk to me privately, soon. But I had to wait until Janko had gone to bed and was safely asleep, out of the way. Finally, Olga came to my room—she was going to sleep in my bed tonight and I on the floor in the kitchen. She began to tell me how the ghetto had come to look. She lived nearby and wherever she went she had to pass near the ghetto, so she saw and heard everything that went on there. Gentiles knew what was going on even before it happened. She told me that on December 8, there had been another akcja. The Germans took nearly two thousand people to Belzec.

"This is the third akcja!" I exclaimed in horror. "How many more can they organize? There can't be many Jews left in the ghetto."

"That's true," Olga said. "Even though they have secret shelters, the Jews are running out of food and water. Most of the people in the ghetto are sick with typhus—they are without doctors, without medicines . . . Life is getting worse each day, and it's even harder now to escape."

"What do the people say?" I asked. "Do they predict the end?" Olga nodded. I could read the answer in her face—words were unnecessary. I thought, *Maybe I should return to the ghetto? Maybe I could be of some help?* I might be able to get Mamma and Rose out and into some safer place; I just couldn't let them stay there and die . . .

Olga continued, "Be glad you have such a refuge, Hania. Frankly, I am surprised that my brother and sister-in-law agreed to take the risk. You know how dangerous it is to harbor a Jew. I see even now they go around like persons under sentence of death—and no wonder! But if you return to the ghetto now, you'll never get out again. The ghetto is surrounded by a high barbed-wire fence and the Ukrainian police stand on guard continuously, day and night. Whoever tries to escape gets shot on sight."

This, then, was the end. Olga looked at me with surprise; I didn't know I had spoken my thoughts aloud. I added hastily, "I don't mean the end of the war, but the end of the Jews in the ghetto."

"I understand," she said and fell silent.

I recalled my mother's last words: "If you survive, don't forget what happened to us." Her words will forever remain in my mind; the sound of her voice still reverberates in my ears. Oh, yes! I did not escape just to save my own life or to better my own condition, but to bear witness to their sufferings—the agony of my people.

After a while, Mrs. Krupka joined us. The house was quiet; Janko and his grandmother were sleeping. Mr. Krupka had had to go on a trip to Lvov; he traveled there rather frequently.

Olga told me that my mother was very depressed, resigned, and was awaiting death any day. She said that after the December 8 akcja, now everyone had the end in sight.

"How do my mother and sister look?" I asked.

"How do they look?" Olga repeated—but did not give me any answer. She went on to say that my mother was afraid that I might be recognized as a Jewess, because she had heard that a fellow was caught in Chodorow posing as an Aryan—she was sure it was Hugo Goldberg . . . I cried bitterly. I remembered Hugo saying, "Wait for me . . ." As I listened to Olga,

I wondered if Goldberg was dead—and thought about the fact that this could happen to me as well. And even as my mother and sister knew that they too were facing death any day, they were still worried about me.

Mrs. Krupka stroked my hair, saying, "Let's stop this talk. I think it will be all right. You fought off your sickness like a tigress, and you're alive. There's a purpose in that, you'll see. But I'm afraid Janko is beginning to suspect something strange is going on here."

"Dear God!" Olga's voice was filled with anxiety. "A nosy child can be very dangerous. And Janko is too smart for his three years. Now when the guests come for Christmas, somebody can readily recognize Hania, if they see her in this house." Mrs. Krupka interrupted. "We've planned for that emergency already. Our superintendent's daughter will be our waitress."

"But perhaps I could help," I said, "if I wore a white cap and apron, like a French maid. I'd like to see how people live and enjoy a good time, to forget even for a few hours . . ."

"See, Olga, what a little devil she is! She'd have the nerve to serve at the table with policemen, Gestapo, and SS men sitting there as guests!"

"I have a soul made of steel!"

"Oh, go to sleep now!" Mrs. Krupka told me. "You know what she suggested to my husband? She wanted him to give her a job in his office! What do you think we are doing, playing with the Germans?"

Hmm, I thought . . . *If I'm Hania, if I'm free, if I'm supposed to be a Christian girl, why can't I live and act like a free person?*

The preparations for the Christmas feast went on; the air was filled with the aroma of cooking and baking. After dinner, Mr. Krupka returned, stamping the snow off his boots and energetically shaking it off his coat. He was lively and talkative after the ride in the sleigh from the station, but when he saw me his expression changed. I was a symbol of danger . . . In Lvov he had heard about various cases like mine. With each day the Jews found themselves in an increasingly precarious situation. Having me in his house was like having a bomb that could explode any day and wipe out his entire family. I could sense his feelings, but I understood perfectly. It was a great responsibility he had taken upon himself.

The next morning, I helped set the tables and clean the silver. Everybody had a job to do around the house. When Mr. Krupka came home from the office, he started to arrange the vodka bottles and liqueurs. Finally, there was the last-minute flurry to get dressed before the guests started to arrive. I ate and was told to be off to bed right away. So I went to bed and they closed the door.

Janko did not miss his chance to ask a question. "Why is Hania in bed?"

"Because she's not well," his grandmother replied.

"That's strange. Ever since she came here she's been sick all the time. Why do you keep her? Why don't you get another girl?"

"Don't you like Hania?"

"Yes, I do. I love Hania. But she's sick too much."

He said it so sweetly that it was impossible to be angry. His grandmother gave him a hug and a kiss and a fond pat on the behind. He stood off from me, knowing that whenever I was sick he must not come too close. But how I would have liked to hug him, too!

Soon I heard the guests coming. I heard the doors opened and shut. There were the usual loud exclamations and greetings, and "Heil, Hitler!" I raised myself and peeked through the keyhole. The ladies went to the adjoining room to fix their makeup, laughing and talking all the while. I recognized the superintendent's daughter, tall, thin, nice-looking. They had outfitted her in a white apron and a frill of white lace on her dark hair. A pretty maid! I was filled with jealousy and tempted to get out of bed. I'd have looked even prettier in a maid's uniform, I thought childishly, and I was younger. I'd comb my long hair up in a sweep off the back of my neck. I'd receive many compliments without a doubt! In these imaginings I sought a bit of satisfaction for my hurt feelings. But I knew they'd never let me come out to meet the guests.

And anyway, who were these guests that I foolishly wanted to serve? Mostly Germans and policemen—SS, Gestapo, and Ukrainian murderers. Suddenly I realized how silly I was to want to go out there and share in their merrymaking. I felt my blood pressure rise. As I squirmed in the bed, restlessly, I heard Mr. Krupka's voice; he seemed nervous and excited. From time to time, I heard the sound of heavy boots, and the hated salute: *Heil, Hitler!* Loud voices were talking in German. Even the Ukrainian police spoke German, though with broken accents. The flow of guests seemed endless.

My heart pounded like a hammer. I thought: What an ironic coincidence! In one room, the German authorities, the Gestapo—and here, in the adjoining room, a Jewish girl. Under the same roof, the haters and the hated! I did not hear many women's voices—mostly men, laughing loud, then singing. From time to time little Janko's treble piped above the rest. Oh, if only he wouldn't get the idea of looking into my room! But I supposed his mother and granny watched him sternly.

It must have been quite late when the door creaked open and Mrs. Krupka entered my room. "Hania, are you asleep?"

"No. I couldn't fall asleep."

"You don't know how lucky it is that you're hiding here . . ."

"Why?" I knew there must be some special reason.

"When I saw who came with one of the Gestapo, my heart almost stopped beating," Mrs. Krupka said. "You remember Nechaika from Rohatyn?"

"Dear God, I can't believe it!" I exclaimed.

"Yes. She told me that he's her friend and that he brought her with him to Brody. We need her in Brody like we need the cholera!"

"Which one of the Nechaika sisters are you talking about?"

"The one who used to work in the grocery store."

"What!" I almost screamed. "That one knows me very well. Her store was close to the bookshop where I worked during the Soviet occupation."

"Now, you see, she has a better job—being a Gestapo's mistress. You ought to see the rings she wears and the bracelets! She looks elegant. But sleep now, Hania. And don't dream of leaving this room tonight! You know, that Nechaika woman has spoiled the whole party for me," Mrs. Krupka admitted. "Even my husband and Olga and their mother just stared, speechless, when they saw her come in. I was terrified that Janko might say something that would give you away! But fortunately, he was a good boy . . ."

Mrs. Krupka went back to the party. After hours of drinking, at last I heard the guests saying farewell. Things quieted down again in the house, and shortly afterward Olga and her mother came into my bedroom, bursting with the news about the Nechaika girl.

The next morning, when the family assembled for breakfast, I noticed that Mr. Krupka looked displeased about something. I could not begin a conversation with him because Janko was present. Later, as they were getting ready to go to church, Mrs. Krupka told the child that I was not going with them because I had to help the cleaning woman. He was bursting with questions, as usual, but this explanation had to satisfy him. By the time they returned from church, their mood was happier and the frown of anxiety was no longer on Mr. Krupka's face. Perhaps he had found comfort in prayer.

On New Year's Day we slept late, but in the afternoon various friends dropped in to wish a happy new year. The superintendent and his daughter were among the first to come. There were also two chauffeurs who only recently had started to work under Mr. Krupka—one, a dark-haired fellow with flashing black eyes, the other, blond and tall—both young Ukrainians. They had heard that there was a young Ukrainian girl at the Krupka house named Hania, and today they would have an opportunity to meet her!

After they departed, Mrs. Krupka joked about it. "Hania, that dark-haired one was making eyes at you! And no wonder; any young buck would find you agreeable to look at. But he doesn't know that you wouldn't go out with him—not even to a movie."

"He's a nice boy," I said, "but I have enough troubles for now."

When Olga went back to Rohatyn she took a lot of food and other goods. She also took, at my request, a large loaf of bread and a few bars of soap for my mother and sister Rose. Olga reminded me that it was next to impossible for her to get inside the ghetto now; she would be afraid to try it, though perhaps she could reach them through the broken wires in the fence or through some other crack in the wall surrounding the ghetto.

For days afterward, my heart skipped a beat every time the mailman came to the house. The Krupkas were also anxious to have news from

Olga, for they feared that she might be stopped on the way with all the foodstuffs she had along; the Germans were very strict with food speculators. But at last a letter came! I tried to contain my curiosity until the family had had a chance to read it, but when Mrs. Krupka started to read it a small note fell out of the envelope. She picked up the paper, glanced at it and handed it over to me. "This is for you, Hania, from your family."

I snatched the paper eagerly from her and nervously began to read, the tears streaming down my face.

"Is it bad news?"

"No, neither good nor bad. It's just as I expected," I said. "If you wish, I'll read it aloud."

> Dear Hania, We received the things you sent us. Thank you very much. The soap especially is a great luxury. Take care of yourself. Don't go out, because we know there has been much snow and it's terribly cold . . . We hear that there is an epidemic of influenza everywhere and many people are dying from it. We also had a hard winter, and we don't go anywhere. We are bored with staying home all the time. Remember, you are most precious to us. We dream of being with you again. We'd like to go to see you, if it were possible. We miss you very much. We are hoping for the day when we can be reunited. All the time I am consoling Mamma (Rose writes) but she cannot accept her fate with resignation. Because it's difficult to obtain remedies, we fear that our wishes will remain only fancies.
>
> Enjoy good health, and don't forget us!
>
> Your loving Mother and Sister

When I finished reading, Mrs. Krupka took the note from my hands and read it again to herself. Her expression was full of sympathy and sorrow. She returned the paper to me and I reread it, etching every word on my memory, in my heart . . . and then I broke into loud lamentations.

The days passed slowly. The little bit of news we got from radio and newspaper was disquieting. There were days when I felt so miserable that I'd have gone out into the street just to be caught and put under arrest. I had had enough of this hiding and pretending . . . Now that Janko's grandmother had also left, I went out for walks with him more frequently. Once I even went with him to the ghetto section of Brody—it was not sealed off here as in Rohatyn. I could not find a shoemaker on the Aryan side who had time to fix Janko's little boots, so Mrs. Krupka told me to go to the ghetto. It also gave me a chance to observe conditions there; perhaps even hear some news. While waiting for the shoes to be repaired, two Jews were holding a conversation in loud voices. Their speech sounded strange in my ears, though I knew Yiddish quite well. The entire surroundings seemed strange to me now, and I wondered how they could stand living in such poverty. At that moment I felt glad that I had escaped from such a life.

Now I could fully appreciate my good fortune in being able to live in the Krupkas' home—which, in comparison with what I had seen in the ghetto, seemed like a palace. As soon as I entered it, I was enveloped in the fragrance of good food. The place was clean, neatly furnished, and comfortably warm. It was a wonderful place for me to hide from the storm! Filled with a humble sense of gratitude, I worked more willingly. If only to live through the winter . . . The spring might bring some change—perhaps even the end of the war!

Then came an incident that I shall never forget. One morning very early, I started the fire in the kitchen stove and went about preparing breakfast. Mr. Krupka had gone to the town of Zlochev the day before, so nobody was yet stirring in the house. Suddenly I seemed to hear the cries of children—not one child, but many, many children. And then the sound of shooting. At first I thought that I must be imagining it, but the cries became louder and nearer. Very quietly, I opened the door to Janko's room. He was sleeping soundly. I returned to the kitchen and again I heard those cries . . . I went out on the balcony that led to the yard; the sounds were louder there, of course, but I could see nothing. When I came back inside, Mrs. Krupka entered the kitchen, looking as though she had just awakened from a deep but frightening sleep. Terror was reflected in her eyes and her mouth trembled. She asked, "Hania, do you hear something—or did I dream it? The crying of children, the shots . . . Where's Janko?"

"He's sleeping," I said. "It must be out in front of the house."

We ran to the windows that faced the street, pulled aside the curtains—and there was our answer.

A mass of people—some with bundles, some with children in their arms—trudged through the snow. The little children, mostly half-naked, hung their heads on their parents' shoulders, clutching them desperately in fear. The people moved forward, some six or seven in a row, along the highway, slowly, step by step, without a word, showing no reaction. Only the weeping of the children broke the sudden silence. There were Gestapo men in helmets, high boots. Mrs. Krupka and I exchanged understanding glances. Words were futile. I hid my face in my hands and began to cry, lamenting loudly. She wept with me, but pushed me away from the window. "Go, go, Hania—don't watch this. Don't cry, please. I don't want Janko to wake up and see this sight. He's still too young . . ."

But though she kept tugging at me, I could not tear myself away from the window. I didn't care if someone saw me from the street. My repressed tears broke through, and I sobbed unrestrainedly. Mrs. Krupka put her arms about my shoulders, trying to comfort me. "Oh, how can God look upon this and remain silent!" she exclaimed. "They are being led like lambs to slaughter."

People had gathered along the sidewalks. They looked on from a safe distance at these thousands of condemned Jews, but the Gentiles did not care. I felt I wanted to go out and join their ranks—or, better, seize the gun from some Gestapo man's hands and shoot him! Maybe I could kill one, maybe two of these monsters . . .

Mrs. Krupka held on to me tightly and finally succeeded in pulling me away from the window. "Hania, you can't help them. There are too many; they are armed. Some of them are leading police dogs with them. It's simply impossible to do anything now!"

Though I knew she was right, I got up from the bed and went back to the window as though drawn there by an irresistible magnet. The mass of people had receded into the distance. On the street below, there were the imprints of their feet in the snow. They were being driven to destruction, just as they were, barefooted, half-naked, in midwinter.

This was the first time I had witnessed with my own eyes an akcja of my people. I had lived through two akcjas in Rohatyn; I had seen *post facto* the results of the massacres. But each time I had been in hiding. Now, however, this day, I had become an eyewitness. I shall never forget that scene to my dying moment. Will my mother and sister be such victims?

Mr. Krupka returned at suppertime. He undoubtedly had heard about the akcja, for they were talking about something in hushed voices at the table while I was in the kitchen. I caught most of what was said. The akcja had not been confined to Brody, but had taken place in several other towns. Mr. Krupka was quite upset. In Zlochev, he had seen posters on buildings, notifying the populace that if anyone was caught harboring a Jew, he and his family would be punished by death. The same posters were in this town, Brody.

Listening, I felt that the time had come for me to break away—but where could I go? They must want to be rid of me—I couldn't blame them. I certainly did not want to be the cause of their deaths. No doubt they would have been shot in the central square, for an example to the rest of the townspeople.

A few days later, the superintendent dropped by for a visit, and the main topic of conversation was the akcja. He was sure that there had been several thousand Jews taken from the ghetto and sent to Belzec to be cremated. He said that one family had wanted to pay him a large sum if he would hide them in his house, but he had been afraid. Now they were gone—dead! It was impossible to stop the superintendent from talking in a loud voice, and little Janko heard everything. It must have reminded him of the Jews he had just recently seen in the ghetto when I took him to the shoemaker . . .

The next time I was dressing Janko, lacing his shoes—he sat on a chair, and I on a low stool before him—he looked at me very strangely. He looked and looked, narrowing his lids. I asked, "Why are you looking at me?" And then suddenly he threw a bombshell at me.

"Hania, you know—you look very much like that Jewish girl, Sheva, who used to come to our house at Rohatyn. She knitted a sweater for me, just like you knitted for me last month. I remember it all now!"

It was as though a bolt of lightning had struck me. And we had thought he was still too young to know the difference or to remember me from the past! Mrs. Krupka, standing nearby, turned to the boy, wagging a warning finger at him. "This is not Sheva, do you hear? This is Hania, Hania, *Hania*! And she is as Ukrainian as you and all of us are. You must not call her Sheva, you must not say she is Jewish! If ever you say that again, Daddy will punish you . . . If ever anyone heard you say that and told the Gestapo, we'd be shot!"

The child's face clouded up with sadness. He said, "I know. This is not Sheva. This is Hania. And I won't say it again, for I mustn't. Forgive me, Hania!" I only hoped that it would never happen again . . . and it never did happen again.

The radio communiqués reported severe losses suffered by the German army at the front, and we knew they had had to mobilize new reinforcements, but that still did not mean the end of the war. We heard there was a shortage of laborers in Germany because more men were being called up to the front. Now they were recruiting laborers from the occupied countries. We heard through the radio how many of these laborers from occupied countries came voluntarily to Germany, because they were given wonderful working conditions and could live in luxury. Occupied Poland was no exception. Polish and Ukrainian youths were sent to Germany. At first they went willingly, but after a short time their families began to receive awful letters. The majority of these young people were sent to factories, mostly ammunition plants. They had to live in barracks, and living conditions were not up to their expectations. The pay was insignificant. Besides, the Germans—who looked upon themselves as being superior to every other nationality—regarded these imported laborers contemptuously. It was rumored that many returned if they could. At any rate, no one now went to Germany to work willingly. Soon the Germans began rounding up able-bodied people for work in Germany.

The winter snows started to melt. Spring was not far distant now; the days grew warmer, tempting people to come out of their houses, stirring them to travel, to new enterprises, new life . . . For that matter, transportation had improved. Trains ran more regularly, and it was easier to go from town to town. Everyone seemed to be on the move, and now that Easter was drawing near there were many things to buy and sell—everyone needed something and went out to get it, whether it was food, or furnishings, or a new spring wardrobe.

Olga soon returned for a visit, and she told me how she had managed to deliver my gift package to my sister. Describing her meeting with Rose, she said that my sister looked very thin; her clothes hung on her bony frame; she was sad, depressed, and missed me very much. Chills shook my body as I listened. Olga said that my sister's large, blue eyes—now sunken into her wizened, fearful face—were her only recognizable feature. She had talked with Rose through the broken boards in the fence separating the ghetto from the Aryan quarter. "Hania, listen to me," she said, seeing the impression her words had made, "you can't save everybody. You must think of yourself. You must find yourself a better, safer hiding place than Brody."

I knew that. I wanted to leave—just as much as they all must have wanted me to leave. But where would I go?

When Olga went back to Rohatyn a few days later, I did not give her anything to take to my mother and sister; not even a letter. I did not want to expose her to any further risks.

One day, my work was interrupted by Mrs. Krupka, who handed me a letter that the mailman had just brought to the house. The letter was addressed to the Krupka family, but when she opened it she saw that it was for me. I jumped for joy, thinking it must contain good news. The letter was from Sal Kreisler, a much respected man in Rohatyn, who knew me well. He also knew about my plan for escaping from the ghetto. Now it appeared that he had received a letter from Srebrnik (whom he also knew) from Dnepropetrovsk, and he was sending it on to me, with a note from himself. The sender of the letter was some Pole from Rohatyn. Sal Kreisler mentioned in a discreet way that people generally were leaving town and that it would soon be quite empty. The letter contained the news that Srebrnik was working very hard, even during the deep frost and snow. Srebrnik said that he was expecting every day to hear from his friend, but he had not yet arrived . . . He would like to know, Srebrnik wrote, if he had changed his mind, and where he was now . . .

I was very glad to receive this letter and to know that Srebrnik had reached his destination and was settled. (Later, after the war, I would see him in Israel.) On the other hand, the news that Hugo Goldberg had not arrived at Dnepropetrovsk was a blow. It seemed to corroborate the rumors I had heard that someone had been caught at Chodorow and shot. I felt sure that this must be Goldberg. Apparently he had been recognized—and killed! As the realization of this sank into my consciousness, I seemed to hear only his voice: "I want to share your birthdays in the future. Wait for me, Sheva!" I was still here, but Hugo was gone. He had saved me, he had helped me to leave, and now he was dead. I missed Hugo; we loved each other. I burned the letter, sobbing my heart out.

Now that warmer days were here, I had to start thinking of getting an identity card that would enable me to go out of the house. I had to provide myself with legal and government papers, no matter what the danger or the cost. It would be impossible to remain within four walls once the summer came. It would certainly have looked suspicious in the eyes of the Krupkas' newly made friends at Brody, and to people like the superintendent and the chauffeurs.

A short time before Easter a letter came from Mr. Krupka's younger brother, who was in the German army, informing them that he would come for the holidays. This was a new shock! I had known him in Rohatyn, though only slightly. He was an intelligent, mild-mannered man, but an ardent German patriot. How would he react to seeing me in their house now—a Jewish girl posing as a Christian? I'd have to lay my cards on the table; I could not turn away from the risk, nor could the family squirm out of the difficulty now. Husband and wife looked at each other in silence after reading his letter. What they may have said later, when I was out of the room, I don't know—but I went through a small hell at that moment. I didn't think he would report me right away, for it meant informing on his own brother's family. But somehow, later on, he might find a way of reporting me without involving them directly—perhaps by claiming that they did not know that I was Jewish. What worried me more immediately, however, was that Mr. Krupka had had enough of me and my troubles! I could read from the expression on his face that I had long overstayed my welcome and that he would be glad to be rid of my presence in his home. No one would accuse him of lack of charity or hospitality—it was a case of self-preservation.

The day of Mr. Krupka's brother's arrival finally came. As in a trance, I saw the door open and, behind it, Franko Krupka, wearing a German uniform. His brother was behind him—I could not see his face in the shadow of the entrance. But Franko Krupka was the same as I remembered him—slight of build, charming, and gracious of manner. My heart beat rapidly at the sight of him—perhaps not so much from fear but simply because of the strangeness of seeing a man with a gentle face wearing a German uniform.

He entered the room with a deliberate step, greeting first his sister-in-law. Then he caught up little Janko and started to throw him playfully up to the ceiling, kissing and hugging the squealing child. Then he turned and shook hands with me. It would be a lie if I said that I did not feel a stranger in this family, or that I looked upon Franko Krupka's uniform with anything but revulsion. Yet he greeted me with a tolerant smile, saying with formal politeness, "How do you do, Miss Hania?" His brother had given him my name.

I forced myself to return his smile. After all, we had to take him into our confidence and ask his advice regarding my problem. My life depended upon him, as it would on so many others. Who could help me better than a man who was with the Germans—if only he were willing to help me? He was stationed with the Nazi army in Warsaw, and had connections.

After the general conversation that the family enjoyed after dinner, and after Janko was put to bed, we began to discuss seriously ways of solving the Krupkas' great problem: Hania. I showed him the birth certificate with the name of the Polish woman, Hanka Buczek, that I had adopted for my own. He read it carefully as I went to the closet and retrieved the coat in which I had traveled from Rohatyn to Brody. Franko raised his eyes and watched me with growing curiosity as I ripped away the lining back of the pocket and took out a passport—the passport that had served me during the Russian occupation. Mrs. Krupka looked at her husband and at Franko, then shattered the puzzled silence: "What does that girl have up her sleeve? She has not one, but two documents in her possession!"

I handed the passport to Franko. He opened it slowly and read: "Ukrainian. Good!" But when he saw the name Bandera, he muttered to himself, "Oh, no!" Then, aloud, he continued, "Not this name." He shook his head in protest and dismay.

His brother echoed his amazement. "Where did this poor creature get such a name?"

Mrs. Krupka laughed. "She has plenty of nerve!" The name of the famous Ukrainian leader, Stefan Bandera, was nothing to play with in any form. I had not chosen the name, but I was stuck with it. Franko examined the document a long while, marveling at the counterfeiter's art in deleting my former name and writing in the adopted name so that the change could hardly be detected. "He's a real professional! It's past believing how he did it!" That was the unanimous opinion as the passport went from hand to hand. And yet, in spite of the perfect piece of deception, the passport was worthless because of the fatal name.

"With such a name," Franko said, "you have a good chance of going straight to jail. Go, take this fool passport and burn it up in the kitchen stove."

So I did. I threw my precious passport into the stove, lit a match, and watched the flame envelope it slowly. In a few minutes the name was nothing but a small heap of ashes. Returning to the room, I said, "The passport is burned . . . and I had had such great hopes, thinking it would be my best means of escape! I felt so much safer, having one extra document—like an ace up my sleeve. And now that is gone!"

"You're lucky that you didn't try to register here on the basis of such a passport," Franko said. "They would have arrested you at once, taking you to be some of Bandera's kin, and then they would have discovered who you really are . . . Yes, your only possible solution at present is to pass yourself off as Hanka Buczek, a Pole, born in Ruda, county Rohatyn . . ." He was reading from the birth certificate before him. "There is a slight problem, because the real Hanka is much older than you."

"Yes," I replied, thanking him for his advice, "there's always some problem."

"Remember, when you go to register, dress up like a peasant girl and try to make yourself look older. Remember!" Franko looked across the table at his brother, as if to say, "Do you know what you have taken on yourself? Do you realize the danger you placed your family in by helping this Jewess?"

I broke into the heavy silence. "And if they start asking me, as I heard from others that they do, who my grandfather and my great-grandfather were, and whether there were any Jews in my family ancestry, and if they telephone to Ruda and learn that Hanka Buczek is living there and I'm only a duplicate—what then?"

"Then you're done for . . . then you've really fallen into a trap. That is what this is all about!"

"Oh, God—and then you, all of you, are lost!" I exclaimed.

Again silence. No one could find anything to say. This was too serious a matter for a ready-made answer.

Franko said suddenly, "Maybe if I could get some other document and send it to you . . . I'll look around. But lately they have little confidence in anyone, even military personnel. Let me think about it." He muttered, as if to himself, "Whom can I trust? I cannot trust anyone with this delicate matter—it's too dangerous . . .

"I am very tired," he said, pushing his chair away from the table and getting up. Mrs. Krupka suggested coffee, but he did not want anything more. After a few words, we went to bed, though I suspect that no one slept very soundly that night.

The tension in the Krupka household grew as the Easter holidays came and went. Mrs. Krupka's nervous condition was bad; she could hardly control herself, though I tried to make things as comfortable as I could, taking most of the work off her hands.

While I busied myself about the house, I listened to the radio. One day—it was April 19, 1943—the musical program was abruptly interrupted to bring news of the Jewish uprising in Warsaw. I could hardly believe my ears. "Oh, my God!" I exclaimed and held my breath, while the commentator told how a Jewish resistance organization had repulsed General Stroop and his men when they arrived at the ghetto. This communiqué about the uprising in the Warsaw ghetto shook me to the core of my being, and tears of joy streamed down my face. At the moment Mrs. Krupka and I were alone in the house; she looked at me and saw pride and happiness beaming in my countenance. "At last! At last!" I cried. "There are some brave souls willing to risk all for the cause of freedom. Kill the Nazis!"

I stood by the radio set as though paralyzed, listening intently. The uprising had been met with firm resistance; Germans in all their might were devastating the ghetto, while awaiting still greater reinforcements.

But at least my people would die with honor, as heroes. Oh, how I wanted to be there with them! Oh, God, how willingly I would have joined their ranks! Great God of our fathers, give them strength, help them . . . and bring peace back to a suffering world . . . show that You have not forgotten us entirely . . .

One evening the superintendent came by, excited and pale. He told us that there was a terrible commotion in town: It was said that the Germans were going to liquidate the ghetto in Brody, and that they were also going to search every house in the Aryan quarter for Jews hiding in Gentile homes. We listened gravely, but we had heard such news too often before to panic. When the superintendent left, we began discussing what to do. If there was an inspection, I must not be found in their house!

After much deliberation, it was decided that I could hide in the provision store owned by a friend of theirs. The lady had gone to Lvov for the holidays and she planned to stay there for some time afterward, so before leaving she had given Mrs. Krupka the key and had asked her to feed her pet cat and to keep an eye on things while she was gone. That would be an ideal place to hide me . . . In case of an inspection, I would have to say that I had climbed in through a window, thus incriminating no one but myself. Olga had come back to Brody for the holidays, and she went with me to the house that night. When we entered, I had the impression that I was in a prison: the three small rooms were cold, the cement floors were frigid and hard. Along the walls hung coils of sausages (kielbasa), smoked hams, other meats—dried or smoked—and rows of knives and other cutting tools, butcher's cleavers and saws, and various machines for grinding or preserving meats.

There was a small cot in one room, covered with a blanket. Olga said that sometimes when a workman or guard stayed late, he would be allowed to sleep on the cot. She did not stay long in that dismal place, which smelled of blood and spicy brine. She said that she was going to padlock the door from the outside and would return in the morning.

I thanked her, and listened to the receding sound of her quick steps in the corridor outside. Quickly I extinguished the lamp, and completely dressed I crawled under the blanket—it was as cold as a layer of ice—and lay on the narrow cot, my teeth chattering from fear as well as cold. It was completely quiet; only the cat meowed pitifully from time to time, scratching itself.

There I was, trying to sleep even if only for an hour—but sleep would not come. When my eyes became accustomed to the darkness, I could make out the outlines of the knives and cutting tools that hung upon the wall. I remembered Olga's words: "Hania, this war will go on for a long time. Every day becomes more and more dangerous. What are you going to do with yourself? Brody is no longer a safe town for you to hide. Where do you plan to go?"

In the morning, when I heard the key turn in the lock, a wave of fear flooded my heart before I remembered that Olga was supposed to come, to bring me my breakfast and milk for the cat. Indeed, there she was—and the cat was already rubbing against her legs. She sat on the edge of the cot next to me and we talked. I was supposed to stay there during the day and, if things remained quiet in town, she would come for me in the evening and take me back to the Krupka's house. I told her that now I really would try to obtain an identification card and go away somewhere. Too many people knew about me by this time, and Brody was no longer safe. Olga added that she too had noticed that her brother's nerves were frayed—whenever anyone called from the police or city hall on routine business, he almost jumped for fear that he had been caught sheltering me.

It was now only a matter of a few weeks, I felt, until I would have to leave Brody for the unknown. I was appalled at the prospect, but I had no choice. Either I went away, or the Krupka family stood in constant danger of discovery and death. But where to go?

That evening, returning to the Krupka household, I must have looked miserable. Mrs. Krupka gave me one look and said, "Oh, you poor dear! Come here, let me comfort you." She put her arms around me and led me to my corner in the kitchen, but would not let me do any work, insisting that I rest and sleep.

Olga and Mr. Krupka left right after Easter, and the house was quiet. A horse-faced German woman—a friend of Mrs. Krupka's who sometimes dropped in for a visit—came by one day to say farewell, for she was being transferred to Lvov where she had been offered a better position with a higher rank. Mrs. Krupka ran into the kitchen where I was preparing coffee and whispered the news to me.

"Get her address in Lvov," I said. Mrs. Krupka nodded her head; she understood fully what I had in mind. A while later I heard her voice in the living room, as she said to the German: "Our Hania would like so much to go to Lvov!"

The German woman replied that she would be glad to help me find a job if I ever went there. When she left, she left her address and promised to write as soon as she was settled. I thought, *This might be the place for me to go.*

I wondered if Mr. Franko Krupka would keep his promise to write as soon as he arrived in Warsaw. The Jewish ghetto was still fighting, according to reports received through the radio. At first it was thought that the Jewish uprising would last only a few days, but with God's help they still seemed to hold on valiantly. Whatever the outcome, I must provide myself with identity papers. Franko had stressed the importance of this, and I realized that even a day's delay could be catastrophic.

The nervous Krupkas finally decided to buy a dog to protect us while Mr. Krupka was at work. It wasn't a big dog, but it could bark with authority. They called him Zeze and he soon made himself a member of the family, our constant companion, and Janko's beloved pet. Zeze was a black, short-haired mongrel, but he at once sensed that he was to be our protector. Now, when we went out for short walks with Janko, Zeze always went with us. The child needed fresh air. He liked the dog so much that he no longer questioned why I did not go with them to church on Sundays; he wanted me to stay home and take care of Zeze so the puppy would not be lonely.

Lying in bed one night, I realized that I had to shake myself of my dangerous sense of relative comfort and security. I decided that tomorrow I must obtain a work card and then a *Kennkarte,* to legalize my presence in Brody. Right after breakfast the next morning I went to the city hall to apply for a work card. On the way I prayed that I would not be recognized as a Jewess. I had looked into the mirror carefully that morning, trying to see whether my features could pass as Gentile. I thought so, but my opinion was not the final word. It depended on luck, or on the sharp eyes and wits of the clerk at the desk. All I had to support my claim that I was a Polish girl was the birth certificate—it was such a flimsy bit of paper! Walking along the street, I felt so lost, so strange, as though I belonged to another world entirely.

When I entered the building, I walked directly up to a table where a secretary was writing. She spoke to me, first in German, then in Polish. I told her why I was there, and she motioned for me to go to another desk. There, a Ukrainian girl took my birth certificate and examined it. My eyes did not leave her face for a moment. In answer to her question, I told her where I was employed as a servant, and I also asked for a food rationing card.

When she heard the Krupka name, she smiled wryly, for she knew that no one under their roof had need of a ration card; they had plenty of food. But she said nothing about that. Taking some forms, she started asking more questions. If my heart had wings it would have taken flight from fear at that moment! For one of the questions was: Is anyone in your family, even remotely, a Jew?

"No, no!" I shook my head.

She looked at me queerly, but kept on writing. I hoped my face was not red. I had never lied so brazenly before—though I soon would become a professional liar. I thought this questioning would never end. I wanted so much to go out and get a breath of fresh air! I seemed to be burning up inside. I heard people coming into the room, passing through, but I never looked around, even when I heard them give the Nazi salute, "Heil, Hitler!"

At last, she finished writing and asked me to sign the form. I did so rather clumsily, for a servant girl was not supposed to be proficient at writing. I also tried to hide the fact that my hands were too well-cared-for for a girl in my humble position. Slowly, I scrawled "Hania Buczek." It was a strange feeling—I had never signed that name before, but I might as well get used to it now. The clerk returned the birth certificate, looking at me closely and, I thought, rather suspiciously. For it was rare for someone in Poland not to have more than just a birth certificate as proof of identity. She told me that I was to bring in two photographs of myself; then I would be sent to the police to be fingerprinted for my Kennkarte. Meanwhile, she handed me a food ration card.

I thanked her in Polish and left. I could hardly believe that the so-called examination was over! My papers would now be sent to the *Landkommissar*, mayor, for his signature.

A few days later, after I had gathered my wits for another excursion, I set out for the photo studio. On my way, I saw large notices pasted on the walls of the buildings, reading—in German, Ukrainian, and Polish—WHOEVER HARBORS A JEW WITH FALSIFIED PAPERS FACES THE THREAT OF EXECUTION. These posters shouted at me, mocked me, and made me shake with horror and indignation. I saw people pausing to read these notices. Apparently they must have been put up only recently.

I felt my knees giving way under me, but I went ahead. I knew the photographer was Ukrainian, so when I reached his shop I spoke to him in his own tongue. When he posed me and told me to smile, I tried very earnestly to smile—for I did not want the picture to betray my suffering and sadness. He asked me to return for the pictures in a couple of days; he was too busy, he said, to finish them the same day. There was nothing I could do or say to change his mind.

A few days later, I mustered up courage to go back for my photographs. I walked along the streets, confidently and almost cheerfully. My elation was short-lived, however. When I opened the door to the studio, I was suddenly paralyzed with fear—for behind the counter stood the Nechaika girl from Rohatyn, who had come to the Krupka's party. We faced each other for an electric second. I could see by her expression that she was no less surprised to see me than I was to see her. Her eyes searched mine, then fell to my sleeve—she saw that I was not wearing the armband that all Jews had to wear. She seemed to be alone in the establishment; I saw no one else. Without a word, on an impulse, I turned around and fled as fast as my legs could carry me! I ran and ran . . . It must have looked suspicious, but I felt that I must run away from Nechaika—as far away as I could! I did not look back to see if she was following me, but I ran through the winding, twisting streets, covering my trail. Before long I was "home." Climbing the stairs slowly, I wondered if I should break the news to Mrs. Krupka at once. As soon as she opened the door for me, she asked: "Have you got the photos, Hania?"

"They weren't ready yet," I lied. I tried to avoid her gaze and busied myself about some work, but the rest of the day I was tormented by the dreadful thought that Nechaika might give my photograph to the newspapers . . . Perhaps she had already guessed with whom I was staying? It would incriminate the whole family, and it was all my fault!

I could not touch any food at dinnertime. I heard Mrs. Krupka tell her husband that I had gone for the pictures but that they were not yet ready. He did not seem to believe it. *No,* I thought, *I can't hold it a secret any longer.* When I cleared the table, I told Mrs. Krupka that I had something very important to tell them.

"Very well," she said, "I'll tell my husband not to go out. Wait till I send Janko into his room to play with the dog."

Though I felt that the words were choking me, I told them what had happened in the photographer's studio. I omitted no detail. Mr. Krupka and his wife exchanged despairing looks. He said in a hollow voice, "This is a tragedy! And now they have her photographs!"

"Yes," she echoed, "that's all we needed! It's the end of the world! We knew that Nechaika had recently come to Brody to live and that she was working evenings as a cashier in the cinema, but we didn't want to upset you, Hania, so we kept quiet. But now she knows you are here, and by putting two and two together, she must guess that you are staying with us. Oh, what a misfortune! Oh, my poor Janko—why must the innocent child suffer because of our folly!"

"Not only the child," Mr. Krupka exclaimed. "We all will suffer."

I was quick to stop him. "I am leaving Brody tonight."

"But where will you go?"

"I don't know, but I am going to pack this minute; I'll just take a few most needed things—and go."

"But you have no papers," Mr. Krupka said.

"I know. But I am going, anyway," I said bravely. "I can risk my life, but I cannot put you in danger any longer. I must leave tonight! In case of a police investigation I must not be found here."

"But you have given our names and address at the police station when you went to register."

"Yes, but I could have done that without your knowledge. Your signatures are not on my application form. As long as they don't find me in your house, they cannot hold you responsible. And if my picture appears in the newspapers, and if I'm caught, only I will be punished—only I will be shot. I am ready for anything."

"Let me get you a ticket," Mr. Krupka said. "But—to what city?"

"I'll go to Lvov."

"Go, Jarema," Mrs. Krupka urged her husband, "go, get her the ticket and find out when the train leaves. Let it be the late train. Then get the superintendent to come with the wagon to take her to the station. Oh, God! God, be merciful to us!" Mrs. Krupka started crying.

After he left, Mrs. Krupka turned to me and said, "Hania, why did this damned Nechaika come here? Maybe she wouldn't inform on you, but can we be sure of that? We can't take that risk in these times and circumstances."

"Life is like a nightmare," I replied. "It's lasting much too long to suit me." I went into my room and took my suitcase out of the closet. Little Janko came in and saw me packing.

"Where are you going, Hania?" he piped, curious as usual.

We told him that I was going to see my mother; that I had received news that she had suddenly fallen ill and needed me. We used the same excuse for the superintendent when he called for me later that evening.

Mrs. Krupka seemed to be more nervous about all this than I. By nature, she was the worrying type and was easily upset. She went from room to room, looking for something to give me. She kept bringing me various items, adding them to my modest possessions—a silk nightgown, some toilet soap, things like that. She also prepared a food package containing ham, sausages, and loaves of bread—she tried to coax me to take it, as though I were really going home to visit my mother. She folded her hands as though in prayer and looked at me sadly. "Hania, when you started packing I couldn't help but think—it's almost six months since we took you into our family. We did not conceal anything from you ever; we had complete confidence in you. Do you suppose that today I can see you go away without my heart breaking? Can I let you go into the unknown?"

"That doesn't depend on you," I replied. "That's how it has to be. You have saved my life, you nursed me through an attack of typhus, and I am deeply grateful. But circumstances are such that now there is no alternative. I must go and leave my fate in God's hands."

She seemed to be listening to her own thoughts, not hearing what I said. "Hania, if you at least had some definite place to go, even to spend a night or two before you leave to go away still further into the world. I'll give you my sister's address—she lives in Lvov, on 12 Piekarska Street. Here, write it down. She will take you in, I'm sure, for she is kind-hearted, like me. Although, on the other hand, they may also be afraid of the Germans . . . But you take this package of food for her, as a pretext. The rest will be up to you. I have faith in you. The rest is in your hands."

I put my arms around Mrs. Krupka and kissed her. We could not hold back our bitter tears. It was hard to believe that all this was really happening.

I took only my summer clothes and what I was wearing for the trip. I would carry my brown sport coat over my arms, in case it was cold at night in the train. I carefully rewrapped the small bundle with the jewelry that Mother had given me. Mrs. Krupka put away my winter clothing, saying that she would send it to me wherever I was next winter. I did not even reply to that; I was not planning so far ahead.

The rest of that evening a pall of sadness descended on the house. We were so preoccupied with our problems that we did not hear or see what was going on just a few streets away. Only when Mr. Krupka came with the ticket for me did we learn that the ghetto in Brody was being liquidated. "What a time Hania has picked for going away!" he exclaimed testily. "The entire railway station is filled with Gestapo men. I got her a ticket for the train that leaves at two in the morning, but how she will be able to get on it without being caught, I don't know. Everybody is being examined. They expect many Jews will try to escape from the ghetto. And she doesn't even have papers!"

"I have a birth certificate," I threw in, "so at least they will know that I was born some place!" Whatever might happen, I decided that I would go. I took the ticket and thanked Mr. Krupka.

Little Janko broke into our conversation. "Hania, when will you return? Come back soon," he said, with tears in his large brown eyes. "Come back as soon as you can." And he cried.

Ah, what a night that was! Though darkness fell at last, no one thought of food or sleep. Now we could hear shots coming more frequently from the direction of the ghetto. Fear chilled our bones. I felt as though I had fallen into a quicksand that would engulf me completely. If I must die, I thought, let it come quickly, without torture . . .

Janko did not want to go to bed—he wanted to stay awake until my departure—but at last sleep won out. Then his mother could speak to me more freely. "Hania," she said, "every day I will think of you. Be careful. Try to find a good, safe place to stay. And after the war, write to us and come."

"I am glad, really, that it happened this way," I told her through my tears.

"Thank God, my conscience is clear," she said. "I don't regret for a moment that we took you in and sheltered you." I knew that every word she said was true. She had done everything possible to keep me and help me, though it had placed their lives in danger. She loved me and I loved her.

"And I'm relieved that I shall no longer endanger you and your family by my presence. Now I have only myself to look out for."

Mr. Krupka came in again. He went to see if my picture had by any chance gotten into the papers. He said that he had arranged with the superintendent to call for me later, before train time. He brought several cartons of cigarettes and gave them to me, saying, "These may be very useful sometime. They are hard to get." I thanked him for his thoughtfulness, and for everything.

A girl we knew, Nechaika, had been the catalyst that suddenly solved the months-old problem of what I should do. But now, one unwary move and I could be lost. Finally, breaking our tense vigil, we heard the superintendent's steps outside, and I began to say goodbye. There was so much that I wanted to say at that moment, but it seemed as though I could not utter a word, except once again: Thank you for everything!

Tears rolled down Mrs. Krupka's cheeks. Mr. Krupka said, "I'm going with her to the station." I understood why: He knew the police and all the authorities in the city, and in case of an inspection we would not be detained.

Quietly I opened the door to Janko's room and whispered, "Good-night, Janko. Goodbye!" But the child was already fast asleep.

The superintendent took my suitcase and the package. Mrs. Krupka said, with great intensity in her voice, "Hania, write me how your mother is—and if she is feeling better, come back right away." She wanted to be sure that the words sank into the superintendent's ears.

"Yes, yes. I will." Once again I looked at her, putting my whole heart into that glance. I leaned over and patted Zeze; even the dog seemed to sense that something was wrong, and kept barking as I went down the creaking stairs. No one said a word.

We got into the horse-drawn wagon. Once more I looked at the house that had sheltered me so hospitably for six months. Mrs. Krupka stood in the window, waving at me. I waved back. The wagon started rattling along the cobbled street.

It was May 22, 1943, when I parted from the Krupka family and left Brody. It was the second parting, and the start of a second journey.

1. *Sheva before the war, 1939.*

2. *Sheva by the river in Rohatyn, 1937.*

3. Rose, Sheva's older sister.

4. The Krupkas with Sheva and her husband in New York, April 1966.

5. *The hospital where Sheva worked for two years, posing as a Catholic.*

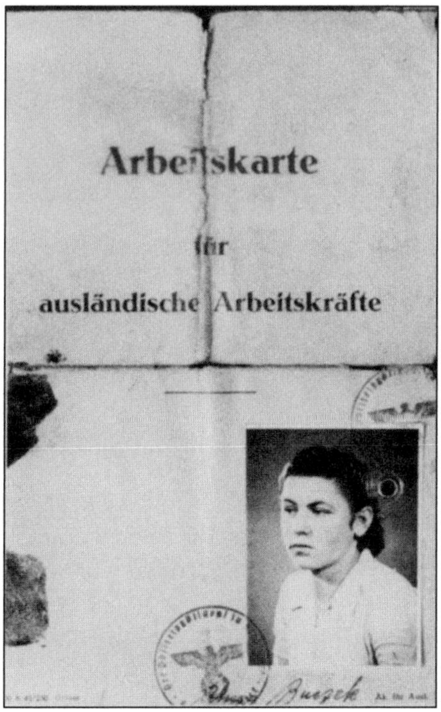

6. *Sheva's working card received from the Gestapo in Stuttgart.*

7. The sisters at the hospital cared for and befriended Sheva.

8. Sheva's first real birthday party, November 20, 1945, with Margie and her American husband. Three nuns from the hospital also attended.

9. *Israel Lederman, Sheva's husband.*

10. *Sheva, now Sylvia Lederman, 1987.*

11. Monument, erected in 1947 in the Hebron Cemetery in Long Island, commemorating the people who were burned alive in the Rohatyn ghetto.

6

Into the Unknown, Alone

NOW THE SHOTS RANG OUT LOUDLY as we approached the railway station. From time to time, Gestapo passed us as we rode along unfamiliar streets. But the town of Brody had always been strange to me, and I a stranger within its boundaries. All I left behind were my tears and my fears; a poor legacy, indeed! The town was quiet except for the ghetto, where even during the darkness of the night the Nazis were exterminating the last traces of human habitation.

The railway station seethed with Gestapo officers and militia. Perhaps they were getting the cars ready to deport Jews from the ghetto. We could hear only the shots and commands, and we knew they were meant for the Jews. We took my things from the wagon and started for the platform and the train. The last farewells, words of gratitude, and I picked up my luggage and boarded the train. It was dark inside, but I could see the silhouetted officers in uniform, flashlights in their hands. I noticed that there was plenty of room in the train. Next to a window sat a Ukrainian policeman, alone; instantly I thought that this would be a good place for me to sit. And without any hesitation I went to him, asking him in perfect Ukrainian if I could sit beside him. Smilingly, he took my baggage and helped me to get settled comfortably, saying that I was a beautiful girl. A moment later the train jolted to a start.

The policeman was curious how I knew that he was Ukrainian. I said, "I can always tell my own kind, and I know the uniform anyway." He seemed quite pleased with my remark. But, I thought, what will he say when the controlling officer asks to see my papers and my birth certificate shows that I am Polish? Well, then I would say that my mother was Polish and my father Ukrainian. It was a plausible explanation from a professional liar . . .

As the train picked up speed, our conversation became livelier and louder. I told him that I was going to visit my aunt and uncle in Lvov. It was my first trip to that city, I said, and I was curious to see the beautiful town.

At the end of the corridor I could see some Gestapo entering from another car. They shone their flashlights into the faces of the passengers, told them to open their luggage for inspection, and demanded that some show their identification papers.

I drew closer to the Ukrainian policeman—even hugged and kissed him—and tried to keep up a running conversation with him. A few minutes more, and it was my turn! I replied to the Gestapo officers' questions with a smile, though my head was splitting and my blood pounding. When the light flashed into my eyes, I heard one of them say to the other: "Here's a Ukrainian policeman with a girl—or maybe his wife. Heil, Hitler!" The Ukrainian replied, "Heil, Hitler!"—and I said it too. And they left.

God, it was a miracle! I couldn't believe it! The Ukrainian kept on talking and I pretended to listen politely. But in my heart I was listening again to my mother's voice, imploring God to watch over me, to help me survive . . .

The Ukrainian said, "The Germans are inspecting all the trains because they are liquidating the Jews, in Brody, everywhere—even in Lvov." As dawn began to break we neared the city. The same Gestapo officers kept walking through the train all night, for it stopped at every station on the way. However, they paid no attention to me and the Ukrainian; whenever I saw them approach nearer, I tried to draw my chance companion into animated conversation. Through the opened windows came fresh, warm breezes, and now that the sun was rising, we could hear notes of birdsongs.

And then another sound—people singing, very faintly, in the distance. I heard what seemed like music—but not an orchestra, nor a military band. As we came to the station, I looked out and saw men in what looked like striped pajamas, standing in rows. Some of them had musical instruments and they were singing a Jewish song. I was so astonished that I almost said something to my Ukrainian companion, but bit my tongue just in time and tried to control my emotions. I had to be doubly careful, for it was daylight now and he could see the expression on my face. Breaking through my silence, he said, "Those are Jews. No doubt they are being taken to the place of execution where they will be shot. They are commanded to sing and dance before they die."

It wasn't necessary for him to have explained the scene to me. I had witnessed similar scenes and knew what was going on. I felt that dizziness come over me. I held on to the window frame, for I thought I would faint.

The group of men—there may have been a hundred at most—marched slowly. The train also slowed down, more and more. In the distance I could see a dragon of fire and I heard shooting. "That is Janowska Street," the Ukrainian said. "That's where they burn the Jews."

As we pulled into the station, more people came to look out of the windows, but not one expressed a word of pity. They all seemed to enjoy the tragic spectacle before them on the station platform—they were smiling scornfully, obviously amused. Now the passengers were getting ready to leave the train. The Ukrainian's words still drummed upon my brain: "They're burning the Jews," he had said, happily.

"Lvov!" thundered the voice of the conductor. The policeman courteously took my baggage off the rack and helped me down the steps. We left together. I kept close to him, for the station in Lvov, as in Brody, was surrounded by Gestapo—only this, being a larger station, had a larger number of Nazis. I saw that my companion was in a hurry and I tried to hold him back, at least until we could leave the station together and reach the street.

"Please," I asked him, "show me how I can get to Piekarska Street. What streetcar should I take?" He said that he could not go with me because he was going to see his wife in the hospital so I suggested that he speak to one of the Gestapo officers to help me. He agreed. Although the idea of seeking help from Gestapo sent shivers down my spine, I felt it would, perversely, give me greater security.

After an enthusiastic exchange of "Heil, Hitler!" the Ukrainian explained, in broken German, that I wanted to get to Piekarska Street, but did not know how to get there—and, he added, I did not know any German. Of course, for me to use it would provoke suspicion. The Gestapo officer obligingly directed me to the tramway, and he told the conductor where to let me off. I thanked him in Ukrainian, using expressive gestures to denote my grateful feelings. So I escaped inspection, thanks to the presence of the Ukrainian policeman, and I did not have to show identification papers! Had I acted timidly and tried to avoid contact with the authorities, I would have been caught. But since I put myself alongside a man of authority, a policeman, no one suspected that I was Jewish . . . one of those whom they were hunting.

I paid for my tram ticket and sat down. I was tired and hungry. The streetcar made frequent stops, though the hour was very early and there were not many people aboard. Everything here was strange to me. The city seemed cold, indifferent. I felt only loneliness and fear . . . My thoughts were interrupted by the conductor calling out the name of the street. As though awakening from sleep, I picked up my suitcase and package, thanked the conductor in Ukrainian, and got off. At the last moment I turned and asked him in which direction I should go, and he politely showed me the way.

My baggage seemed to weigh more heavily, but it was only because I felt so weak and tired. At last I found the house where Mrs. Krupka's sister and brother-in-law lived.

Mr. Tarashkewitz was a retired professor, and they had no children; that was all I knew about them. The hour was still early, and I wondered whether or not to ring their bell. On the other hand, I did not want to stand out in the street. I made my way slowly up to the second floor and looked for their name on the doors. I could imagine how surprised they would be to see such an uninvited, unnecessary, and dangerous visitor. I rang one, timidly, and waited. When no one answered, I rang again, this time pressing the button harder.

A frightened voice asked through the door, "Who is there?"

I waited till the door opened a crack. "Mrs. Tarashkewitz?"

"Yes. Who are you?"

"Hania. Hania from Brody."

They knew about me, who I was. Mrs. Tarashkewitz said nothing, but let me in. For a while, she appeared dumbfounded. What to do? What has happened? I could see that I had gotten her out of bed, for she was still wearing her nightgown; her husband was still asleep. She brought me into a small room and told me to sit down. She did not resemble her sister, Mrs. Krupka, at all. She was tall, rather stout, with a full, round face and a deep voice. But the kind expression on her face reminded me of her sister. We spoke in whispers, so as not to awaken anyone. Besides her husband, her niece—a student at the Lvov Polytechnic Institute—also made her home with them; she was still asleep, for it was a Sunday morning.

I told her that I was very sorry that I had disturbed their sleep so early, and I tried to find words to explain my visit there in such a way as not to cause her alarm. I started by telling her that I brought a package from her sister—Mrs. Krupka thought they could use the extra supplies of food. Then, in a whisper, I told her what happened to me in Brody—my meeting with the Nechaika girl . . .

As I talked, I watched the expression on Mrs. Tarashkewitz's face and saw that she was frightened and groping for the right thing to say to me. Tears welled up into my eyes as I begged her to let me stay for a few days, or even for a day or two. After a short silence, Mrs. Tarashkewitz remarked that it was a great problem, indeed—that along the streets everywhere there were posters announcing that whoever gives shelter to a Jew will be punished by death. Especially now that the ghetto was being liquidated in Lvov and in other cities, every strange person was suspected. Even the neighbors, as soon as they saw a stranger, could—and very willingly did—report it to the Germans, for they were rewarded for it. She said that lately she and her husband had tried to go out as infrequently as possible and to preserve the quiet of their lives.

I saw that not even the package of food was any inducement to Mrs. Tarashkewitz to keep me, but I saw so much kindness in her face that I felt that she would not turn me away in spite of her fears. I said that if she would only let me stay for a day or two, it would give me a chance to look around for a place to live. My latest experiences in Brody made it imperative for me to leave that town. And here I was, a frightened, small slip of a girl . . . In a big world, among millions of people, alone and without a roof over my head. Whom should I ask? Who would answer my plea? If my mother had only known . . .

Quietly, Mrs. Tarashkewitz went into the kitchen and made fresh coffee. The wonderful aroma filled the entire apartment. She also gave me something more substantial to eat, setting the breakfast before me in the small guest room. I noticed her hands were shaking.

The room I was sitting in had heavy drapes on the window, and it was impossible for anyone to notice me from the street below. After some time we heard soft footsteps in the adjoining room. Mrs. Tarashkewitz motioned for me not to speak. She went out, closing the door after her. "She's just like her sister," I said to myself. "Always trying to smooth things out, to present a problem in its rosiest aspects." I could hear whispers in the kitchen. She was telling her husband about the unexpected guest. No doubt they were deliberating what to do with me, I thought. Then suddenly the door opened and they both entered the small room.

The words of explanation and apology for having intruded on their household so early in the morning, for causing them so much trouble and anxiety, died on my lips when I saw Professor Tarashkewitz—for I knew he understood completely. When I was introduced, he greeted me with a kind smile. I liked him at once. He was of medium height, slight of build, very gracious—in manner and appearance every inch an educated, cultured gentleman. What a wonderful feeling it gave me when I saw their mutual willingness to help me and to understand and sympathize!

They asked me not to disclose to their niece my real identity or my reason for coming. When she awoke, they would tell her that I was some distant relative—their families were widely branched out. Besides, she was so busy preparing for exams that she would probably not even stop to think about me. They did not suspect that she would denounce me if she knew the truth, but it was best for her to know nothing. (Incidentally, that niece is now living in the United States, with a highly responsible position—and when I met her recently at the Krupka's house and reminded her of this incident in Lvov, she laughed heartily and confessed she had no idea then that I was not really her relative, but a Jewish refugee.)

The Tarashkewitzes occupied a large and comfortable apartment—it was so spacious, in fact, that there were several rooms I never entered. I used only one entrance that led directly to the kitchen, and from there to the small room, where I found temporary shelter.

They had only so much food as they could receive on their ration cards; I knew that they could not afford to overeat, and now they would also have to share their meager rations with me. Fortunately, I had brought plenty of food with me, donated by Mrs. Krupka, and it would last a week or maybe two. A larger problem was how to preserve me from falling into a trap—and drawing them into it along with me. Each new arrival in town had to be registered within three days and had to obtain a ration card. For this, one needed personal documents—a passport or identity card. Since the ghetto in Lvov was liquidated, numerous rumors had circulated that the authorities would go from house to house, checking on possible Jewish stowaways.

And here were these two quiet, elderly people who until now had lived peacefully, though with limited means. They had tried until now not to transgress any laws so as to not get into trouble. And suddenly I had appeared, destroying their peace! I fervently hoped I would not have to stay at their home longer than just a few days . . .

After breakfast, they went to church and asked me not to answer if I heard a knock on the door or someone calling. I remained sitting on a chair, all alone in the room, a prey to my thoughts.

My light dreams were not interrupted until the return of the Tarashkewitzes from church. Mrs. Tarashkewitz went into the kitchen to start dinner. Her husband came into the guest room and talked a while with me. With sympathetic understanding, he advised me to look in the newspaper for job openings. I told him that tomorrow I would look up Mr. Kowalski, whose address had been given me at Rohatyn—he might be able to place me somewhere.

Their niece did not join us at the dinner table, having been invited to some friend's house. The food was plain, but prepared tastefully and served in an attractive manner. Mrs. Tarashkewitz did not even let me help with the dishes—partly, I suppose, because she still regarded me as a guest, but mostly because she was afraid that someone might see me in the kitchen window. So I spent all the time in the small guest room, with the drapes and shades drawn. Time dragged. I could hardly wait for the next day, thinking that if I could get in touch with Mr. Kowalski, he would be able to help me, in return for money or jewelry. I went to bed right after supper. Just one more day, two at most, and I would not be here to complicate the lives of these good people. I lay awake for hours, making plans of one kind or another. Without hope, I could not exist.

But the next day, I found that my hopes were without foundation. I went to see Mr. Kowalski only to learn that he had been taken by the Gestapo, and I myself was almost taken captive by one of his housemates; the woman wanted me to wait, but I escaped. The day was a total waste. In the evening, Professor Tarashkewitz went out and brought me a newspaper. He showed me an advertisement for the state employment bureau; they wanted girls and young men for various kinds of work. He advised me to try the next morning.

So, armed with fresh courage and energy, I went there the next day, trying to forget that I was Jewish, that I was hiding under a false name. I tried only to think that I was Hanka Buczek, a Polish girl, and that I had every right to seek work and live like all the others. Holding my head high, I entered the building where the bureau was located. The waiting room was filled with people queued up in long lines. First, I quickly looked around, checking if by any chance there was someone I might have known from Rohatyn.

The woman behind the desk spoke to me in German, but I pretended I did not understand. Then she directed me to another clerk who asked if I spoke Polish or Ukrainian. "Yes," I said, "either language." We continued the interview in Ukrainian. I gave her my name, my place, and date of birth. "Show me your Kennkarte," she demanded.

I tried to explain that I did not have it with me, because I only wanted to get information about job opportunities. "I did not think I'd need a Kennkarte for this," I said, "but if necessary, I'll go home and bring it."

She eyed me up and down and then whispered something to a man who was standing near her desk. They talked in German—she repeated her conversation with me, thinking that I did not understand, but I did.

After listening to her, the man went to a telephone, and I could hear him plainly tell someone at the other end that he has a suspicious character here. I knew immediately that he was telephoning the police station or the Gestapo. It was too late to run away, for I would have been caught at once. I feigned complete indifference and leaned over to ask the woman if I could go to the washroom. She pointed to a door at the end of the room and I went in that direction, but instead of going into the toilet I bolted out the door and into the street. Fortunately, because of the crowd of people in the employment bureau, my escape was not immediately noticed, and I reached the car stop and took the first tram that came along, not caring in which direction it was going. When the streetcar stopped near a park, I got out. I did not know where I was; I sat down on a bench. It didn't matter. I had lots of time, and nowhere to go . . . I sat, totally resigned to my fate.

My musings were interrupted by sounds that beat like hammers on my consciousness—sounds of heavy, measured footsteps, sounds I had heard so many times before that I instantly knew what they were. I looked in their direction, and saw several Gestapo coming toward me. They seemed to be in a hurry. Were they looking for me? It made no difference now! But to my astonishment they did not even glance my way.

I remained on the park bench for several hours, until I was roused from my inertia by the sight of a Gestapo officer in the distance, dragging a young boy after him. The lad—I thought he was Jewish—tried to pull away and run, but the German simply gripped him harder. Suddenly, I heard a shot—and the boy's dead body lay sprawled on the sidewalk. Even then, the Gestapo officer kicked him as though he wanted to push him off the sidewalk into the gutter. Then he left.

It all happened so quickly, without an outcry, without tears. If it were not for the shot, no one would have noticed the incident. A few passersby stopped for a second. Their whispers reached my ears: "He must have escaped from the ghetto," they were saying. "A Jew, no doubt. He wanted to hide."

I thought: *Who knows? In an hour, a few minutes maybe, a few days at most, this same fate can befall me.* The sight of the dead boy sent a chill up my spine. I got up from the bench at last and, slowly, reached the streetcar stop.

By the time I arrived at the Tarashkewitzes' house, it was dark—and my stomach at last had started to protest against being starved all day. I had no sensation of hunger until then; fear had taken away all craving for food.

Piekarska Street was dark, quiet, and empty. The Tarashkewitzes were probably very worried about me by this time, and feeling a pang of conscience for having caused them this anxiety, I crept up the stairs like a thief. As soon as I knocked on the door, in the special way we had decided upon earlier as a signal, I heard Mrs. Tarashkewitz call out, "Hania! What happened?" She let me in, plying me with questions. "Did you work today? No? Then, where did you spend the whole day long? Did you eat?"

And when I shook my head negatively, she started to fuss about the kitchen, warming up some food for me. Her husband remained in the small living room—which had become "my" room—reading a paper, for he had already had his supper. When I entered and said "Good evening," he put the newspaper aside and asked me to give him an account of how I had spent the day. As he listened, his face showed his disappointment.

When I was summoned by Mrs. Tarashkewitz to come to the kitchen, I sat down and ate everything she put before me. After I had had my fill, we returned to the small room and they both put the question to me: "What do you intend to do now? Where will you go?"

Three days had elapsed since my coming to Lvov, and I knew that I should register with the police. Even non-Jews had to register in the place where they intended to take up permanent residence. We sat up until late that night, discussing my situation, trying to make plans for the future. Even when at last I went to bed, I could not sleep. The events of that terrible evening finally came fully alive in my mind. I was aware of what was happening around me; I realized the precariousness of my existence. Where would I go tomorrow? Although I bit my lips until they bled, to keep from crying aloud, I could not hold back my sobs—even though I trembled in fear, knowing that the Tarashkewitzes' niece was asleep in the next room. Louder and louder became my spasmodic cries, and at times I called out, "Mamma, O Mamma, help me!" I was absolutely unable to control myself.

Suddenly the door to my room opened and Mrs. Tarashkewitz came in. She took my hand and said gently, "Hania, Hania, try to be calm. What has happened? Please, stop crying."

But instead of stopping, my cries became louder and more despairing. She placed her hand over my mouth and stroked my hair, which was as damp as if I had just come out of a bath. My nightclothes and the pillow were also wet with tears and perspiration. She gave me a glass of cold water, and I finally quieted down a little. I said nothing. I felt as weak as a fly. The emotional reaction to the events of the preceding day had at last taken their toll. Mrs. Tarashkewitz covered me with a blanket, signed my forehead with a cross, and left. I knew that she felt for me, but what could she do? To keep me in her home meant risking all their lives.

After a long and dismal night, I managed to get up, wash, get dressed, and eat breakfast. I was exhausted. I could not go anywhere that day. I read the newspaper carefully, noting places where I might apply for work. Then it occurred to me that I had the address of the German woman who had been transferred from Brody to a better position in Lvov. Hastily, I opened my suitcase and found her address. It was a spark of hope; perhaps she would take me to work for her as a servant, simply for my food and lodging. But when I went by her apartment that day after lunch, she told me quite abruptly that she needed no help, and that she could not stop to converse. Once again, I felt sunk in despair.

Again, I turned to reading the newspaper ads for employment opportunities. The days passed, each one more dangerous than the last. Public notices, radio broadcasts, papers—from all sides one could hear only one cry: *"Judenrein!"* or *"Judenfrei!"* Get rid of the Jews! Now Professor Tarashkewitz bought several newspapers a day, all the papers he could get. At last we found one advertisement: Girls and young men (Gentile, naturally) were wanted for work in Germany. This seemed to fit our needs. We paused to analyze the pros and cons. I would have to apply at the camp on Janowska Street—the same street where a Jewish ghetto was located. On the other hand, once in Germany, I could try to lose myself, achieve some degree of anonymity. Germany was far from Lvov, or Rohatyn, or Brody. Ironically, that made it safer than remaining in Poland.

We read further. What would I need? A work card, of course; clothing, and a certificate of good health—they did not want sick people. My problem was how to obtain a work card. Where? From Brody? I had submitted my papers there, at the city hall; that was the only place. We had

had no news from the Krupka family. Though the Tarashkewitzes were saddled with me, they did not want to take the risk of writing to Brody; but the letter could not be put off any longer. They would have to write—very obliquely and diplomatically of course—and yet so that the Krupkas would understand. The Professor helped compose that important letter. After many tries we finished it and sent it off. Now we impatiently waited for a reply. Meanwhile, I did not look for employment, for we had decided it would be safest for me to make an application to the work camp and to leave these parts of the country for good. So I became a guest of the Tarashkewitzes, not for a day or two as I had expected and as they had hoped but for a considerably longer time. I was really sorry for these people who, because of my presence in their home, had to live in mortal fear.

At last the month of May drew to a close. Each day we looked for the mailman to bring a reply from the Krupka family, but in vain. Our fears increased; we supposed any number of evil things might have happened, for this silence was disturbing, and in such critical times one could only look for the worst.

At last, I asked them to send a telegram to Brody. I gave the Professor some money to cover the cost of the wire, and he went to the post office to take care of it. Just a few words: WORK PAPERS NEEDED URGENTLY, followed by the Professor's name as the sender. I hoped that this telegram would bring quick results.

Three days after sending out the telegram, much to our relief, a letter came from Mr. Krupka in Brody. Enclosed was a card showing that I was officially registered for work and checked out from Brody. Our faces shone with joy! We passed the small card from hand to hand—it was about the size of an ordinary postcard, maybe smaller. Just an *Arbeitskarte,* a work card, but it was the card of salvation. It saved the Tarashkewitzes more of this strain, and it saved me especially—it was my hope for a future! I pressed the card to my heart as though it were a precious treasure, as indeed it was.

I began to get ready. My suitcase had, except for a change of clothes, remained packed since my arrival in Lvov. I decided to wear my dark green suit and the blouse that my mother had made me—it might bring me luck. While I was repacking my things, the Tarashkewitzes held a conference in the kitchen; they were worried about how I would get to the work camp. It was finally decided that Mrs. Tarashkewitz would accompany me there. I thanked them for this lovely gesture, and accepted her kind offer, though it would still be risky. Suppose someone should recognize me?

How good it was of Mr. Krupka to send me the work card! No doubt he had had plenty of trouble getting it. I guessed that he had used his influence in obtaining this document for me. But, in any case, he must have assumed a great risk. I wished that I could show my gratitude . . .

When I threw the last things into the suitcase, I came across the small packet of jewelry, and an idea came to my mind. I opened the packet and considered what I should leave for Mr. Krupka. They had shown me so much kindness—thanks to them, I was still alive. They took care of me, nursed me through a siege of typhus—without any compensation. Fear and troubles were their only reward. I looked through my valuables and picked the gold watch that had once been my father's. It was many years since my father was killed in World War I, and although the remembrance was precious, I felt I could part with the watch. And I wanted to hold on to my mother's jewelry as long as possible—maybe someday I might be able to return it to her.

When Mrs. Tarashkewitz called me, I went to the kitchen and placed my father's large gold watch in the center of the table. I saw the amazement in their eyes as they exchanged looks across the table. Perhaps they thought that I meant it as a gift for them; perhaps not. I asked them to be good enough to give the watch to Mr. Krupka if he comes, as a token of gratitude. I was sorry, I said, that I could not give them anything now, but in the future I might be able to express my thanks better. They guessed that I had a few things left, but they also knew that the road ahead of me was long. As a matter of fact, I did not know for certain whether I would get anything to eat when I reported at the work camp. I said goodbye to the Professor, who blessed me like a father, and said that he wished I could come back to visit them after the war and tell them about all the experiences still ahead of me. I thanked them for the shelter they had provided me, and asked them to forgive me for causing so much anxiety and trouble.

Now I left with Mrs. Tarashkewitz, talking with her in Ukrainian so as not to draw any attention if someone should meet us in the hall. Armed with the work card, I felt more sure of myself. We waited at the car stop.

The streetcar, when it came, was almost full, but we managed to find seats. We said little, looking out of the window at the passing throng. It was a warm, beautiful day—the second of June—and I was somewhat too heavily dressed. I felt like I was melting, but in my case it was not just the temperature but rather my nervous reaction to this new adventure that made me perspire uncomfortably. For here I was again setting out into the unknown, risking everything, not knowing what the morrow might bring. To give myself courage, I repeated my mother's parting blessing—"O God, give her strength, watch over her!" and I prayed to my father.

Gradually the character of the streets changed, grew shabbier, and after a long ride we came to the last stop outside the city limits. We still had a distance to walk to reach the work camp on Janowska Street. We had to cross railway tracks and follow an unpaved, sandy road, frequently stubbing our shoes on the protruding stones. I changed my suitcase from one hand to the other as I grew tired; it hit against my legs, and I often had to stop and rest. The sun was very hot, and I was wearing a coat.

We hardly met a soul on the way to the camp; once we saw someone crossing the railroad tracks in the distance. I pitied my companion, for she was bathed in perspiration and her clothes were covered in dust. This was no pleasant promenade for an older, stout person! But at last we discerned the gates of the camp; it was surrounded by a wooden board fence, quite high, and guards were posted at the gates. The camp was big.

At the gate stood a Ukrainian policeman and a Sonderdienst man. With pounding heart, I gave them my name and said I was reporting for work in Germany. They took my work card, showing I had been registered in Brody, and told me to go inside the building. They showed me in which direction to turn to find the right office. I parted from Mrs. Tarashkewitz at the gate, telling her in a loud voice—so the guards would hear—that I would write, and asking her to give my regards to "everyone." With tears in our eyes, we embraced and kissed, but tried to keep our emotions under control. We couldn't let the sobs that shook us inside burst out and betray our deep fears.

Now I was alone . . . I walked toward the large building straight ahead, carrying my suitcase. The camp was composed of several such buildings, some frame and some brick, in a desolate area outside the city. I saw signs in three languages above the door where I was to enter; Application Office, Medical Commission. As I looked around, I saw people going in and coming out of the various buildings—civilians and militia. Before I pushed the door open, I wondered if this might be my last step . . . The whole camp and its surroundings did not portend anything good to my mind. There were too many "authorities" in this camp; the whole air seemed to smell of danger. But there was nothing I could do now. My knock on the door was answered with a gruff "*jawohl.*" I entered.

At that moment I felt like I must have been made of iron, indeed, and my heart of stone—otherwise, I could not have stood up on my own legs and faced the two men behind the desk. One of them was wearing a white coat, like a doctor, and the other was in civilian clothes. The civilian asked whether I spoke German. "No, I speak Polish." And he continued his questioning in that language, asking my name, birth date, occupation. I showed him my card; on it was stated that I was a servant, from Brody. "How did you happen to come here?" he asked. I told him that I came of my own free will. That must have aroused his suspicion. Who ever came here voluntarily? Though he kept on writing, he constantly looked up and observed me. The other man, while he was busy looking through some files, kept an eye on me, and his ears seemed to be ready to catch every word. It wasn't often that I had to lie about my identity or occupation, but this was a matter of life or death for me. I had no other choice but to resort to lies.

When the interrogator wrote on my application "*freiwillig*"—volunteer—I noticed that the other man was singularly impressed. He stopped going through his files and looked at me from head to foot. Well, that one word, at least, was not a lie: I was a volunteer . . . And yet, it was a dangerous word, for no Polish or Ukrainian girls volunteered to go to Germany as workers. On the contrary, the Germans had to hunt them down and catch them, either in their homes or on the streets, to send them to Germany. Yet here, supposedly, was a Polish girl volunteering for work! Instantly they must have thought that I was Jewish, that I was trying to escape from the ghetto this way, to find shelter. But it was too late to go back. And even if I tried, what could I do? Where would I go? I stood there, trembling, yet anxious to look calm, waiting for further questions.

When the man had finished writing, he sent me to the one in the white jacket. They sat at the same table, but the table was long and there was a considerable space between them. The white-coated one picked up my card and started writing on another form, asking me (also in Polish) about my state of health. Did I ever have any serious illness? Operations? I told him that as far as I could recall, I had only measles as a child, and occasionally the grippe—but that was all. I did not mention that only recently I had been sick with the typhus. It might have increased their suspicions, because typhus was prevalent in the ghettos.

The doctor—for now I understood that that was who he was—asked me to step up closer. He looked into my eyes, looked me all over, and said, "I don't think you will be able to work in Germany. You look anemic, too thin. It would be a shame to send you there, because they would not accept you. And I think you are running a temperature."

While he was saying this, the other official kept looking both at him and at me. I tried to protest that I was healthy and strong, and that if I had a high temperature I would certainly know it. "I am just warm because it is a hot day and I'm dressed too heavily for it," I said. "It was a long walk from the car stop. And saying goodbye to my aunt upset me. That's all. I'm sure I am not running a temperature."

But he insisted that he was right. Meanwhile, some young German Sonderdienst man came in and said something in German that I did not hear. He left a list on the table. That gave me a moment to catch my breath—though I almost stopped breathing at the sight of his hated uniform! After he left, the doctor said to me, "Take your suitcase and come with me to my office. It is next to the camp hospital and I have all my instruments there. I will give you a thorough examination."

I followed him out of the building. Now I could see that he was quite tall, about thirty-five, and that he limped slightly. He walked slowly, as though pushing himself forward. I felt like I really was beginning to run a temperature. I did not know where he was taking me; if it had been any further, I'm afraid I would have fainted—black spots floated before my eyes. As through a mist I could see now how large the camp was. It was under the strict surveillance of German and Ukrainian military authorities. People were swarming all over the place. And to this place, I, Sheva Weiler, had to come! I came as though I had wanted to save them the trouble of hunting me down!

We stopped in front of a small building and he opened the door. Although it was a bright day, the interior was so dark and damp that he had to put on an electric light. The room was furnished with old equipment: a table, some chairs and benches, metal closets, files. A few doctor's instruments were spread out on the table. He asked me to sit down, and I dropped into the nearest chair, for my legs would not hold me up any longer. He sat opposite me and seemed to be lost in thought. After a moment he opened the door to another room, looked inside, and closed it again. He asked me in a voice hardly above a whisper, "What is your name?"

"Hanka Buczek," I replied suspiciously.

"Miss Hania," he addressed me graciously, "you've come here to find help, but you've only succeeded in getting deeper into trouble—quite deep. I intentionally told you that you have a fever, because I wanted to get you out of that room—and, if possible, to help you get away from this place altogether."

Listening to his unexpected words, I thought that my heart would stop beating. I knew now definitely that he recognized who I was. I was trapped! But I did not want to admit it. "I don't know what you're saying, Doctor," I said in return. "I just don't understand anything."

He got up from the chair and went to the front door, opened it a crack, and closed it again. I thought, *now he will go and report me*—but he returned and sat down across from my chair. "Admit it," he said gently, "I only want to help you. Many girls have tried to escape this way since the ghettos in Lvov and other towns have been liquidated. They try to escape to Germany to work, posing as Polish or Ukrainian girls. But the Ukrainian criminal police come here frequently, looking for Jews, and they catch them like flies. I cannot look on while they torture them and send them to the flames—I cannot stand it any longer. For God's sake, Miss, believe me and go away from here!"

And yet I did not trust him completely. Who knows how much he was paid for each Jewish head he turned in? I knew that the Germans used various methods of catching us. I still thought that it was some sort of game he was playing, and I firmly refused to make the admission. If he really meant what he said, why was he working here—with those German murderers? But he kept on persuading, imploring me to believe him.

"I am a Pole," he continued, "a former air force pilot. I was wounded in the leg at the outbreak of the war—and I'll have this souvenir for the rest of my life. I have two brothers who were captains in the Polish army, but they are now in a German prisoner-of-war camp. Actually, I am a veterinarian, but I work here as a doctor-nurse." As he spoke, he put his hand in his pocket, pulled out a Kennkarte, and showed it to me. "See, here's my name, Dr. Jagoda, a Pole, from Kalisz." Quickly, he took the card away from me and put it in his pocket. I was almost convinced, but not quite. I would not yet admit who I was.

"Do you think that I like working here?" he went on. "It costs me a lot in health and nerves to see the secret police take those girls and lead them to the camp at the other end of this street, on the hill, and cremate them. But before they are killed, these girls are tortured and raped. Some are thrown into the flames alive. These girls come here voluntarily to register for work—and that is the first thing that makes them suspect. And so did you, when you registered for work voluntarily—you aroused their suspicions."

I knew the story was true. On the way from Brody to Lvov by train, I had heard about the camp on Janowska Street from the Ukrainian militia man who sat in my compartment. He had told me that the Germans try in every way to find out who produces the false passports and identity cards. They torture the Jewish suspects until they either confess who their contacts were or perish under the interrogations. All this corroborated what the doctor was telling me. I saw tears in his eyes as he spoke. I listened mutely, still undecided, for I could not understand why a stranger should want to help me at the risk of his life.

While I hesitated, he added: "The next transport will not leave before the Pentecost holidays, so you would have to remain here for ten days, at least. I feel sure that in that time you could not avoid being questioned. You do not look like a typical servant; you seem to be too young for that; certainly younger than the birth date given in your work card. Your appearance is too pretty and refined—and anyway, when they read the list and find the word 'freiwillig' next to your name, they will guess you are Jewish. Polish and Ukrainian girls try to run away when they're brought here by force; they already know how hard they would have to work in Germany, for next to nothing, so they don't want to go. You came of your free will. Now that the Judenfrei campaign is on and the ghettos are being liquidated, the Germans and the Ukrainian police are on the lookout for escaping Jews. I will give you a pass, you will go home for the holidays, and when you return—I will try to put you on the next transport to Germany. So now, go with God, Miss Hania. Believe me, and please trust me!"

After these words, tears started rolling down my face. Then I said, "Doctor, you know the truth about me. It's useless to pretend further. But I have no place to go. Wherever I turn, I run the risk of death—no less than here." In a few words, I told him everything—how I was recognized at Brody—everything. "Besides, I have no Kennkarte," I concluded despairingly.

As I talked, I could see compassion in his face. He said, as if to himself, "This is a tragedy . . . I must think of some solution. We have been sitting here so long, it may look suspicious."

He thought for a while, then got up energetically. "Come quickly into the next room. You will get undressed and get into bed. I will give you a pill that will make your temperature rise, and I'll report that you are sick. They do not have the right to come in to inspect my patients, and that will give me a little time to consider what would be best to do. You will find another in that room, she is a Polish patient—but don't talk to her much. She is a real Pole. Besides, you will have a fever, so she will not be tempted to draw you into a conversation." Taking some pills from his medicine cabinet, he gave me one with a glass of water. I swallowed it obediently.

"Now, go with God, Miss Hania!" he whispered and opened the door to the ward. In a louder voice he said, "You will be fed later. But you must stay in bed, and with such a temperature you will not be able to take much food."

I entered the ward like a thief, unobtrusively. It was a large room with about ten beds arranged in a row along one wall. On the opposite side were benches. Ordinary, old wooden closets lined the third wall—it all looked like a third-rate, old-fashioned clinic. I noticed a young girl lying in a bed near the door—a pale, blond creature, with blue eyes. She smiled wanly.

The room was rather dark and damp; there were only two windows on one side. I began to undress, feeling that the pill was already beginning to take effect. Despite the dampness and chill, my body burned with heat. I decided to pick the bed furthest away from the girl.

She spoke timidly: "Are you Ukrainian, or Polish?"

"Polish," I answered. I gestured for her to understand that my head ached and I couldn't talk.

"Oh, that's good," she said, disregarding my gesture. "I am also Polish. They brought me here several days ago and I sprained my ankle. Did they catch you, too?"

"Yes." I put on my pajamas and put the rest of my things in a closet near my bed. I got under the covers quickly, for I felt really feverish now; my body shook, my cheeks burned, my whole head seemed afire. I heard a knock on the door; it was a woman, who brought us something to eat. The Polish girl ate greedily, but I could not touch the food. I could not even move. Either the pill was so potent, or my emotions were so tense, or it might have been a combination of both—but I lay there helpless. I heard the girl say, "She is running a temperature."

The woman who had brought the trays must have been Polish or Ukrainian, for I heard her say, "Oh, she is a new one—and already sick."

My head was bursting with pain. I wanted so much to sleep, but was unsuccessful. One thought tortured me: Why does this stranger—seeing me for the first time in his life—want to endanger his own life to help me? He knew very well that if anyone overheard our conversation, or saw him hiding me in the ward, he would be faced with death. I awaited that end every minute, as a final eventuality, but he was safe—he had a good position here—why should he take on this responsibility? Despite the pain and fever, my poor head could not leave the thought alone. Who is this Dr. Jagoda from Kalisz? Was he also, like myself, a Jew using Aryan papers? It was possible. Perhaps this doctor lost his family by the Germans, and now wants only to help others?

Another thought also bothered me: Was his attitude only a trick? Perhaps tomorrow the Ukrainian criminal police would come and take me to

Janowska Street—to that hilltop where I would be burned alive? But my thoughts were interrupted by a knocking on the door. Dr. Jagoda came in at my bidding and approached my bed. He was wearing his white coat this time. He felt my forehead and said aloud so it could be overheard, "You have a high fever and you must remain in bed for several days." He looked at me with great compassion. As our eyes met, he whispered, "Goodnight, dear child," and went over to look at his other patient, Halina. He looked at her ankle and remarked that in a day or two she would be able to walk again. Before turning out the light, he turned toward us and said cheerfully, "Goodnight girls!" and left.

Outside the window the next morning was bright and sunny. This was June 3, 1943; the date was fresh in my mind, because only yesterday I had registered and filled out my application. Our room faced the north, so the sun did not come into our windows directly; the room consequently was still gloomy, but I was sure that the air must be warm and pleasant outdoors. I could hear the voices of passersby—men's and women's voices, laughing.

After a while the woman who had brought us food the night before came in with our breakfast. I must have looked rather awful, because as she approached my bed she gave a start of surprise and exclaimed, "You are really sick!"

"That's for sure," I replied with more spirit than I felt.

About an hour later, Dr. Jagoda came in. Until now the whole situation seemed fantastic to me, like a legendary happening. But now in the broad daylight I could see his face and study his features and convince myself that he was real. His eyes were large, dark, and expressive; his face rather flat and thin, its pallor bespeaking sufferings and yet, perhaps because of this, creating the impression of goodness, of great kindness. Yes, I knew I could trust him implicitly.

He took my pulse count and said, "You must stay in bed at least another day. Probably tomorrow you will feel better." This he said aloud, then bent closer and very softly added, "Everything will be all right. Don't worry, Hania."

He went over to see the other patient and told Halina that she could get out of bed. She threw her coat over her shoulders and began to walk around a bit, limping slightly. He said that she should try to get out into the air for at least an hour each day. Now I knew that she was a Polish girl with her own, unforged and true, papers—for she expressed her delight at being able to visit the barracks where other members of her group were quartered, awaiting shipment to Germany.

Dr. Jagoda came to my bedside again, told me to try to regain my strength, and promised that he would drop in to see me again that day. "What an angel," I thought, watching his receding figure. Though moving about was difficult for him because of his leg injury, he went on his round of duties, trying to help others, forgetting his own pain.

Halina lay down to rest before dinner. Our "dinner" was some watered-down soup, a piece of sausage, and tea. But it was enough for me. Food no longer seemed very important; besides, in my feverish condition I was afraid to eat heavily. I drank the tea eagerly, though it was only colored water—I was thirsty, and this brought me some relief. We rested all afternoon. My companion tried to keep up a conversation, but I closed my eyes and pretended to be asleep. But I could hardly contain my impatience, counting the hours until evening when Dr. Jagoda would come in to see me.

Since the days in June are long, I reckoned that it must have been already nearly nine o'clock before it got dark outdoors. At last Dr. Jagoda came! He stopped to look at Halina's foot, then came and took my pulse and put his hand on my forehead. I looked at him with astonishment. I would have liked to ask him where I would go tomorrow, if I left the sick bay, but I did not dare say anything before a witness. However, from his expression I felt that he had already reached some decision. *I must be patient,* I thought, *and wait till tomorrow.*

"Goodnight, girls," he waved to us as he left.

I thought that the doctor seemed a bit nervous, but how could I know his reasons and plans? My companion bubbled with joy that she would be able to rejoin the others in the main building tomorrow, for she disliked loneliness and enjoyed their company and laughter. I said "Goodnight!" and put out the light near my bed. I desperately tried to sleep. Who knows where I would have to go, or what plans Dr. Jagoda had for me?

After breakfast the next day, we waited for the doctor to come—but he did not. I worried whether something had happened to him; my existence depended entirely upon him now and on the success of his plans. I tossed with impatience, but stayed in bed. Halina had gotten up, dressed, and gone out. She did not return until lunchtime; she said that it was beautifully warm outdoors. After lunch, she started to pack her things into a suitcase. She asked me why I did not get ready—we were supposed to go to camp barracks today, weren't we? But I answered that I would wait until the doctor checked me out of the ward. She shrugged her shoulders. We waited. It might have been around three o'clock when at last I heard the doctor's footsteps in the first room, between his office and the ward. Dr. Jagoda knocked and entered our room. He saw one of us already packed and ready to leave—so he asked Halina to come with him to his office where he would give her a check-out card. She gaily waved to me, picked up her valise, and left. After a few moments, the doctor returned, giving me a sign not to speak loudly. He looked up and down the hall, to make sure no one was eavesdropping, then whispered, "I have a place for you. It is a small room, very simple, but for a week it will do. It is in one of the buildings. When I check you out, I'll say you are going home for the holidays and will return later. Since you registered as a volunteer worker, I can do this; they know that you will return. When it gets darker, you will leave by the main gate and show this pass to the guards on duty there. Then you will go to the left of the camp until you find a place where the fence boards are broken and loose, back of some shrubbery. I broke them. Crawl in through the openings and I'll wait for you there and take you to this room. But you must be very, very careful. Just a moment—I'll come back with your check-out card."

Dr. Jagoda left and I remained alone in the ward—alone with my thoughts. After a while, there was a knock on the door and the serving woman came in with my supper. I thanked her and she left. There was rice boiled in water, and bread with tea. I tried to eat all of it, for who knew when I would get another meal? For that matter, it might very well be my last . . . Now, with beating heart, I began to get dressed for the transfer to my shelter. The ward was cold, and in my excited state I felt chills shaking my body. Though it was the fourth day of June, summery and warm outside, I put on a woolen dress with short sleeves—I remember it was a sapphire blue, my favorite color, with a flared skirt; I chose it because the free cut of the skirt would permit easy running or jumping over fences or bushes. I got ready my brown sport coat, which was dark and would not be visible at night. I pulled out my suitcase from the closet and felt around to see if the precious packet with my mother's jewelry was there intact—my only treasure salvaged from a happier past. I packed away the rest of my things and waited. It was still light outdoors. I could hear muffled voices. Oh, how nervously I waited for the evening to come! I cannot attempt to describe how long each minute of waiting seemed to me.

There was a knock on the door and the serving woman came in to clear away the dishes. She turned on the light and saw me sitting there in my clothes, ready to leave. "You're also well now?" she asked, wrinkling her forehead.

"Yes," I replied shortly. "It's late. I'm sleepy." I half-closed my eyes and put my hand up to my head. "I have a headache," I said to forestall further questions. I did not know what to tell her if she asked me anything more. She went out of the ward, leaving the light burning. I looked through the window. It was completely dark outside—but a summer night, clear and cloudless, is never really dark. At last I heard knocking at the door, and Dr. Jagoda entered. He was not wearing his white coat, but a dark civilian outfit.

My heart started beating like a hammer. "Are you ready?" he asked and I nodded my head.

He told me to go to a corner of the room where the clothes closets blocked off the view from the windows. There he took out a pass from his pocket. My hand shook as I took it from him, but I noticed his hand was shaking no less than mine. He also saw this and said, "Miss Hania, please try to control your nerves. You must go out of here feeling very sure of yourself, just as you were when you came here—otherwise it might look suspicious. Now, listen! You will leave by the main gate and show this pass to the guard or the militiaman on duty. Then, slowly, you will go to the right—in the direction from which you came the other day. Just before the end of the camp enclosure you will look around to make sure there is no one nearby. Then, carefully, very carefully, bending over, you will go around the camp to a spot where there are some bushes—there, making no noise, you will look for broken boards in the fence. When you push them apart, look out for sharp nails. You will get back in the camp area through that opening in the fence. Push your valise inside first, then crawl in yourself. I'll be waiting at that spot. We will not walk together; it would look suspicious—but I'll go ahead and you will follow me at a distance. The most important thing you must remember is that if a militiaman, or someone from the Sonderdienst, notices and stops you—you will say you lost your way. That's all. It was dark, you will say, and on the way to the railway station you became confused and lost your way. That is the only explanation you can give. If I notice any danger, I will hide at first and then go away. You must promise me that you will not get me involved, because I would have to pay for it with my life, and I would not be able to help you anyway. We have no more time to lose. You understand everything?" I nodded my head. "Now I am going back to my office. Go with God, dear Hania," he said.

"Thank you, doctor," I whispered. I threw on my coat, took the suitcase, and with tears in my eyes left the room. It may have been about nine o'clock. Oh, God, what a dangerous undertaking! Oh, dear mother, if you are still alive—or wherever you are, pray for me and help me reach safety.

I walked out into the yard. There was a building to the left of the small hospital. I walked straight ahead, turned slightly to the right once and then again. The inmates of the main camp undoubtedly were asleep already. At the moment no one was to be seen. I trembled with fear, looking at that ominously dark building, the largest one in a row of low barracks—there were lights in some windows, but most were dark. I directed my steps toward the gate. It was a long way off, and I tried to gather my courage. *I must have self-assurance,* I told myself; I knew that already from past experience.

As I neared the gate, I made out the silhouettes of the guards and their rifles. A few steps away from them I drew the pass out of my pocket to have it ready. Again, there was a man from the Sonderdienst and one Ukrainian militiaman, though not the same that had admitted me to the camp. I held out the pass, wondering which one of them would take it.

They simply stared at me. Finally, I turned to the Ukrainian and spoke to him—after all, I was not supposed to understand German, it would have seemed suspicious.

I spoke to the Ukrainian in Polish (both languages were understood in this part of the country) and he translated my words into broken German for the benefit of the Sonderdienst officer. Handing him my pass, I said that I was going home for the holidays. (Pentecost was ceremoniously observed in Poland.) I explained that it would seem a waste of time to wait in the camp for the next transport to Germany, when I could spend the next ten days with my nearby family. I would return after the holiday, I said, and added hastily that I must be off or I'd miss the train. He made a mark on my pass and gave it back to me. Straining for self-control, I smiled and said "Goodnight!"

They let me go. I walked out of the camp enclosure and still did not believe it. Was I foolish, or were they simply stupid? They believed me! Lying was now to become part of my existence . . . I went straight ahead, fighting down the impulse to look back to see whether they were following me. I did not hear any steps—and surely I would have heard the sound of their heavy boots if they were behind me. I dragged the heavy valise; it seemed heavier than it was, because I was so weak. After I had gone some distance, I stopped to rest. That was quite normal, I thought, and should not awaken their distrust. Standing still, I pretended to unbutton my coat and at the same time I turned around. I saw that I had covered quite a bit of the road. I saw no one; it was very quiet. In back of me stretched the huge camp, dark and ominous.

I picked up my valise and started walking again. I wished that I could be older by an hour, even half an hour, just to have this ordeal over with. Again I was risking my life . . . Fortunately, I saw that it could not be very far to the turn in the road. But suddenly I noticed someone—a civilian, but not Dr. Jagoda, for this man was of shorter stature and he did not walk with a limp. Fear paralyzed me—for a moment I imagined it might be a plainclothes agent. Oh God, help me! But the man kept on walking; he seemed to be in a big hurry and did not even see me. I was on the right side of the road—he on the left, walking in the opposite direction. I stepped off into the sandy shoulder, bending over as I held my suitcase.

I was awfully uncomfortable, so I clutched the valise in both hands and held it in front of me. Already I could see the shrubbery near the fence; the summer had covered the branches with thick green foliage. Crouching low, I neared the fence to look for the broken boards. My knees were giving way. I shifted the valise from hand to hand, feeling its growing weight. At last I found the place and stopped.

From a distance I could see a tall figure silhouetted against the sapphire night—Dr. Jagoda. Every moment was precious and important; I must quicken my steps, not keep him waiting there. More and more rapidly I approached the fence. I put the suitcase on the ground, and, like a cat, I crawled through the opening. Luckily I was slim. I gathered up the coat in front, so as not to tear it, and got back inside the camp. Dr. Jagoda stood at a distance, watching. When he moved forward, I followed him.

It was quiet. No one was stirring. Apparently, the nearest buildings were empty—there were no lights anywhere. Reaching a left turn, he stopped to be sure that I would not lose the way. I saw him enter a building—and now quickly I entered after him. A long, dark hallway led from the door to the interior of the building. There was a musty smell, as if it had not been inhabited by anyone for a long time. Once inside, Dr. Jagoda gave me his hand and we walked in silence until we reached another door. He took a key out of his pocket and opened it.

As we entered, he did not turn on the light. The room was small. One window, covered by an old rag, let in just a glimmer of moonlight, and in the darkness I could discern the shape of a table. I felt around me and touched a metal clothes closet; there was a single chair, and also what seemed to be an army cot covered with a rough blanket.

Dr. Jagoda started to give me instructions, keeping his voice down to a whisper. I must try to remain seated in one place as much as possible, so as not to make even the slightest noise. There was always the possibility that someone might come around and hear and guess that there was a stowaway in this room. I must never make a light. If anyone should knock or call, I must not answer. "I will take the key," he said, "and I will try to come here every day to bring you something to eat, but not more than once a day. So that you will know it is I, I will hum the "La Palona" as I approach the door."

I asked the good doctor if it wasn't too big a responsibility that he was taking on himself, risking his life for a stranger. Wouldn't it be better if I just returned to the ghetto in Rohatyn? At least there I would be with my mother and sister. I just did not feel that I had the right to leave them and try to survive without them.

He replied, "Stop torturing yourself now, Hania dear. You must think of life, not death. In these times one must fight for life as long as possible. Somebody has to survive—and you will, even if only to be a witness to these crimes, or to tell the world how the Germans destroyed innocent people and children. So, you try—for those that went to death already." He began to hurry, and he told me he did not live at the camp but in Lvov. "Goodnight, dear Hania. Good luck! I will see you tomorrow." And he went out, locking the door after him, leaving me in the darkness, alone.

7

A Perilous Refuge

FOR A FEW MINUTES I remained standing in a state of utter confusion and shock. I could only wonder why Dr. Jagoda was risking his life for me. I was a total stranger—yet he had inexplicably decided to help me.

I sat down on the cot and folded my hands tightly, trying to steady my shaking body. Would I be able to live through this war? How I longed for my dear ones—my home—the normal life we once knew!

I could not control my emotions any longer and began to cry bitterly. I covered my mouth with my hands to stifle the sobs; I was choking . . . but I had to cry. I was very, very tired. Without removing my clothes, I crawled under the blanket and tried at last to sleep. The pillow was hard, as if stuffed with rocks. No doubt it was filled with straw or chopped feathers; it hurt my aching head. I wanted so much to sleep, but was afraid that I might cry out in my dreams of terror. However, weariness took its toll, and after some time I must have fallen asleep in spite of my caution. A squealing noise wakened me; I shook with fear, for I felt something creeping along the blanket (the cot on which I slept was quite low, almost touching the floor). I was afraid to turn on the light—if there indeed was a light in this room. I could now feel that something was jumping all over the cot. I drew up my legs till they touched my chin; I wanted to cry out but suppressed my screams.

When my eyes had grown accustomed to the darkness, I could make out some small creatures—rats! Yes, rats! Oh, God, how would I live through this night? Why did I agree to come to this awful shelter? I slid out of bed and in the darkness I felt around until I found the chair—from the chair I jumped onto the table. Curled up into a ball, I covered myself with my coat, pulled the collar over my head, and in this fashion spent the rest of the night. Oh, if my mother should see me suffering so in this black hole infested with rats!

I could not get used to the sound of those squealing rats, even though I pulled the coat collar tighter about my ears. In a wave of hysteria I thought I would start screaming so loudly that the whole world would hear me. Why must I suffer only because I'm Jewish? It was stifling hot in the hole—the window was closed and curtained, I was completely dressed and perspiring from excitement, unable to catch my breath. And I was afraid to stir . . . Oh, if only day would come! As soon as it grew light outside the rats would disappear. Crouched atop the table, at last I saw the pale light of dawn breaking through the heavy rag-like drape that covered the window—after what was surely the longest night that I had ever known. The squeals quieted down—the rats ran back to their holes as soon as they saw the light. It must have still been very early. Somehow the date remains clear in my memory: June 5, 1943.

At last I could look around and see where I was. The room looked as though no one had occupied it for a long time—there was much dust on the furniture and cobwebs hung from the ceiling and walls like lace curtains. The floor was strewn with empty bottles, and an unwashed soldier's mess tin lay under the table. It was the first container that I could use—and I availed myself of it.

Quietly I returned to the cot, lay down, and drew the blanket over me. I hoped that I could sleep even for an hour, and I shut my eyes and lay still—but sleep would not come. It was so hot in the room. Quietly, I brushed off the dust that settled on the coat when I was huddled atop the table. I could hear footsteps outside, and voices, so I lay back again on the cot and remained motionless. Though the window was covered, the cot stood directly under it, and I had to be careful. I lay there and waited. Who knew when Dr. Jagoda would come—or whether he would? I wanted badly to wash myself. Whatever I touched smelled of rats.

My thoughts were interrupted by the sound of footsteps—one step slower than the other—in the corridor. I guessed that it must be Dr. Jagoda. Then I heard a low singing outside my door: the melody of "La Paloma."

Then a very soft knock, the key turned in the door, and—with my heart beating rapidly with joy—I saw Dr. Jagoda. He had a jacket thrown over one arm, hiding something he had brought me. He placed a warning finger to his lips, and put the food on the table—the table had already been cleared of dust by my coat during the night. He had brought me coffee, bread, some sausage, and biscuits.

Taking the chair, he sat down. I noticed that he was very pale. I told him about the frightful night I had. Compassion was visible in his eyes, but he could not find a word of comfort. I drank the coffee and ate a piece of bread, leaving the rest for later. The doctor noticed the bottles and the tin mess can on the floor. "I'll take these," he said quietly, though he must have seen my grimace of embarrassment. He listened a moment at the door, then went out, taking the filled utensils with him. "There's no lack of empty containers here," he said, looking back at me with a smile. Obviously he wanted to make me feel more at ease. "Until tomorrow," he whispered, shutting the door after him. "Be brave, dear Hania!"

I took the rest of the food and put it on top of the high metal closet, then lay down again on the cot. The rays of sunshine managed to steal into the room a few at a time, reminding me that it must be a beautiful, warm day outside, a time for flowers and joy. Ruefully, I thought that my solitary confinement here would be easier to endure if the weather outdoors were nasty; this brilliantly sunny day made it hard to take my imprisonment patiently. I had to resign myself to a terrifying boredom. Was it time to eat again? I felt hungry, but at the sight of all the dirt around me in this horrible room I could have thrown up in disgust.

Outside I heard footsteps, firm and heavy—they must have belonged to a Sonderdienst man in military boots, one of the young Germans who were employed in this camp. If he only suspected that a Jewish girl was hidden here! In my imagination I could see his face contorted with hate, with revenge . . . Oh God, help me! Very quietly I reached up for the food package on top of the closet and broke off a morsel of bread and dry sausage. I ate, chewing the food slowly, not caring whether I enjoyed the taste or not—I ate simply to keep alive. Then I put what was left back on the closet top; I would finish it a little later—or else my roommates the rats would finish it themselves!

There was nothing else to do but wait. Lying on the cot, I tried to sleep, to forget everything. I don't know how long I slept, but I dreamed that something horrible was happening in the Rohatyn ghetto. I was standing on the Aryan side, screaming from a distance, seeing them murdering the Jews. Don't kill them! I called out: Mamma! Rose! The Gestapo were holding me back. Then I heard my own cries and woke up; I was bathed in perspiration. Something jumped scarily near the cot. At first, I could not remember where I was. I began to look around me. Then I wiped my forehead and realized that I had had an awful dream. God only knows whether someone at that moment had heard my scream! And that scurrying, that must have been a rat frightened at the sound of my voice, running back to his hole. My head ached like an open wound. I felt extremely weak; there was a sharp pain in the region of my heart. I thought that I could see Mamma, her long hair streaming down her back, as she struggled to free herself from the hands of the Gestapo. In spite of the struggle, she seemed as beautiful as always, in a tragic sort of way. I wanted to go help her—I cried "Mamma!" But there was no sound—and at last I broke out in spasmodic weeping.

The morning dawned at last, and again I wished that I could wash myself—a bit of water would have done me so much good. But I could only dream of such luxury. When the doctor had come to visit me the day before, I did not have the temerity to ask him to bring me a bottle of water—I thought it would really be too demanding on my part. But I hoped that he would think of it himself and bring me some today. I waited as patiently as I could—not so much because of the food but because he might bring me some news. Anyway, it would be good to chat with the doctor even for a few minutes. My loneliness was driving me mad. I liked human companionship—and here I had only myself to talk to, yet even that was forbidden.

It was full daylight when again I heard the almost-whispered singing of "La Paloma." It startled me only because I had not heard the doctor's footsteps in the corridor; he must have walked in very, very quietly.

Dr. Jagoda stood in the doorway, carrying a package under his jacket. "It's very warm here," he said. "Warm outside, too."

I could see that he wondered how I could stand being cooped up in this stifling room, but he did not say it. "You are pale, but beautiful," he remarked, studying my face carefully. "Were you frightened by something?"

"I had an awful dream and it wrung me out emotionally. I hope nobody heard me screaming."

He shook his head. "This building is vacant, there's no one here—unless somebody passing the window might have heard you." The doctor looked around to see if there were any containers to take away. He did not want to talk; apparently, he was depressed.

"Is anything wrong?" I ventured to ask.

"No," he replied. He seemed disgusted with something. "But have courage, dear Hania!" He picked up the filled container and left without another word.

True to his promise, the doctor was doing all he could to help me, assuming the gravest risk. My admiration and wonder were as great as my gratitude.

Sighing, I poured some coffee over my hands in an effort to wash them. I dried my hands with a piece of paper in which the sausage had been wrapped. Today, I noticed, he also brought me a piece of cheese. The dark bread and cheese with coffee would make a good breakfast; the sausage and bread I would save for later.

June 6—there were still six days before I could leave this room. After I finished eating, I lay down on the cot. If only I could rest peacefully, stop thinking . . . ah, that would be so good! But this beautiful, sunny day brought back so many poignant memories of my home and of my beautiful past in Rohatyn.

Eventually, I slid off the cot and helped myself to a piece of sausage and bread. After having lost myself for a while in thoughts of the past, I now felt as though I had come back from another world—and in a sense, I had indeed. It occurred to me that I'd love to look into a mirror, just to see if I still resembled the former beautiful Sheva of happier days . . . It was difficult to believe that I was still the same person.

I watched the shadows gradually deepen in the corners of the room. Soon it would be night. Oh, if I could sleep the whole night through, I would feel better—but there were two fears which made sleep almost impossible: fear that I might cry aloud in my nightmarish dreams, and fear of my co-tenants, the rats. If they were to bite me, I'd be finished; if someone were to hear me cry out, I'd be done for, too. It was safer not to sleep, but to be constantly on the alert. When at last it was totally dark, I pulled down the package with the remaining bits of sausage and bread and ate all that was left. But the sausage was salty and made me thirsty. There was nothing to drink, so I tried to forget about it. I put the wrapping paper back on top of the closet, to make use even of that . . . I lay down on the cot, and after a while I dozed off.

I don't know how long I slept, but it must have been late at night when I was awakened by the sounds of shooting. I jumped up and sat on the edge of the cot. No wonder the rats had not been molesting me—the shooting must have frightened them back into their holes. I wanted to look out of the window, but did not dare. So I sat there, shaking as though in a fever. I tried to guess what was behind the shooting. Various ideas suggested themselves to my mind. The most comforting, indeed miraculous, solution would be that there was some change in the war—perhaps the front had moved up closer to Lvov? But that would have been too good to be true. It was more likely that the shooting was taking place in the ghetto. Hadn't I heard that ghettos were being liquidated everywhere? They were shooting the remnants of the Jews that still clung tenaciously to life—yes, that was the only answer. It seemed to me that the sounds were getting closer. I could hardly remain in one spot, but I dared not move. So I crawled under that dirty, smelly blanket and pulled it over my ears so that I would not hear the horrible staccato barking of dogs and of the Nazi guns. I impatiently waited for morning to come, so that I could get some news from Dr. Jagoda.

In such a time of dreadful fear and loneliness, it is easy to eat one's heart out with reproaches of conscience. I was tormented by the thought that maybe I should have done thus and so, that maybe I had no right to leave the ghetto. Should I have remained with my loved ones? Should I have remained in Brody, taken that risk? That one word "maybe" drove me to despair.

I lay in a pool of sweat, perspiring copiously from fear as well as from the warmth of the covers. After a while, everything was quiet again outside. Slowly, I pushed the blanket away from my face. It was beginning to dawn . . . I counted the days off my fingers; yes, my third day in this shelter. I waited impatiently to hear the tune of "La Paloma" sung outside my door; for it was to me not only a password, but a paean of hope in this cage. As if to mock me, the golden rays of a summer sun that filtered through the dusty windowpanes reminded me of the beautiful day outdoors and of other days, days of blessed freedom, that I no longer knew.

I could hear voices outside, but at a distance. I could also hear the sound of heavy, measured steps—booted steps of the Sonderdienst and the Ukrainian militia. There seemed to be more noise and commotion than usual. Was it because of the shooting last night? Soon I would be able to satisfy my curiosity. I was counting each minute toward the arrival of Dr. Jagoda, but he did not come. Time went by so slowly . . . My stomach demanded some food, something warm; my throat was parched and dry. I was sure it was already past the hour when the doctor was supposed to come—but I saw nothing, heard nothing. Waiting made me very restless; I was sure now that something must have happened. I curled up on the cot, afraid to move, and hours seemed to roll like a heavy wave over my head. It surely must have been noon! I should have kept some of the food for today, instead of eating it all the night before. But how could I have known? In my thoughts I tried to talk to God and to convince Him that I did not merit this misery.

Suddenly, the silence was rent with cries. They became louder and louder, and reminded me of the cries that I had heard in the ghetto during the akcjas.

A woman was shrieking, "*Nein, nein!*" No, no!

My teeth began to chatter. At that moment I forgot about my hunger and thirst. Something must be happening, something dreadful . . . Did the woman's cries have anything to do with Dr. Jagoda? Why hadn't he shown up yet today? The woman's cries stopped, but loud sobbing went on for quite a while.

My hole of a room was almost dark now. I remained on the cot, afraid to stir. Even when nature urged, I did not get up. I think this day was the worst in my life. When it became totally dark, I slowly, quietly crept to a corner of the room and relieved myself—I could not help that. Then I went back to the cot. Somehow I fell asleep and when I opened my eyes again it was daylight.

What would this new day bring? Each day had its own variety of fears and dangers. I felt my nerves were fraying and I was afraid that I would suffer a collapse. If I lost my will to live, I might do something rash, so I tried to bolster my own spirits as much as I could. The hours passed. My hunger pains gave me a terrible headache. If only I could do something, busy myself with something, I might forget that I was so hungry—but now I had only idle time in which to think about it. What a long day it seemed to me—and again the doctor did not appear. Now I felt certain that he would never come. What could I do? Where could I go? And I was locked in—how could I get out of here?

Darkness was again descending upon the earth when I suddenly heard the melody of "La Paloma" sung very, very quietly. As the voice grew louder, however, I realized that it was not Dr. Jagoda—nor were the footsteps his. Though at first I had sprung forward eagerly, now I hesitated, for certainly it was not he. My heart began to pound. They must have discovered my hiding place! Perhaps they had tortured the doctor into disclosing our song . . . Now the voice was right at my door. Should I try to hide? And where? Or should I jump out of the window? There was no time for anything. I heard a light rap on the door. Someone in a low voice said, "I am a friend of Dr. Jagoda."

I heard the key turn in the lock and the man stood before me. He was of medium height, middle-aged, and pale from fright. He carried a package under his arm. He said that the doctor had had to go to Przemysl for a day; he had wanted to come see me yesterday and bring the package, but it had not been safe. They had caught two Jewish girls that had escaped from the ghetto and had come here to apply for work in Germany under assumed papers. They were taken to the Gestapo by the Ukrainian police.

Just hearing the news took away from me all desire to eat. My expression must have reflected my feelings, for the man said, "Don't be afraid of me. I will not betray you. I am the doctor's friend. He will be here tomorrow." The man had a kind face and was very polite towards me. I believed him, thanked him—and he left immediately.

I looked inside the package. There was the usual sausage and bread. I broke off a piece, but could not force it down my throat; so I wrapped up the food again and covered it with the blanket, to prevent the rats from nibbling at it. I lay down and waited, thinking about what the man had told me. Yesterday they had caught those two; tomorrow, or the day after, they would catch me. What the doctor said was true: I should run away from here, as he had advised. Struggling with these thoughts, I dozed a while until a squealing woke me up. I had gotten used to the rats by this time, however, and was not afraid of them.

It must have been about the middle of the night—I had no idea of the exact hour. I sat on the edge of the cot and began to eat. The rats stopped squealing. I put away about half of the food for the next day, and having satiated my hunger, I fell asleep again. When I awoke it was daylight. I wanted to drink. The shelter was hot and evil smelling. My only comforting thought was perhaps today Dr. Jagoda would come. Maybe he would have some good news for me? Perhaps at last there was some hope of a change for the better?

I never knew what hour it was, but when it grew darker I knew the day was almost over. And after a night, there was another day. True, I had Mamma's watch on a gold chain, packed away with the other things in my suitcase, but I did not want even to touch it.

This was my eighth day in the shelter. If all went well, in two days I should be able to leave it and report officially at the work camp. This day I thought so intently about Dr. Jagoda that I must have drawn him, for at last I heard his voice singing "La Paloma"—and his characteristic walk, one firm step and one light and shuffling, as he pulled his crippled leg after the good one. He opened the door and entered, smiling encouragingly. My eyes fell to the package he held, covered with a white coat, and I noticed he had brought me something to drink. Thinking that I was very hungry, he urged me to eat right away, but I pointed to the package his friend had brought yesterday, still only half-touched, lying atop the closet. However, I opened the bag and pulled out a container of coffee—I began to drink eagerly, until there was none left.

We talked in whispers—almost, one might say, in gestures and signs—rather than words. He said that he had to go to Przemysl on business. The news that he brought back, though not unexpected, hit me like a bombshell; the Nazis had liquidated all the ghettos and had announced the *Judenfrei*—the successful extermination of the Jews—in all Polish cities. "That means in Rohatyn too?" I asked.

"Everywhere!"

"And what did they do with them?"

He did not reply to this question, but looked at me wonderingly, as if I had dropped out of another world. It was a foolish question, for did I not know what the Nazis did with the Jews? "They burn them alive, or take them to the concentration camps . . . The methods might differ in some cases," the doctor said, "but officially Jews have no right to live, to exist."

He got up, looked around, and noticing the container in the corner of the room, picked it up and hid it under his white coat. "Goodbye," he whispered, "until tomorrow, Hania dear." As he left, he seemed more than usually depressed. I could see that he took the situation very much to heart, as a man of conscience. There were not many like him . . .

Now my thoughts centered about the ghetto in my native town. Were my dear ones still alive? And, if so, did they know that I was alive—did they have faith in my return? Would I ever see them again? Though my imagination painted all sorts of pictures, I could do nothing but sit quietly and wait—and I cried and cried . . .

So I lived through yet another day and night, and saw another dawn. Now I counted the hours until I would again hear "La Paloma" hummed outside the door. (That melody will remain forever in my mind.) Then again, I heard it, and when the door opened, there was Dr. Jagoda as usual with his package. Yet his face was a picture of tragedy! My face probably reflected a similar attitude.

His voice lowered to a whisper, he started to give me directions and instructions for tomorrow's departure. I felt cold waves going over my body as I listened carefully. Dr. Jagoda said that the next day at ten o'clock in the morning I was to leave the shelter. It would have been better to do so at night, he remarked, but then it might look strange. He took everything into consideration and reasoned it out. If I were to leave the shelter at night, I would have to spend the rest of the night hidden in some bushes nearby—and that would be dangerous. On the other hand, in the morning everyone was busy about some task, and so the probability of my being noticed would be lessened; besides, the window, being on the side of the house away from the barracks, was not observed and the building was quite empty. Also, the way I was to go was not visible to the office or other buildings in the center of the camp. It still was risky business, of course, but I had to take that chance. There were no half-measures, no mercy. He left, saying, "Good luck! And be ready for tomorrow, dear Hania."

I wondered what the Krupka family was doing now—and how little Janko was. Oh, if they could see how I spent this miserable ten days in hiding! I missed Mrs. Krupka, for she had shared my troubles with me. Here, I had to struggle with my problems all by myself.

At least the rats would be happy when I left. Just one night more, and I would have to retrace the dangerous route and stand again before a new and unknown danger when I reported back to the camp. A few hours more; eager as I was to leave this place, I trembled with fear at the thought.

I looked down at myself; even without a mirror I could see that I was a fright. So many days without washing, without changing my clothes. I decided at least to change my dress, for the one I had on was like a rag, crumpled and soiled—it adhered to my body and disgusted me. I put on my green suit-dress, cleaned myself up as best I could, and again sat down on the edge of the cot and waited.

Next day, at last, the moment arrived. For the last time I heard the melody of "La Paloma"—a melody that had become to me a sort of battle-hymn, a call to courage and hope in a hopeless existence. And I heard the doctor's steps, a little faster today than before, betraying his nervous excitement. The door opened and my savior stood before me. He looked anxious and pale, but he had kept his promise and came at the appointed time. And again I heard the same words: "Are you ready, dear Hania?"

"Ready," I answered.

"Dear Hania," he said, "if someone were to catch you on the way to the camp now, or during your stay in the camp, remember—not a word about me. Hold your head up high and have courage. That is very important."

Tears came to my eyes, but this was no time for sentiment. I merely said, "Thank you, Doctor Jagoda."

Gently he said, "Go with God, Hania!"

For the last time I looked around at my shelter. True, it was an awful place, but it had protected me during these tense and endless ten days. I clambered up on the cot and reached for the window above it. Carefully I pushed aside the curtain, thickly powdered with dust, and stole a quick look outside. Everything was quiet. I saw no one. Then, slowly, I opened the window. My heart started to beat rapidly and I felt as though someone had stuck a knife into my side, but I managed to slide through the open frame and pull the valise after me, which the doctor handed to me from below. I did not look back. I knew Dr. Jagoda would close the window once I was on the other side. When my feet touched the ground, I walked quickly in the direction from which I had come to this place ten days before.

The sun's hot rays were piercing. I felt pain in my eyes, unaccustomed to such bright light. I hastened my steps, not looking back—I did not know, nor did I want to know what was happening behind me. Yet all was quiet. When I reached the broken fence-boards and squeezed through to the other side, I took off my coat. It was hot and I would have looked strange wearing a heavy coat in June, and a crumpled and soiled coat like that, besides. Now it was easier to walk, and I went faster and faster until I came to the other side of the camp. In my thoughts I thanked God for helping me get out, and now asked Him not to abandon me but to stay with me in this tragic situation, to give me the strength to survive, to put the right words in my mouth, and to lead me along a safe and sure path. As I walked on, I told myself that there must be some Power leading me; Someone with me. This gave me comfort. And perhaps my mother was watching me . . .

Now I had circled the camp and I saw from a distance the guards at the gate. I had to greet them with a smile—to prove that I came back willingly! I quickly took the pass from my pocket; it was somewhat creased, but that did not matter. Assuming an artificial gaiety, I handed them the card, saying—in Ukrainian, to the Ukrainian policeman—that I had come back after spending the holidays with my family. These were not the same guards who had seen me leave the camp, but that was perhaps all the better. The militiaman narrowed his eyes after scanning the pass, then returned it to me, saying—partly to me, and partly to the Sonderdienst officer—"After the holidays she looks like hell!" Then, turning to me, he asked, "Were you sick? What's the matter with you?"

I sized up the situation quickly and replied, "During the holidays the whole family got together, ate, drank, and—I'm afraid my stomach had to pay the consequences. I worried whether I'd be able to get back here in time, but now I feel better."

Whether my reply satisfied them or not, or whether they actually believed me, I did not know. Trying to avoid further questions, I nodded to the guards pleasantly and went on inside the camp, following the sandy path—shimmering now in the hot sun—that led to the main office. I still anxiously pondered the meaning of the Ukrainian militiaman's expression. *Maybe he just let me in,* I thought, *because he knows that in here I'll be trapped.* I could not help but feel that he was suspicious of me. But there was now no alternative; I must be patient and be prepared for anything. Wrestling with these poisonous thoughts, I reached the office.

There was the same man who had registered me the first day. I gave him my pass, and he directed me to the main building, where all those who were to be sent to work in Germany were gathered. I did not see Dr. Jagoda anywhere—not in the office, nor in the yard outside. He might have been hiding someplace, so as not to be a witness in case I was caught.

I crossed the courtyard and turned left towards the building that housed the workers. It stood next to the hospital where I had spent the first few days, but was considerably larger. To go inside was a dangerous step, for here I might meet someone from my part of the country, perhaps even from Rohatyn. But I pushed open the door—a large, heavy door, like a gateway to a fortress—and went inside.

The eyes of those who did not happen to be busy with something at the moment all turned in my direction. It's easier for me to write of this experience now than it was to live it. At first glance I could not discern all the faces and could not see whether there were any there whom I knew or who could recognize me. There seemed to be a lot of girls and boys in that large room. It gave me such a strange feeling, as though I were a child just learning to walk and not knowing in which direction it might be safer to turn, ready to fall out of fear and uncertainty.

It was a very large room, or hall, with cots lining two walls. In the center stood long tables with benches. It was dark and gloomy; only two windows illuminated the room—and these were at the further end. I approached the nearest bench and put down my valise, sat down, and waited for someone to speak to me.

It was not long before one, and then another girl came up to me—followed by some young boys, mostly Ukrainians—to find out where I came from and how I got caught. They did not even guess that I was a voluntary victim, over whom the death penalty hung if I was discovered—trying to find help here. Looking around, I wondered myself how I could expect to find help in this place, among people from so many districts and localities. My eyes searched the faces to see if there might be someone I knew from Rohatyn—but they were so far all strangers to me. Thank God for that! But they kept plying me with questions, and I had to answer them. Where did I come from? From Brody. Where was I caught? On the street. Again, I lied like a professional.

When they heard the name of the town I supposedly came from, they began to look around to see if there was anyone else from Brody—but there was none. They could not know that I did not know Brody, that someone from Brody would not know me any better than they did. My fear was not that I would meet a Brody inhabitant, after all!

I could see that almost all the girls here were wearing peasant skirts. Some had kerchiefs, and some wore their hair in braids falling down their back or wound atop their head. They were walking around barefoot, having taken off their boots to be more comfortable, and they seemed gay. The boys also looked as if they had come straight from the village. They were joking, singing—most of them in Ukrainian. I listened more than I talked, avoiding all the conversation I could.

I hoped that I would be able to sleep that night. My constant fear was that I might cry out in my dreams, and that some harm might come to me from my strange companions. I had to be very careful not to give my identity away. I had to be careful also in my lies—for it was not at all easy to have to live a lie twenty-four hours a day.

The noisy chatter quieted down when two ladies came in, bringing our lunch. Everybody reached for a bowl and a spoon and tried to get a portion of the food. I was also handed a bowl and spoon. It was very plain food, but now that was not important: soup, some kind of pudding, black bread, and tea. Some voiced their complaints, others cursed—but all the bowls were emptied. With the addition of a few jokes, even this miserable food tasted better.

The cans were soon emptied. We threw in the bowls and spoons for them to take away to be washed. Now came the tea. That was best; it was for me a real luxury and delicacy. There was still plenty of time after dinner before we turned in—too many hours, indeed, in which I might be questioned and studied. I trembled to think that each moment in this crowd was potentially dangerous. Yet I tried to appear in the best of humor. I forced myself to believe that I was really that Hanka Buczek, caught by Germans on the street and taken to this work camp. I was beginning a new life.

I shoved my suitcase under the cot and mixed with the crowd, taking part in their jokes. I talked mostly in Ukrainian, because most of the youth here were Ukrainians. They did not know that I was posing as a Polish girl—they would not see my identification papers. They were here in the same category as I, I thought. If they knew that I was supposed to be Polish they might want to avoid me, because Ukrainians did not like the Poles. I knew Ukrainian perfectly. Why shouldn't I be able to pass for a Ukrainian in this camp?

I talked with everyone that came my way. Some were swapping funny stories, others were singing, still others were playing chess or cards. It was a pleasant, congenial atmosphere. At last someone started to play his mandolin and a group formed around him to sing. I knew all the songs, so I joined my voice to theirs. There were moments when I really forgot about everything; I felt one with them. I suggested some songs of my own—"Houtzulka Ksenia" and "Loneliness." The words were suited to this place and time. A few around me knew the songs. Some of the girls had tears in their eyes as they listened. Now I felt no longer alone; I had others to share my tears. The singing helped to assuage my pain somewhat; it was like a balm to my shattered nerves.

Our singing and merrymaking was interrupted by suppertime. Again, we had a thin soup, like dishwater, some sausage, and bread. But our humor was improved and even our appetite was keener. I was surprised, and—I will confess—pleased that some of my companions were actually concerned about Hania. "Here's soup for Hania, here's some sausage, here's bread for Hania!" I was the prettiest and they gave me compliments. I did not know whether to take it as a good or an evil omen, but for the present, everything was going smoothly.

After our coffee, we got up from the bench, feeling quite pleased. The cans and dishes were cleared away, and we returned to our little groups. Everyone seemed to feel as though we had known each other for a long time, and many expressed the wish that they might be sent to the same city in Germany. Of course, Hania must go with them!

"I hope we'll stay together," I said, but in my thoughts I prayed that it would be otherwise. My plan was to get lost somehow in Germany, to go it alone. If I stayed with these Ukrainians, sooner or later they would discover who I really was. And I knew how their friendly attitude would change suddenly toward "Hania" if they knew who she really was . . . a Jew! The Ukrainians were the real murderers, and these happy youth would be the same . . .

It was dark, about nine o'clock, when the guard came to tell us to put out the lights and go to sleep. Slowly, we broke up our groups. As I lay down, I did as I saw the others do—I made the sign of the cross and whispered a prayer. My prayer was different from theirs. I asked God to perform a miracle, to show the world that He had not forsaken me and my people. "Send down a curse on these Germans," I prayed, "and free us from their clutches. Give me strength and confidence to see that moment. Save those who are still alive . . . Thank you, God, for protecting me until now—for I could have fallen into a trap many times. But I am not alone, there are still thousands, thousands asking You for help—even my Mamma and my sister Rose, if they are yet alive." Such was my prayer and petition. Tears were rolling down my cheeks, but it was dark and no one could see my crying.

The night passed slowly. Light was beginning to come through the window before people began crawling out of their cots. Everybody seemed to have a complaint. Amidst complaints, I heard a voice quoting an old Ukrainian proverb: *Ne chotily Zydy manujisty, naj hiwno jidat*—The

Jews did not want to eat manna, let them eat crap! To this fairly common proverb, someone else replied mockingly, "The Jews aren't even eating crap any longer—they don't exist anymore. They've been turned into manure—and the Germans were smart to do it! Who needs the Jews?"

There remarks caught me by surprise. I knew that sooner or later the subject of the Jews had to come up, but this happened so quickly that I was stunned. The night passed away in the morning.

Luckily, the breakfast was brought in just then, and they did not talk about Jews any longer. But the incident was just another stab at my heart. I had been present before during such scenes of Jew-hatred . . .

When we got up from breakfast, I noticed how awful we looked. Our clothes were crumpled, like rags. We looked at each other, seeing ourselves as in a mirror. Someone quipped that when we arrived in Germany we'd receive complete new wardrobes and that our pockets would be filled with money. Someone else added, "And all the boys will get a German blonde!" Then, seeing how the Ukrainian girls were listening to this talk with frowns on their faces, a boy said: "To hell with German girls! We have our own."

As the day went on, some played chess, others cards. One group just sat and complained about everything. Some listened to a mandolin player—this was the quietest group, perhaps the most cultured—and I joined them. But they did not remain still for long. Someone noticed that at another table sat a middle-aged woman, rather stout and wearing a flowered kerchief on her head, who was telling fortunes from cards. Two or three girls had gathered around her at first, but the group grew larger as more people became interested. Everybody was eager to have his or her fortune told—and when she told them the truth as she saw it in the cards, they often exclaimed in surprise or embarrassment.

The woman seemed to have the gift of guessing everything about a person's past and future. Soon people were whispering about her talents, saying that she was no fake. And so the line grew; they swarmed around her like ants, sat down for a while, listened, and walked away dazed. But at last there were no more volunteers. Shortly after, I noticed the fortune teller was going around to the bashful ones, offering to read the cards for them in private. When they shook their heads, she insisted until she had convinced them. This made me wonder if she was not some sort of spy—maybe the Germans or the Ukrainian police had planted her among us purposely to pry some information out of us. A lot would depend on my decision now. If I remained the only one who refused to have a fortune told, it would look suspicious, but if I let her read my cards—if she really had the gift of mind-reading or foretelling the future—she would learn too much about me. No matter what, it was a bad spot for me.

She came up to me, and—because I simply could not avoid her, or perhaps because I was really curious to know what lay in the future—I agreed to let her read the cards, but somewhere in a corner privately. It would be false to say that I was indifferent to the outcome of this sitting. But just as I was about to walk over with her to a quiet corner, we suddenly heard loud cries and weeping, growing louder and louder each moment. Everyone jumped up. The same question was on all lips: What's going on? Without thinking, everyone pushed toward the door to see what was happening. There I saw a scene of horror that made me wish that I had died sooner than witness it.

A tall girl with loosened braids was being dragged along by two Ukrainians, one grasping her hand and the other pulling her lovely blonde hair, while she struggled with them and cried to high heaven. She was barefoot and wore a torn dress that exposed a breast. Her face had a wild expression; saliva dribbled from her mouth in a thin froth. Then I noticed that one of the men—a policeman—had a revolver in his hand . . . Like a trapped animal she struggled, her cheeks inflamed, her eyes bulging with terror . . . I shall never forget the sight!

Some of my companions looked on in silence; others whispered guesses that she must be a Jewess. "She deserves it," they said. We turned away slowly. When dinner came, I tried to eat, but it was almost impossible. While sitting at the table, I heard some remarks about a similar incident that happened here a week ago; apparently, it made little impression on them. I did not doubt that the girl I had seen was Jewish, but I wondered where they had caught her—and where were they taking her now?

After dinner, I cleared away the dishes from the table. Again the fortune teller came up to me and diverted my thoughts. She pulled me toward a corner. She apparently was more interested in my future than I . . . with beating heart I sat down. She studied my expression and observed me so intently that I expected her to lay down the cards and say, "You are Jewish!" After all, Dr. Jagoda must have uncovered my identity at our first interview. Now she could see my features close up—just as I could study her face, too—though to tell the truth, her facial characteristics were more Semitic than mine.

Narrowing her eyes, she compressed her lips and began to lay out the cards with energetic gestures of her hands. When they were spread out on the table, she again looked at me. I did not like this whole procedure, but I sat quietly, trying to conceal my impatience, wondering why it took her so long to get started. Somehow she seemed to need time for inspiration in my special case. Her expression became very serious as she began to shuffle the cards, then she told me to divide the pack into two halves—and she began to lay them out, one by one, shaking her head. I was really worried now, and thought, *What kind of a devil is this?*

At last she stopped, and fixing me in her gaze, she said, "You are living through a great deal. You had an important decision to make before you came here. You wanted to volunteer, and yet you did not want to . . ."

I nodded my head, and interrupted her. "They caught me. No one wants to volunteer to go to Germany."

But she motioned me with her hand not to disturb her. "Your thoughts are back home with your family. I see something here that is not very clear—but something is burning, maybe a house; there are screams, people, some great misfortune, fire, fire most certainly—or maybe somebody is critically ill, somebody will die."

I felt my whole body freeze. I noticed that people were observing us from a distance—so many eyes turned in my direction! From time to time, someone would come up to our table, but she would wave them away. This experience was surely an unnecessary supplement to all my adventures! Was this to be the last move, the last play?

She continued to speak: "Don't go back there. They are in danger. I see something red—like blood. Don't go back," she repeated. "Nothing good awaits you there." I knew that, of course, but did she really know, or was she only trying to draw me out? Was she playing a game, a terrible game with me? Trying to divert her, I asked, "Maybe they are also catching members of my family to send to work in Germany?"

"No," she answered, "not for work. I don't want to distress you, but I see death. A terrible death, fire, a burning house—and someone in the house. It isn't very clear, but I see fire and death. People are in a fire."

I felt like I would faint. I must have been very pale, for she remarked about my changed expression and tried to quiet me. "Don't take it so hard," she said, comfortingly. "Sometimes the cards can be mistaken. Or maybe the fire is only in the neighborhood of your home. Maybe your family lives near the Jewish ghetto? For you know they are liquidating ghettos everywhere . . . the Judenfrei . . ."

This was the final blow, the final thrust to the heart. "No," I answered, trying again to appear calm, "we live outside the city, in a village. Maybe the fire was in the village—maybe a barn burned down?" But she did not even listen to my reply.

She kept on saying that what she saw was very interesting. "You will go through a lot yet in this camp. You have some valuables with you; I don't know exactly what, but some money and something else of value, jewelry. They will take that away from you. I don't know exactly who, but you will have trouble—I see the authorities, the authorities," she repeated and again looked significantly at me.

"I don't have anything with me," I said brazenly, "except a few rags." Yet I thought that she must know what she was talking about; I still had the jewelry and money. Now I believed that she knew everything. I would have gotten away from this woman if I could, but she seemed completely engrossed in what she saw. "You will get out of here. You will go abroad with much trouble—but you will go," she said, "but you will not have your valuables with you. You will find many difficulties en route, too—I cannot tell clearly just what." She paused for a while, then continued. "There is a change; afterwards it will be well, very well for you. You will work with women. I see a large building and many women there, almost nobody but women, many of them in uniforms, and yet you will feel very lonely. Yes. Loneliness will be your constant companion, despite everything. You will work hard; work, work, work. You will be worried, sad—but you will be all right. People will like and respect you."

The woman was so involved in telling my fortune that the tears coursing down my cheeks and falling upon her cards did not distract her. I tried with all my might not to cry, but I was not made of iron. I felt like I wanted to hug her for this good fortune she saw in my future. There would be a tomorrow for me, after all! It was a faint spark of hope. I waited for her to tell me more, but she was mumbling to herself—I could not understand a word. "What is it?" I finally asked. "What do you see now?"

"It's good," she said, "but nothing very gay. Work, loneliness. You will feel all alone."

"Maybe I'll go back home? Maybe I'll be given a vacation?"

"No," she replied firmly. Then she looked at me and asked, "What do you think about all this that I have told you?"

"There's some truth in it," I replied evasively, "but not all."

"I only told you what the cards showed, and my cards do not lie," she retorted.

Fearing that I might have offended her, I said no more, but simply thanked her. I added, "Of course, you will keep this all a secret!"

"A fortune teller does not peddle other people's secrets," she said. At that, as if awakening from a dream, we both breathed easier.

I went away, and another girl took my place at the table. Several people tugged at my arm, saying, "She knows everything, doesn't she?"

A guard entered the hall and announced that the next day, after breakfast, we would report to the medical commission, since the transport was probably leaving for Germany that day. After he left, the room was immediately filled with commotion and complaints.

The afternoon passed swiftly, and after supper we spent some time talking. Then I said my prayers just like most of the others did. This promised to be the last night spent in the camp. A long and frightening night.

At last the morning came. Quickly I got up from my cot and crossed over to a water basin. I freshened up a bit, straightened out the wrinkles in my dress—the two-piece green dress—and smoothed down my hair. It was not long before everyone was up and ready to go; they packed their belongings, complaining all the while.

During the last breakfast in camp, everyone seemed anxious to show as much friendliness and courtesy as possible. They passed the plates of food with smiles, sharing it equably. Everyone knew that after we passed the medical commission we would be separated and sent in different directions in Germany. Whether we would be able to choose our destinations, we did not know. Still, our appetites were good, and the bread vanished rapidly, along with the coffee. After breakfast, most of us remained where we sat on the benches, talking.

At last our chatter was broken by the appearance of a guard in the doorway. He was a tall, robust civilian in high boots. First in Polish, then in Ukrainian, he gave an order to take our suitcases and line up in double file. We did as he commanded. I picked up my suitcase, tied a kerchief around my head, and took my place in line.

8

From the Jaws of Death

WE FORMED A DOUBLE FILE. The girl at my side was sighing deeply, and from time to time a curse escaped her lips. "Devil take it," she muttered. "Who knows where they will take me, or for how long. Who knows if I'll ever even return home!" She set her valise down on the floor with an angry thump.

The sudden gesture drew my attention to her luggage. It was more like a cardboard box than a suitcase, and it was held together with leather straps. Comparing it with my own suitcase, which matched my green suit outfit and my kerchief and which still looked quite presentable, I realized for the first time what a mistake I had made. It was made of a fiber like leather and looked too prosperous—even luxurious—next to the girl's battered box and the luggage that the other peasants had. I should have borrowed some old suitcase from the Krupkas when I left Brody. With this one, I looked as if I was going away on a vacation to a summer resort! It had to strike someone as being suspicious—but now it was too late to worry about it.

The line grew longer behind me, two by two. For the last time, I turned back to look at the main hall of the camp—and I saw that the line now stretched almost to the end of the enormous room. The hall looked even darker and more ominous, it seemed to me, than during our last few days there. Perhaps it was by contrast with the dazzlingly bright June morning outside. The rays of sunshine streamed through the open door, and I could see the courtyard bathed in golden light. In only a few moments we would be outdoors! I felt like a butterfly coming out of a damp, dark, and smelly cocoon into a new life of freedom.

Step by step we moved forward. Everyone breathed deeply, trying to fill his lungs with the clean, fresh air. From many lips came cries of joy at the sight of this bright, summery morning. As the line moved outdoors, I saw in front of the building in the courtyard that there was a sort of roofed porch where several men sat at a long table, on a bench—like judges. There was a stack of papers on the table—no doubt lists with our names.

As I came nearer, I recognized Dr. Jagoda among the men. Our glances met—and I could see that he also was surprised. I don't think anyone could have noticed it, but I saw his facial expression change. He must have seen the astonishment in mine. And at that moment we must have had the same thought: God, help her get out of this place!

The first ones in line were already at the table of the commission. Dr. Jagoda began to examine them. Those that appeared healthy were passed. He said something and wrote down his remarks. After the inspection they received some papers from the commissioners and then were conducted to a room on the right. The girls entered by one door, the young men by another. I heard whispers: they were being sent to the shower rooms.

Ah, I thought with relief, at last I will be able to wash myself! How long since I had had a bath? Long enough. Since I left the Tarashkewitzes' house two weeks had gone by, two weeks without washing, without even taking off my clothes. But in these times it did not matter too much. Nothing mattered, save one's life . . .

The line was getting closer and closer. I kept watching Dr. Jagoda from a distance. *What a noble soul,* I thought. *How happy he will be—what a happy moment for both of us—when he sees me leave with the transport.* It was only thanks to his assistance that I had been able to survive all this. I would try to whisper "Thank you" while he was examining me . . .

My heart beating wildly, I felt again that I was under the protection of someone who cared. My throat choked up with unshed tears. Oh, how I would have wanted to cry aloud—this time with gratitude and joy!

Suddenly, unexpectedly, this moment of exalted confidence and hope was broken by the sound of heavy steps. I heard voices directly behind me, and as I looked back I saw that others in line were also looking in that direction. Three civilians in dark clothing, their trousers tucked into high boots, grasping large ominous-looking knouts, were looking closely at everyone in line. To me they seemed like demons sprouting out of hell. They all had guns: Ukrainian police.

Their sharp eyes scanned every face, coming closer to where I stood. One was short and stout, the other thinner and of medium height, and the third one tall. All of them evoked in my mind the vision of doom. I stood petrified with fear, feeling that my death sentence would soon sound in my ears. These were the same men, I was sure, who had dragged out the fear-maddened girl a few days before. Their knouts would soon descend upon my back—I knew those whips well from my ghetto days! There were only two people before me, waiting to be examined by the doctor. I cast one last glance at Dr. Jagoda. All color had drained from his face as his eyes met mine. It was as though he wanted to say, "Yes, it was from this that I tried to save you. Now I cannot do anything."

I could read in his glance that if these policemen wanted me, it would be the end. He knew them and their tactics well. And they were coming closer . . . Seconds more, and they had stopped in front of me. And this lovely, sun-filled morning turned dark in my eyes. I felt as if I would faint—the whole courtyard seemed to be whirling around before my eyes. And then I heard a voice in broken German:

"You, you there, in green!" I opened my eyes and saw that it was the taller of the men who was addressing me. For a moment I was mute. That voice sounded in my ears like a bomb bursting in the sky. While I stood there in silence, the shorter one approached closer and pointed his finger straight at me. There was no doubt that it was me they wanted. I took a couple of hesitating steps forward, dark spots wavering in front of my eyes. He shouted at me again, in broken German: *"Dein Rantz, dein Rantz!"*—he wanted me to pick up my suitcase. But as I did not turn back immediately, he thought that I did not understand, and angrily he repeated the words, "Your suitcase!" Then I went back and took my valise. That gave me a chance to look up again at the doctor—in my thoughts, at least, I reached out to him for help. He sat by the table, his head lowered, not seeing me.

I took my place between the three policemen. *"Juden!"* the taller man muttered under his breath, in German. "Dirty Jewess!"

I wanted to reply, but I seemed to have lost my voice. Yes, I was a Jewess—and I had no right to exist. These men and their leaders had the right to deprive me of my life. To whom could I turn for justice?

I walked slowly; I could hardly move my feet. The suitcase weighed heavier, so that I could scarcely hold it up. They pushed me angrily. "Hurry up, you! Where are your papers? Your Kennkarte?"

"In my suitcase," I told them. They led me into one of the buildings in the corner of the courtyard. We passed through a long corridor, then they opened a door, and I found myself in an office in which a fourth plainclothes policeman sat at a desk. A big, burly man. He lifted his head as soon as they brought me in and eyed me coldly from head to toe.

The first thing they said was, "Jewess!" The word came as a shout from both of them, like an incontrovertible accusation. Then the one at the desk shouted, "Show me your papers!"

My fingers shook nervously, but somehow I managed to open my suitcase and take out the birth certificate—the one I had obtained from Hanka Buczek, and now my only proof of identity. They looked at the paper, then at each other, and the one at the desk said impatiently, "This is a forged document. Where did you get it?" He began to read aloud: "Hanka Buczek, born in Rudy, county of Rohatyn, Poland. That's false! Where did you get this certificate? Where is your Kennkarte, if you are not a Jewess? Look at that birth date," he said, turning his eyes back to the certificate he held in his hand. "It doesn't jibe. She can't be as old as it says here."

"I left my Kennkarte at Brody," I answered. "That is where I worked until recently, and I came to Lvov from there. All my papers remained in the city hall at Brody. If you want to, you can check with them." This was the truth, after all.

"What were you doing in Brody?"

"I was working as a domestic."

They exchanged amused glances. Apparently I did not look at all like a typical servant girl. Again, they began to insist that I tell them where I got the birth certificate. One of them suggested that they get in touch with the authorities in Rudy and find out about it. I tried to defend myself; I said that I had obtained the birth certificate from the parish priest just before I left for Brody. They had my work card here in the camp, I reminded them, the card that I had been issued at Brody.

Perhaps I should have been in a greater panic, but somehow fear left me when I saw the end approaching. A reckless courage took over and I was determined to die bravely. I began to defend myself, and in so doing I gained self-confidence. The louder they shouted at me, the greater my courage grew.

"I have no idea what you're talking about," I retorted. "I don't know the reason why you have brought me here."

"Yeah—all of them have the same answer, all of them deny being Jewish," they sneered. "We have caught many just like you and have sent them to the fires."

The short one added, "But after a while under interrogation, every Jew or Jewess admits it—if not here, then at the Gestapo. *There* they don't ask too many questions." He held my birth certificate in one grubby paw, the document that until now I had considered to be my greatest treasure, my defense. With his free hand he opened my suitcase and started to throw the contents out, angrily, upon the floor. When he saw the silk nightgown and scented toilet soap, he became infuriated. "So, you're not a Jewess?" he bellowed. "A maid with a silk nightgown?"

The taller policeman also helped throw my possessions around, and finally came upon the bag with my mother's jewelry. He pulled the cord and spilled everything upon the table. He gritted his teeth and looked at me with wild eyes, piercingly, as though he would have liked to tear me apart in his rage.

Now I could say nothing. I knew that every subterfuge and every defense would be useless. It was better to admit to being a Jewess. I counted now not minutes but seconds before he would empty the bullets in the revolver at his belt into my brain.

At that moment I was indifferent to everything. Had there been only one of them, I might have tried to grab his revolver and shoot him and then myself. But I had no chance against these four. They stood before me, motionless, looking as though they had caught me in the act of stealing something.

At last the short one screamed, "A servant girl from a village!" He spat with disgust. Then they began to examine each piece of jewelry, to see if it was really of value, as though they feared being cheated. I could see that my jewelry impressed them. The big one who looked like a bandit began examining my birth certificate again.

"Born in Rudy, county of Rohatyn, residing in Brody for six months," he recited in a monotone, as though to himself. "All this can be checked out. We will telephone the police at Rohatyn, they will get in touch with the village authorities in Rudy, and all will be explained."

I kept silent, for I knew that all this could be done and very easily, too. In that way they would certainly find out that I was the false Hanka Buczek. The real Hanka, for her good deed, might pay dearly—for they would know that the real Hanka Buczek was still living in Rudy and was the housekeeper for the parish priest.

While he spoke, the other kept throwing my belongings around like wild animals. They found the cigarettes among my things. The short policeman came upon a beige duster that I had packed away. He liked the checkered pattern, and he exclaimed, "This will be just right for my wife!"

They began to divide my things among them. Observing them closely, I saw that they were puzzled and did not seem to know the right solution. At last the short one said, "There aren't enough valuables here for us to set you free. Do you have more gold?" His statement anticipated what I had had in mind. I could hear, and yet I could hardly believe what I heard. Then there was a possibility of a future for me? He added, "Besides, there isn't enough here for the four of us—we must divide everything."

Then I felt that there must be some higher Power protecting me. It was a feeling of great relief that I could cast aside the burden of fear and lies and could now talk openly. Confidently, perhaps a bit naively, with tears in my eyes, I told them that I also had a gold watch, a very beautiful man's watch that my father had owned, and I told them where I had left it. But I hastened to say, in defense of the Tarashkewitzes, that the people with whom I had left the watch were completely unaware of my true identity and were strangers. They didn't know I was Jewish. I told the policemen not to say anything about me, but simply to demand the return of the watch. They wrote down the address.

The policemen stepped outside the room for a consultation behind closed doors. In a few minutes they returned and said, "Now we will allow you to go to Germany—to let the Gestapo find you and shoot you as a Jew . . ."

I could not believe that I truly heard these words from his lips. Were my ears deceiving me?

"To Germany—to the Gestapo," I said and left the room, my head lowered, going directly back outside to the camp. A miracle of God! Couldn't they have shot me? I had to believe—believe strongly—that only God's will saved me. Not my words, nor their fears—for only one bullet and I'd be done for. No, it was the Lord of Hosts who had saved and protected me; it was my mother's blessing and prayers that were with me every moment in every danger.

I entered the main hall and found a dozen or more people assembled inside. Shortly afterward they brought the dinner pails in, and after we had eaten we were told to report to the office. We started to move forward. A few words were spoken now and then, but everyone was busy thinking about himself. These people had arrived here only recently and had not had time to become acquainted. We left the building.

Impatiently, I yearned to stand before the commission again. We were nearing the same place where the shadow of death had fallen across my path before. When Dr. Jagoda saw me in the line, he must have thought I was a ghost from another world. I knew that he could not believe his eyes. He looked closely at my face, probably thinking that it was someone who happened to resemble me. But when I stood in front of his table and said, "Hanka Buczek," the name must have sounded incredible in his ears. Oh, how I wished I could tell him about everything! How I wanted to share my experience with him! But alas, I could only stand there in silence. Only just as I was turning to go, I managed to whisper "Thank you."

Those were my last words, my last look at that man to whom I owed my life. Would I ever see him again? Would I ever be able to thank him properly?

We were handed our papers and told to go to the shower rooms—girls on one side, the men on the other. There were only a few girls in this group. A matron told us to undress quickly, put our clothes on a bench standing against the wall in a corner of the room, and pass through a door to the showers.

Without a murmur, we began to wash ourselves, and I saw the grime rolling off my body—the soapy foam was black, not white. I thought wryly that this was the first time in my life that I stood naked before strangers, or anyone. It gave me a shock. Never had I completely undressed even in the presence of my own mother or sister—yet here, at a given order, each one of us quickly threw off all her clothes and stood under the shower. Everything was done in a flash, without protest, without shame.

At last we lined up, dressed and clean, ready to leave. The sun greeted us in the courtyard and dried the last drops of moisture from our faces and hands and hair. The boys were already waiting outside. Each of us received a package of food and were told to march to the railroad station.

Now at last I had to believe that these were my last moments and my last steps in this transit camp on Janowska Street; the camp where, for two weeks, my life hung upon a thread—where I was in the maws of a lion that could swallow me at any time.

My suitcase in one hand, the food package in the other, I marched along with a girl at my side. We exchanged hardly a word. After what I had been through here, what could I say to her or to anyone else? I would take my recollections of the Janowska Street camp and all my experiences there with me always, even to the grave. I felt a wave of pity for Dr. Jagoda, that he had to remain here, witnessing these scenes of misery and suffering, and only rarely able to help.

At the gate, the guards sized us up arrogantly. *"Heil, Hitler!"*—those words were the last I heard as I left the camp. It seemed to me that they were the same guards I had encountered on entering the camp. I lowered my head, hoping that they would not recognize me, and with the others I quickly made a right turn into the road. It was a long way to the station. The sun was hot, and the stone-paved road was tiring. My suitcase at least was not heavy now, for the jewelry and most of my other possessions were gone. At least they had left me the sport coat! I was glad of that, though the coat was badly wrinkled because I had slept in it during the time I was hidden in the shelter, to protect me from rat bites. Now it looked like a rag draped over my arm, but it might be useful yet.

It took us about half an hour to reach the railway station. The entire area swarmed with people. Life here seemed almost normal—passengers with packages and luggage, hurrying in different directions either to or from a train. The guard in charge of our group told us to wait at the gate to the trains, and he went to get our tickets. I sensed danger in every extra minute of waiting, and it seemed an eternity before he returned, holding the tickets in one hand. He told us to follow him. We went along the station platform, pushing our way through the milling throngs of people, until we reached the spot where we had to wait for our train.

Everyone was curious to know where we were going. We learned that we were bound for Vienna. As I looked around, carefully, trying not to attract attention, my heart suddenly skipped a beat. At a distance from us, in one of the entrances to the station platform, I noticed a girl from Rohatyn whom I knew quite well. We had been classmates in our schooldays. She was turned in profile to me, so that while I could study her features carefully, she could not see me. Quickly, I sat down on my suitcase and turned in the other direction. "Oh, how my feet hurt!" I said to the girl at my side. She smiled and also sat down on her suitcase. "You've got the right idea," she said. I felt every nerve shaking in my body.

We had to wait a long time, but I did not look back again. I sat on my suitcase until we were ordered to move on. A train had pulled up to the station and we were told to board the open cars. This was a great shock and disappointment to us—usually such cars were used to transport cows and cattle—and we were supposed to ride in them ourselves! The commissioner who escorted us to the station now gave our tickets to the oldest of our group. Once more, as we boarded the train, he called out our names—there were eighteen of us. How strange it sounded in my ears when he called "Hanka Buczek!" I nodded my head, my heart pounding wildly. When he left, the sliding door of our car was closed. We heard the train whistle, and with a rumbling jolt, the cars began to move.

The barred openings of the car were placed high, so all we could see was a strip of sky. Now, as the day waned, the red rays of the setting sun penetrated the gloomy interior, as though to reassure me that Heaven was watching over us. With each turn of the wheels, the country and the towns that I knew began to recede into the distance. The town in which I was born and in which I had lived my whole life, where I left the memories of happy youth, would remain only in my memory now as the tomb of hundreds, thousands of corpses.

On this day in June, 1943, I was going out into the unknown—into the land of our murderers, our destroyers. There, ironically, I would try to find shelter and a haven among our enemies.

After a frugal meal, we talked a little among ourselves until it was too dark to see. With nightfall, there came a drop in temperature. I was glad they had not taken away my coat—I needed it now to keep warm. I wrapped it around me, huddled into a corner, and tried to sleep. Many others did likewise—they pulled out extra clothing from their suitcases to keep warm. But it was not easy to fall asleep surrounded by the noise of the locomotive and the rattle of the cars. Whenever we stopped at a station, there was an unearthly squeal of iron against steel and a conductor's gruff voice announcing the name of the town.

We tried somehow to live through the night. Our first stop was to be Krakow, where we were to change trains in the early hours of the morning. From time to time someone snored. The train made frequent stops, some of long duration. The day was already whitening the sky when we heard "Krakow!" in Polish and in German. Now we had to gather our things together and leave the train. We would have to wait several hours at the station, they said, for other connections to Vienna. As I got up, I felt as though I were collecting all my broken bones into a unified whole. Everything ached, every nerve still felt the hard boards of the car, every muscle twinged from the rough jolting of the wheels. We stood up and stretched, but our leader began to urge us to hurry, as this train was pulling out very soon and we had to be quick to all get out in time.

One by one, we began to scramble down to the station platform. There were very few people in the station, considerably fewer than at Lvov. The railway station in Krakow was very old and neglected, and looked as though it had seen a war.

When we returned to the station after a long walking tour of the city—where again I saw the signs JEWS AND DOGS FORBIDDEN—we were astonished to see that the train was already waiting for us. We quickly picked up our things and boarded the car that was reserved for us. To our relief, we saw there were two long benches in our car, and we sat down to rest our tired feet. The train was soon moving on towards Vienna. Whether it was the fault of the track bed or the construction of the cars, this train gave us a more uncomfortable ride than the first; it felt as though we were sitting directly on the wheels. Soon the shadows of evening hid the landscape from our eyes. We huddled as best as we could upon the floor of the car and began to open our food sacks. Though it was but bread and sausage, we ate hungrily, then talked a while and finally bedded down. Some of us quietly said prayers, and I joined in.

Next morning, we were told that we had passed the border and were now in Austria. My head felt dizzy from having been bounced around all night long. As we took in the situation and looked at one another, we began to make fun of our disheveled appearances. Though my body ached all over, I felt a constant pain in my legs—I looked down and saw that my feet were so swollen that my stockings seemed ready to burst.

This was the first time in my life that my feet had swollen up. I was afraid—but even more afraid to say anything about it, because I might be sent back as unfit to work. And, after all, I had no home—no place that I could be sent back to! The Germans wanted only young and healthy people for work.

We looked forward impatiently to our arrival in Vienna. We ate our evening meal without washing our hands (we had no water), spreading our provisions out on the dirty benches. Afterward we spent some time straightening out our clothes; what we were wearing looked like wrinkled, untidy rags. The girls began to comb their hair, trying to make themselves appear attractive—probably hoping that they would get better employment if they looked neat.

Our train slowed down as we approached the Vienna depot. I could not believe that I actually succeeded in coming such a long distance, that I was here. Maybe here at last I would be able to live through the rest of the war quietly . . .

The doors were rolled back on one side of our car, and when the train came to a full stop we began to jump down to the station platform. One by one, we were counted—like cattle. As we entered the station, we were surrounded on all sides by German sounds—the language grated in my ears.

The station was rather quiet, however. We saw mostly military uniforms, with only a sprinkling of civilians and a few women. What irritated me almost beyond endurance was the martial step of army boots and the continuous salutation, "Heil, Hitler!"

Our leader, after a quick consultation with the conductor, ordered us to follow him and we fell into step, two by two, like sheep. Some wanted to know where he was taking us and he replied, "To the employment bureau—the *Arbeitsamt*." We were so tired that we dragged our feet; we must have looked to passersby like tramps.

My legs seemed to have turned into numb posts—my feet ached with every step. *My God,* I thought with alarm, *what is happening to me?* If they noticed my swollen legs at the Arbeitsamt they might turn me down and send me back "home." I sighed with relief when we reached the office: it was staffed mainly by German women seated at desks in the large hall. One of them looked up as soon as we came in and greeted us with a sardonic smile. The others exchanged mocking glances. Then began the questioning: name, date and place of birth, and so forth. Because none of our group spoke German, I also pretended not to understand the language. Our leader tried to help out in these interrogations, though he himself spoke only broken German.

When the registration was completed, they began to allot us places where we were to stay temporarily and to assign us various jobs. Some of the group requested to be sent to the same place together, but I did not ask for that. I preferred to be alone—that was safer. They told us that in a few days we would be sent to residence camps for foreigners; this news did not please me one bit, for who knows whom I might run into in such a place—and whether I would be recognized. But, of course, I had no choice.

Some of our group were assigned to work in restaurant kitchens; that was my lot. And for the next few days I was to live with an old German couple and pay them out of my earning for room and board. Since the clerk was not sure whether these people were at home, she had to get in touch with them first. It turned out that I could not go there until evening, and I had the rest of the day at my disposal, it seemed. They led me and a few others into another room where we could leave our things. We were doled out the usual sausage and bread, but to our amazement we were also given cake and coffee and some cups to share. We were so thirsty that we set to drink like wild animals. The coffee was freshly made and good, but even if it had been vile it would have tasted wonderful to us. We had eaten only dry food for such a long time that something hot to drink was indescribably delicious. After we had sated our thirst and hunger, we started to compare the addresses—where we were to work and live. They all promised to visit whenever possible and to try to be assigned to the same camp later. I could not be the exception; I also promised to keep in touch.

What would we do now with our remaining hours of "freedom?" One of the group had heard about a beautiful park and palace called Schönbrun and proposed that we go there. We decided to follow his suggestion, especially as our leader said that he would get information about the place and accompany us on the tour. Although I was glad of the opportunity to see something new, the condition of my legs made walking a painful experience; nevertheless, I could not hold back from the group. I tried to cover my legs as much as possible by wearing my tan sport coat, saying by way of explanation that it might be cool by the time we returned in the evening.

It was a warm—no, it was a hot day. My legs burned like fire. When I looked down, I saw with mounting fear that they were as red as beets. I would have taken off my stockings, but then my swollen legs would have been conspicuous. So I gritted my teeth and marched on in silence.

The park was indeed beautiful, but I was glad to begin the walk back that afternoon. My legs felt as though they did not belong to me . . . On the way everyone exclaimed over the beauty of the park and exchanged promises to meet there whenever they could. But then, all at once, one of the group noticed that I was hardly able to walk.

"For God's sake!" she screamed. "What happened to your legs?"

They came to a quick halt, thinking that I had been bitten by some insect. I smilingly assured them that it was nothing—my legs were like that normally; it was nothing new.

"And they took you for work—with such legs?" They could not believe it.

Our leader overheard the conversation. He wrinkled his forehead and began to examine my legs. "All over her body she is thin," he muttered as though to himself, "but her legs are like an elephant's."

"And they're so red!" one girl exclaimed.

"That's because I was in the sun all day," I tried to explain. "Besides, I'm not used to wearing stockings—that's why."

The girl nodded her head as if to say, "If you're not complaining, why should we bother?"

And so, talking and laughing, we reached the Arbeitsamt. We were late; they were waiting for us so that they could close the office. Each one took his belongings. I picked up my suitcase, exchanged a few addresses with the girls, writing down my own new address in a shaky peasant (or so I hoped) scribble. They instructed us in which direction to go, and we left.

Walking slowly, with my suitcase in my hand, I passed many streets and back alleys before I found the house where I would stay for a few days. It was a large apartment building, four stories high. The street was quiet. With pounding heart I pushed open the heavy door leading to the main hall. I took out the slip of paper on which the name of the family was written and compared it with the names on the mail boxes. I found it—on the fourth floor. There was no elevator, so I started the climb up the stairs, dragging my suitcase after me. I felt my legs swelling up more and more. The staircase was filled with the aroma of cooking, probably from the restaurant nearby. I wondered if I would get something to eat; despite my condition, I was hungry.

At last I stood before the door of the apartment and rang the bell. An elderly gentleman opened the door. His face was pale and emaciated and his hand shook as he read the paper the Arbeitsamt had given me. With a grimace of displeasure, he let me in, calling out to his wife in German, "Already they have sent someone to us."

His wife, also well on in years, looked me over from head to toes and guided me to a small room furnished with a bed, table, chair, and wardrobe. "This is your place," she said and went away. I took stock of my surroundings; from what I could see of the apartment it seemed large, but gloomy, neglected, and poor. I took off my coat and shoes and sat down on the chair. Oh, how I wished that I could bathe or just wash myself, cleanse my feet of the dust and dirt of the streets. They ached so! My hunger was growing more intense, but I guessed that I would have to wait. I did not dare ask for anything. I could read from their faces that I was not a welcome guest; they took me only because the authorities had forced them.

However, in a little while, the old lady came in and asked if I wanted some coffee. "Yes, thank you!" I replied and followed her into the living room, in the center of which stood a huge table with equally large-looking chairs. She gave me coffee and a few slices of bread with marmalade. I had appetite enough to eat it all, but I saw that it was meant for three people. I sipped my coffee slowly—it tasted as if it had been boiled several times. At least it was hot and helped wash down the bread—for once, bread without sausage.

I hesitated, wondering if I should let them know that I understood German—they might feel more kindly disposed towards me if I did. On the other hand, it might be dangerous, especially if the leader of our group came here to check on me and discovered that I knew German.

Somehow they tried to make me understand that they were living on a retirement pension and that they found it hard to exist. All food was rationed. Gathering up courage, I asked if I could wash myself. The woman took me by the hand and showed me where the bathroom was, and she also gave me a clean though threadbare towel. Nothing could have made me feel better! Now I could at last wash my swollen legs and soak my feet in a basin. Afterward I felt like I could sleep soundly for not one night or two but rather a whole week without a break. But the woman had told me that she would serve supper later on, so I went to my room and waited.

Somehow I lived through the miserable meal and through the following night. Getting up very early, I left my sleeping hosts and eventually found my way to my place of work—a restaurant in a side street. Entering, I handed my employment card to a man who presumably was the owner. He told me to follow him. In the kitchen he introduced me to a girl and a boy who also worked there—Ukrainians from the Lvov area. They set me at once to peeling potatoes, and I was told that later I would wash dishes and pots and clean up the kitchen.

We worked through the day. As I was leaving, the girl—who had taken a liking to me when I told her I was Ukrainian—assured me that in two or three days I would be transferred to a camp where only Ukrainians and Poles lived. Little did she know that this was the last thing that I wanted to have happen! Thus far, my goal had been simply to cross the boundary—to lose myself in a foreign country where no one would know me, no one could recognize me, and where at last I could find some rest and quiet until the war's end. But as it happened, from what I learned at the Arbeitsamt and from my coworkers in the restaurant, in a few days I would now have to go to a camp where I would live among people from Poland. That again would place me in danger. Living with the others, I would have to go with them to church, pray with them, observe their holidays—and although I knew all the prayers and traditions, there was always the chance that among so many people there might be one who might recognize me. And another thing: living among these people, I would have to be constantly on guard—especially at night. I would be afraid to fall asleep lest I begin talking aloud—it had happened before—and someone might understand something of my wild ranting. Now I had to consider well what I ought to do . . . and again, as usual, I had no one whose advice I could seek. I was alone, and whatever I decided, it had to be at my own risk; it had to be thought out with my own intelligence.

After finishing a hard day's work, I barely managed to walk "home," for my legs were swollen even worse than before. With difficulty I climbed up to the fourth floor. My legs did not seem to belong to me anymore; they refused to obey. If I still had some remnants of energy and the desire to live, my legs did not share it—they seemed to be in rebellion against me. I knocked on the door, and the old lady opened it, greeting me with her by-now-familiar hostile expression. If the world hated me, she must have hated me the most, even without knowing who I really was . . . The atmosphere of their apartment was like that of a cemetery. Her husband sat in an easy chair in a dark corner and seemed to be muttering to himself—though I had the impression that he was cursing me. I could understand German well enough, but I did not know all the swear words—they did not teach me those in college. With lowered head I had to slink past him into my "doghouse." I was tired, very tired.

Never before in my life, not even when I was with the Krupkas in Brody, did I have to work as hard as I had to that day—peeling so many potatoes, scraping vegetables, lifting heavy cans and pots and then later scouring them. Oh, if my mother could have seen me—I thought—she would have wept. I was so lonely . . . I lay down on the bed and closed my eyes, resting. Now I had to plan how I could get out of Vienna. Neither the city, nor the job, nor the prospect of living in a camp suited my needs.

My legs were now really a problem and I had no idea when the swelling would subside. As I sat pondering, the old lady called me to have some coffee. We sat at the table, not saying a word. She—with her gray hair pulled severely back, her sunken eyes, her lips so thin that one could not even see them (I knew that people with thin lips are mean)—resembled in some way the rats that ran over me in the shelter in the camp on Janowska Street. Her husband, too—a wizened, shrunken figure—looked at me, shifty-eyed, as though he did not trust me. Eh, those rats were more pleasant company!

The old couple drank that watery coffee and said nothing, but their glances were eloquent enough. Perhaps they thought that I was some secret agent, not to be trusted. I got up from the table and said, "Goodnight." Lying in bed, as I tried to formulate my plans, some instinct urged me to get away from Vienna. At last I decided that during my lunch break the next day, I would ask the restaurant owner to let me go to the employment office. I would tell him that I had received a card from the employment bureau to report there, and if he wanted to see the card, I'd tell him that I left it at home. All night long I thought about my plan, trying it out in every which way—while I turned from side to side during those sleepless hours. I arose early in the morning, quietly, and tossed my few belongings into the suitcase. I did not want to have to rush at the last minute, because the pain in my legs was increasingly worse. Even putting my shoes on in the morning was a torture that made me almost faint. I never removed my stockings now, afraid that I would not be able to put them on again if I did.

Very quietly, like a mouse, I left the apartment and went downstairs. The street was empty and peaceful—the tall buildings seemed like sleeping giants guarding the thoroughfare. Once in a while someone would pass by, but no one paid any attention to me. I had to walk to work, for I had not a cent to my name.

When I arrived at the restaurant they wondered why I had arrived so early. Did they think that I loved my job so much? I, in turn, was amazed at the quantities of vegetables, onions, and potatoes that they had already prepared for me to scrape and clean and pare. After a quick breakfast, I set to work. I tried to keep my legs hidden behind a tall can so that no one would notice how they had expanded overnight. Pretty soon they would burst through my stockings, and then my shoes. Near me sat the Ukrainian girl, who tried to describe the life I would have in their camp. She said that she already had a boyfriend lined up for me. She talked on and on, while I was thinking my own thoughts. At last she noticed that I was not paying attention. Why? I explained that I had to report to the Arbeitsamt. I had to receive a card from the employment office, but had left it at home. Would she, since she speaks German so well, would she please talk to the boss and ask him to let me go there during my lunch period? It would save time if I could go then.

She agreed, and after we had worked together a few hours, she went with me to the employer and told him my story. I naturally understood every word of their conversation and knew that he was not pleased that I wanted to have time off from work. Perhaps he was afraid that he might lose one work horse—and it was not easy to get another. My Ukrainian friend, however, went on to say that the Arbeitsamt demanded my appearance to complete some formalities they had forgotten to take care of, and the boss would just have to comply and let me go. I saw his greasy, perspiring face twist into a grimace of displeasure, but he nodded and waved his hand. She turned to me and said it was all right. "Thank you," I said. I knew that I had a friend in this girl, but I also knew that it would not last long.

I ate a hearty lunch, for I needed strength for this enterprise. The Ukrainian girl explained how to get to the employment office, adding that it was a good distance away. Thanking her again, I left. I had no money for the train, and had to walk far. Even with her directions, I had trouble finding my way. At last, I reached the Arbeitsamt. As I stood before the building, I sighed deeply. I must now consider well how I was to begin—otherwise I might fall into a trap of my own connivance. I only prayed that I would not run into anyone from my part of Poland—or my city—one could never be too sure of that. With beating heart, I entered. There were lines, but not too long, and in a little while I stood before one of the women clerks, explaining to her—more with gestures than with words, for I was still afraid to own up that I understood German—that I was a village girl, that Vienna was a big city and I was not used to city life. I was afraid of the tall buildings . . . She asked me my name, and hesitantly I gave it to her—Hanka Buczek . . . She obtained my dossier from another clerk, and after examining it, she said, "You will go to a camp, anyway, and won't have to be in the city except to work."

Desperately, I told her that my parents would be very dissatisfied when I wrote and told them that I was working in a big city. And as I spoke, my eyes filled with tears. She looked at me with some surprise, but said, "Wait, we shall see."

Taking my file, she went to a man who seemed to be the chief. After talking to him, she returned and, to my amazement, asked where I would like to go. Still pretending not to understand German very well, I did not know what to answer. She took out a map and asked me a second time where I would like to go . . . Meanwhile, I felt that the people in line behind me were getting impatient. I said, "*Klein, klein*—a small town." She mentioned the names of a few towns, among them Stuttgart, Munchen, and Frankfort am Main, but she added that Stuttgart—though it was far away in Germany—was a lovely town with many gardens, parks, and trees.

"Good," I said, "it will be like a village." I agreed. The fact that it was far away was all the better, I thought. She gave me a referral slip to the Arbeitsamt at Stuttgart and also a pass that entitled me to a free railroad ticket to that town. I was to leave tomorrow morning. I thanked the clerk effusively. The stares of the impatient people lined up in back of me stabbed me like knives, but I did not care now. I left in a state of elation.

Outside on the street I looked through the papers she had given me and I was content. I felt that I had done well, and it gave me great moral satisfaction to know that I had lied to them and that they had believed me completely. I was proud of myself.

I said my goodbyes to the people in the restaurant and to the unpleasant elderly couple. The next morning I took my suitcase and went quickly to the station, where I exchanged my pass for a ticket. There was no trouble; the ticket seller handled the matter efficiently and courteously. My self-confidence increased with every moment. Now I had official papers with me—like a legal citizen!

Then suddenly a voice boomed, *"Nach Stuttgart—Württemberg!"* I picked up my suitcase and boarded the train, choosing a seat near the window. It was another lonely, sunny morning. I removed my coat and tried to make myself comfortable in the compartment. Soon we were on our way. There were few people on that train—a clean, comfortable train. Looking out of the window, I felt that the further away I travelled from home the lonelier I would be, the more my heart would ache. And where was I now going? Into Germany, paradoxically to hide from Nazi hatred! It seemed to be the only way—to go as far away from people who knew me . . . I closed my eyes and thought, *Someday perhaps I shall return, and then Mamma and Rose will run out to greet me with joy. They will cry, "Sheva! Sheva is alive—she has come back to us!"* Will this ever come true? Though I doubted it, I still tried to find comfort in this hope.

Many hours passed, but I did not mind. The train arrived at Stuttgart before nightfall. As soon as I left the train I found a different world. At the station one could hear many languages: French, Ukrainian, Czech, Polish—and many others I could not understand. A large sign proclaimed Stuttgart to be "The City of Foreigners" and it seemed to be just that!

I left the station and, with some difficulty, found the employment office and entered. They told me to report to a camp and to return the next morning. When I did so, the clerk in the office said that I had a choice of working in a factory, a private home, or a hospital with thirty nuns. To give myself time to think, I began to repeat slowly what she just told me, as though I did not understand it. I decided that a hospital would be the safest choice, so I told her, *"Krankenhaus."* She motioned me to wait on the side, while she telephoned the hospital to send someone over to fetch me.

After a considerable time, a nun entered the room, and the clerk at the desk introduced her to me as Sister Maria. She was of rather short stature, her slight figure garbed in a religious dress of royal blue and a white cap. She smiled at me, the smile lighting up her delicate features from within, and immediately she picked up my suitcase, saying, "Let's go." Although I protested, she insisted upon carrying it. We nodded pleasantly to the clerk and left the Arbeitsamt.

Outside on the street, Sister Maria told me that it was quite a distance to the hospital and that we'd have to take a trolley. I was sorry that I did not have any money to pay my fare, and in broken German I explained my situation to her. She smiled and said, "Don't worry. You are now in our care." What a wonderful feeling it was! I began to live again in this aura of confidence and security. On the way to the car stop, we chatted in a friendly fashion. It was not long before she noticed the swollen condition of my legs and wondered how I could stand it, for the work at the hospital would require me to be on my feet all day. But I tried to assure her that it was only as the result of my long train trip that my legs had swelled up so badly.

Sister Maria asked me to repeat my name. I said, "Hanka. Hanka Buczek—but at home they call me Hania." Now she wanted to know where I came from and if I had left any family at home. I replied simply that I came from Poland, from a village called Rudy, and that I had left behind my parents and one sister. I lied constantly.

We caught the trolley, and it left us at Hohenheimerstrasse. A little distance up the street, after we had passed several houses, the sister pointed to a building on the top of the hill in a well-kept garden surrounded by an iron fence. One entered by a small gate on the left; there were wide stone steps and above them, in the wall, a plaque with the words: Albrecht Krankenhaus, Hohenheimerstr. 21. It was a luxurious hospital.

The sister said, "This hospital was always called Bethesda Hospital—a biblical name—but since our Führer came to power we had to change it, for he did not favor the religious connotation."

Inside the gate there was a winding staircase leading to a higher level of the garden and orchard. It was truly beautiful. A few more steps and we found ourselves in one of the hospital corridors. For me, it was like the entrance to Paradise in the company of an angel. Everything had a dreamlike quality; I could not believe that it was all real.

The corridor was wide and stretched a long distance. As soon as we entered, I was assailed by the odor of disinfectants. Sister Maria explained that on the left-hand side was the surgery room, on the right the admissions office; an X-ray room was located near the surgery, and the doorway beyond led to the office of the *Oberschwester,* the Superior. The stairway opposite the entrance took one up to the other floors, as did the nearby elevator. There was absolute silence in the corridor, though from time to time some door opened and a smiling sister appeared, hurrying on her errands. I noticed that some of the sisters wore white gowns and white aprons, of a style that in Poland used to be called "cobbler's aprons." I guessed, and later was told, that these sister-nurses were assigned to the operating rooms.

The sister took me to the Verwaltung, the administrative office. In response to our knock, a gentle but firm voice answered, *"Herein!"* We entered. I saw a sister seated behind a desk, a woman a little older than Sister Maria. I was introduced as Hanka Buczek and I felt her keen eyes observing me. The sister in Verwaltung said that I looked very tired, and Sister Maria quickly explained that I had been on a long and wearying journey. She added, "I think Hanka is homesick." She stroked my hair and left, leaving me with the sister in Verwaltung. She asked my name and wrote it down in a file, along with the place and date of my birth, and where I had come from. I gave the sister the card I had received from the Arbeitsamt. She noted everything and let me sign the paper on the line next to the date of my admission for work in the hospital: June 22, 1943.

She then put a few more questions to me: Was I regular in church attendance? The sisters, she said, were very strict on that point; they expected us to go to church every Sunday at least. The sister mentioned that Nastya and Katerina, the two Russian girls who worked in the hospital, also went to church and that I'd be able to go with them; I would find them good friends to have. However, she was assigning me to a room with a girl from Holland, whose name was Lena. I must do my share to keep the room in neat condition, for the Sister Superior often inspected our quarters. I would have to rise at 5 A.M., because punctually at six I would have to be at my work station and would need at least an hour to get myself ready and my room in order.

Glancing at the signature I had just affixed to the paper, the sister complimented me on my fine handwriting. "It's much neater than Nastya's or Katerina's," she added. Then, as an afterthought, she asked if I had left any relatives behind in Poland. "My parents and a sister," I replied.

"That is all the information we need," she said quietly, "but in three days you will go with one of the sisters to the police station to be registered there. They will fingerprint you and give you a work card."

This last piece of news startled me a little, but I should have expected some such formality would be required. The sister now reached for a bunch of keys and told me to follow her—she would show me to my room. We went out of the hospital building, crossed the big, beautiful garden and up a few steps to a small house or villa, like a pretty summer cottage set on a slightly higher hill among trees. The view was breathtakingly lovely from this point. My room, however, down the end of a corridor, was rather small and disappointingly gloomy. There were two beds at right angles to each other along the walls, a plain oak wardrobe, two chairs, a dresser, and a small table. A mirror hung on one of the walls. Two windows let in the pale daylight, filtered through the dense foliage of the trees outside.

Sister said, "Lena, the Dutch girl, occupies the bed on the left; the other bed is yours. You will share with her the use of the dresser and clothes-closet." Then she showed me a sink in the corridor just outside the room where I could wash myself. Under wartime conditions, and especially in my situation, this seemed like a palace. I could not believe my good fortune. I felt that I could stay here contentedly until the end of the war, if they would let me.

Sister told me to remain in my room until I heard the dinner bell; I would have until about one o'clock to wash up and rest. She pointed through the window in which direction I should go to reach the dining hall, and she started to leave but, turning around at the door, said, "I hope you will be satisfied with us here."

"Danke schön," I smiled, and thanked her sincerely. *Oh, may this be my last stop indeed,* I thought. I felt now that I had made a good and fitting decision in choosing this place to work. In my circumstances I could not have done better.

I looked around the room, then went out into the hall to wash myself. What a luxury—hot and cold water from the faucets! I soon returned to the room, where I was briefly visited by a Sister Gertrude, who wished me luck. I then took a short nap.

My rest was broken by the short, quick rings of the dinner bell. I had to get up and find the dining hall, as the sister told me. I smoothed my hair and changed into a dark blue skirt. What a shame that my legs didn't match the skirt's slenderness! I could hear steps now in the corridor. I waited until the others had left their rooms, for I did not want to be the first to answer the bell. Pushing open the heavy entrance door, I went slowly down the stone steps into the garden. The midday sun blazed above, bathing the idyllic landscape with golden light. The sight of so much beauty brought tears to my eyes. Reaching the main hospital building, I entered by way of a glass door, and immediately caught a strong odor of iodine and disinfectants coming from the second floor.

The dining hall was on a lower level, and when I reached the end of the corridor I had to descend some stairs to the first floor. I let the sisters around me all go in ahead and waited at the door for Sister Maria, the one who had brought me from the Arbeitsamt that morning, for I did not know at which table I should sit. One of the sisters approached me and asked if I was waiting for someone. I told her.

"Oh, you're waiting for Sister Maria!" she laughed, and pointed her out to me as she was coming out of an elevator nearby. In a few moments Sister Maria was at my side and took my hand. It seemed that everyone had a special seat at the tables, and she guided me to mine. My place was on the left of the entrance, the third chair from the end, facing the room—so that I could see everyone and in turn everyone could see me. I felt as though hundreds of eyes focused in my direction.

The dining room was huge, with windows on two sides; long tables lined three of the walls. There was a silence. After a few minutes a gentleman came in and took his place at the upper end of the hall at the Sister Superior's table. He was of medium height, middle-aged, with a round, genial face, and was dressed like a civilian. The Sister Superior at his side looked older than most of the others and she appeared different, for she was wearing a black uniform, whereas the others were in dark blue with blue-and-white checkered aprons. We sat down and they all folded their hands in prayer. I, too, lowered my eyes and whispered some words.

The food was served in large platters and bowls, and everyone could take as much as they desired. I helped myself to only a small portion, for although I was hungry I felt choked up inside and could hardly swallow. Besides, I was ashamed to eat too much the first day—I wanted them to see that I had some manners.

My companion on one side looked like a German girl; the girl on the other impressed me as being either Polish or Ukrainian. During the meal, however, no one talked. Everyone ate with good appetites and the bowls were soon empty. My neighbor on the left must have realized that I was a newcomer and she whispered, "Why aren't you eating?" From her weak attempt at German I guessed that she must be one of the Ukrainian or Russian girls that the sister had mentioned. I replied that I had lost my appetite.

"You must be homesick," she sympathized. "During my first days here I also could not eat or sleep, but I got used to it. It will pass." (I later learned that she was Nastya, a Ukrainian, who spent a great deal of time with another Ukrainian girl named Katerina.)

My neighbor on the right was a tall and strongly built German girl who occasionally made some remark to the girl alongside of her, looking askance in my direction. She smacked her thin lips over the food as she ate greedily. First, there was soup—I understood that it was made of bread and vegetables—then a potato salad with meat loaf, and a pudding for dessert.

When dinner was finished, the gentleman at the Sister Superior's table arose and again they folded their hands and prayed. Afterwards, he announced in a gentle, well-modulated voice, "We have been given a new coworker today, assigned to us by the Arbeitsamt, who comes from Poland. She will work with us in the hospital."

At these words, everyone looked in my direction. I thought that I would faint; I trembled all over and my eyes filled with tears. I must have looked like a corpse, for I felt the blood ebbing from my face, but I clenched my fingers, digging my nails into my palms so as not to collapse. If I could just hold on a few moments more!

He continued: "Her name is Hanka Buczek, and she will be assigned as an aide to Sister Maria at the *Wochenstation,* the lying-in ward on the second floor. We hope she will be happy here." Then he told me to get up. I don't know how I managed to stand on my feet, for I swayed feebly—but somehow I arose, nodded, and sat down.

The room was filled with the clatter of some sixty or seventy chairs being moved back at once—thirty nuns, and the rest working girls like me. As the sisters filed out of the dining hall, each one gave me a kind look and a smile. I waited on the side for the "Little" Sister Maria (so called to distinguish her from the other Sister Maria, to whom I had just been assigned), but instead a taller sister came up to me. She was of about middle age and very pretty, and I thought that she looked like an angel, for she reminded me of someone close and dear to me—my mother.

Extending her hand to me, she said, "I am Sister Maria Schumacher from the Wochenstation, and you have been assigned to work with me there." Her handclasp was warm and sincere; I don't know why, but the long-held tears started coursing down my cheeks. Her eyes, I noticed, were also moist with sympathetic understanding. Where we waited for the elevator, the gentleman who had introduced me to the entire group now introduced himself as the inspector of the hospital. He said, "You look sad; but this is only the first day, and you feel strange here. Soon you will feel at home among us." He smiled and again wished me good luck.

His words made me thoughtful. How could it be that he was a German and yet so kind? Would he still treat me with kindness if he knew that I was a Jewess? Or would he become like the other Germans who had persecuted and murdered us?

Sister Maria noticed my pensive mood and said, "Your name is Hanka, yes?" I nodded in reply. "Hanka, at this moment your thoughts were very far away. Maybe you did not hear what the *Herr Inspektor* just said?"

"Yes, I heard. He is a very kind gentleman," And again, for no apparent reason, I burst into tears.

"Herr Inspektor is a Lutheran minister," she explained. Then she said, "Probably you are missing your father. The minister can be like another father to you if you want to tell him what's in your heart."

I loved this Sister Maria from that moment and I felt that I would find in her not just a supervisor of my work but a maternal and protective friend in need.

The sister took me to her department. Each floor had a small kitchen adjoining the wards and the patients' rooms. There she introduced me to a group of girls who worked on her floor and also to some sisters who were on duty at that time. One of the girls in this group was from France; she was older and not very pretty. Another was from Alsace, a vivacious brunette named Elsa. And the third was a German, Marie, from München—short but shapely, a pretty blonde with blue eyes.

Here I met Sister Gertrude again, and some eight or ten other sisters who were just changing their shifts of duty. I was told that my duties would include cleaning, making beds, feeding the patients, taking temperatures, and in general assisting the patients whenever they wanted anything (which they signaled by a light over the door). If a sister did not notice the light, we were to answer it, or at least to look into the room to see what was needed. We also had to give bedpans and help wash the patients; in short, we were nurse's aides.

Among the duties, Sister explained, was assisting in moving the patients from the operating room to their ward. Sometimes we would change dressings. Sister Maria assured me that she knew it would be hard for me in the beginning, especially (she smiled) when I would have to scrub the floor with a coarse brush. "But you will get used to it," she consoled me, "and I will try to make things easier for you."

Each girl had her own pail and broom, scouring brushes, mop, and large gray rag. We had to report for work at six sharp each morning, and our own rooms had to be in perfect order before we left them—for if the Sister Superior found anything to criticize she would do so openly, in the dining hall, before everyone assembled. I shuddered at the prospect!

Our workday did not end until eight in the evening, with one hour off in the afternoon. During the week, on Tuesdays or Wednesdays, we were given half a day free—and a Sunday every two weeks.

That first day I worked only a few hours, but my legs increased in size—and I heard the sisters and the girls remark that unless the swelling went down I would not be able to do a full day's work. I still tried to put the blame for the swelling on the rigors of the long trip, assuring them that it would pass soon. But I was really worried. I could hardly wait until the evening when I could retire to my room. We were given a coffee break at three o'clock—coffee and bread with marmalade—in a small kitchen where the girls from my floor gathered and chatted. I took an instant liking to Marie Kraus, who, although she was a German, was a warm and friendly person.

After the break, she showed me how to arrange trays for the patients. The food was sent up to our floor by a dumbwaiter in the kitchen wall. At a given hour, when the bell rang we had to pull it up, tugging on the heavy rope. Her instructions were clear and simple, but my head was still confused and I doubt if I got things straight the first time. At six o'clock we were to serve supper trays to the patients; we would eat at seven. Before suppertime, however, we had to look in on the patients and help them wash up or bring them something to drink.

Before I retired for the night, Sister Maria reminded me that we started work at six in the morning. Should I happen to oversleep, Lena would wake me—she was already going on her second year at the hospital and knew the routine. When I went to our room, Lena, my rather noisy roommate whom I'd met at the break, was not there yet, so I lay down on my bed and gave my thoughts free rein. My brain was still hyperactive, always caught up in the web of having to scheme, lie, pretend to be someone I was not—just to keep alive. Was my life worth so much trouble? I really did not know the answer.

When Lena came in, her full, round face showed signs of great fatigue. Frowning, she removed her glasses and wiped the perspiration from her forehead, cursing the Germans, the hospital, and her job. She looked at me sharply. "You think maybe I'm cracked? What?" she said gruffly. Without the glasses her eyes squinted even more. "You speak German?"

"Yes," I answered. Her whole attitude was so strange that, in spite of all my troubles, I felt like laughing—but I bit my lip. As we prepared for bed, she plied me with questions, asking me why I had come, where I had come from, and so forth. When I pulled off my stockings, she screamed when she saw how red my legs were. "Why didn't you show them your legs?" she shouted. "Maybe those beasts would not have sent you here."

"But my legs were perfectly normal then," I said. "They were slender and shapely. They just swelled up on the way from Poland."

"Don't tell me such stories," she insisted. "You must have had such legs all your life!"

I didn't say another word, but got into bed and pulled the covers over me and tried to sleep. It was a long time before my nerves could relax, and even when I did fall asleep, I had horrible dreams. In the morning, Lena asked more questions. "What happened—what was wrong with you last night?" she said. "I could not sleep all night because of you. You were calling, 'Mamma, Mamma, Gestapo!' You were crying. It's not enough that I must put up with many things during the day, you have to keep me awake during the night as well! I could not shut an eye. You talked in so many languages that I don't know now where you come from and what tongue you really speak. I'll go to Sister Superior today and ask her to put you with some other girl. I must have my rest and peace at night. I work in the kitchen and it is hard work."

So I had another problem! I told Lena that I didn't usually have nightmares like that; it was because I was so exhausted from the day before. It brought back, subconsciously, the memories of that time when I was hunted on the street—and how my family lamented over me. After all, I was still new here—it would pass. "You say you are an *Ausländer* yourself," I tried to plead with her, "so why not have some understanding for me—a foreigner here just like yourself. Why can't we live in friendship? You yourself said that the Germans hate us, so—if I get assigned to a room with a German girl, you know how hard it will be on me!" I begged her to have patience, and if it should happen again, she should wake me. Somehow I must have reached her compassionate sense, for she promised to give me another chance. She must have seen that I was on the verge of tears and she stopped her tirade.

We began to dress, and she noticed my suitcase. "Is that all you brought with you?" she said. "After a few months you will be going around naked. You will ruin all your clothes here. For this kind of work we should have dresses of iron, not cloth"—and since I looked at her oddly, she thought I did not understand. "Iron!" she repeated, and hit the radiator with her hand. "They won't give you a thing, though. Only the

Germans get clothes." She was talking so loudly that I began to tremble. Every word pierced my aching head, but I kept silent. I was used now to keeping silent. I was only afraid that someone might hear her ranting.

"It is getting late," I reminded her, trying to interrupt her stream of words. I had heard enough to know how she hated the Germans from the depths of her being—but I certainly did not want to get into trouble because of her.

A little before six we left our room and walked through the garden and down the steps to the hospital building. On the way I inhaled great draughts of the pure morning air, rejoicing in the beauty of the flowers and sunshine. It was still quiet in the building. I went along the corridor until I reached the kitchen, where I found a sister just going off night duty. In a few minutes the other girls, as well as the sisters, came in. I said "Good morning" to all, but perhaps in a special way to Marie Kraus and Sister Maria.

Sister Maria asked how I had slept, and I said, "Just wonderfully!"

My legs were hurting terribly. I felt as though they did not belong to me, but I tried to believe that this would pass. Again, the girls instructed me on how to arrange the trays for breakfast, and Sister Maria took me by the hand and showed me which rooms were my special care and where I had to clean. She added that if I had any questions I should come to her and she would be happy to explain in detail.

Thus began my first full day of work at the hospital. At seven, after I had cleaned the washrooms and corridor assigned to me, I helped bring basins of water to the patients. Then I had to take their temperatures, help some of them down from bed, change the linens. They were served their breakfast trays meanwhile, and at about eight we—the girls and sisters—went to the dining hall for breakfast.

Again, a prayer. For breakfast we had the usual coffee and bread with jam or preserves. A short prayer, and off to work—cleaning the rooms and wards, cleaning the rest of the corridors. In some of the wards there were only three or four beds, and some semiprivate rooms had two. Private rooms were occupied by very special patients. Then, there was a large nursery for the newborn infants, a large delivery room, and a smaller labor room for the expectant mothers. Since we were in the obstetric department, our patients were women only. As we busied ourselves around their beds, each one tried to ask us questions or to air her complaints. The common gripe seemed to be that their husbands were in the army or with the SS forces or Gestapo in other countries, and could not be with them when their time came—an understandable complaint. Each patient had her own special story to tell, and I listened whenever I could, for I was curious. Here I had the opportunity, in my free moments, to hear from them what they thought of the war. Did they share Hitler's ideas? Or was what was happening to the Jews entirely his doing? Did the German people consent willingly to his crimes? Naturally, I had to seek their opinions very discreetly and carefully. It took time and a certain degree of cold-bloodedness. In no way did I want to betray my real identity.

There was a practical side to my curiosity. Whatever I could learn in this way might someday be useful, I thought.

The patients in our department were discharged usually at the end of a week, unless there were complications; that was the reason it was called "Wochenstation." All the patients realized immediately that I was a foreigner, because of my accent. I knew that the Germans were arrogant and looked down upon all foreigners; with their slogan, "*Deutschland über alles*," they regarded themselves as a superior race. Consequently, the attitude of most of the patients toward me and the other foreign girls was rather unpleasant. They knew me to be Polish, and they had a grudge against Poland because that country had the effrontery to fight back when invaded by their armies at the beginning of the war.

On the other hand, since the patients needed my help, they had to accept me. After a while, they even began to like me. I tried to speak German brokenly to them, so they would not suspect I knew the language fluently, which might very well have seemed suspicious to them. I told them that I thought I must have some German blood in me, thinking that this would make me appear more acceptable in their eyes. They often nodded, saying that I looked like a German girl, and adding that in a short time I would be speaking German as fluently as they.

It was far from easy to continue this play-acting on my part. I had to watch every word and to keep myself under control at every moment. It wasn't enough that others watched me constantly—I also had to watch myself! I could not forget, ever, who I was—though I did try to be "Hanka," and to live and think the way a Polish peasant girl would. For I knew that my assumed identity would not be just for a day, a week, a month—but it would have to endure until the end of war, at least. It was not easy to survive, but it was my duty.

9

Hanka, the Nurse's Aide

THE WORK WAS HARD, requiring a great deal of physical strength and energy. I was not used to scrubbing, waxing, and polishing floors until they shone like glass. This had to be done day after day. Then, there was a routine of making up beds and going from room to room to see what the patients needed. Frequently they would throw up when recovering from anesthesia, sometimes into our hands, but we had to perform even the most unpleasant duties without a murmur. From early morning till evening, we lived with one eye on the red light above the door of each ward. If it flashed, we had to quickly see what some patient wanted.

To satisfy the sisters, I worked intensively, applying myself to each task with complete absorption. I knew that Germans were exact and they insisted on cleanliness, especially in a hospital. And so I kept the wards assigned to me spotlessly clean. The sisters were perfectionists. They expected it not only of their workers but also of themselves—giving of themselves conscientiously to every duty and service.

The wards had to be in meticulous order before eleven o'clock in the morning, when the doctor made his rounds of the patients. The doctor in charge of our wing was a gynecologist—tall, stout, deep-voiced, but with a quick smile. When he said *"Guten Morgen,* Hanka!" the walls seemed to shake with the vibrations of his voice. He was always accompanied by his assistant, a petite blond woman physician who looked like a small poodle trotting at his side—a likeness further intensified by her short, curly hair. When the gynecologist appeared at the end of a corridor, all the sisters stood at attention—or ran to the wards under their care. He would stop to read each patient's chart, and the sisters would always add something of their latest personal observations.

The gynecologist liked to joke with the patients, and he was generally admired and respected. His visits usually lasted until about noon, and right after he left we served lunch to the patients. Our lunch was at one, then we had to wash the patient's dishes. After that we took turns, both the sisters and the girls, at an hour of relaxation. These free hours we almost invariably spent in our rooms, because there was always something that needed to be washed or mended—some little chore to be done—before we could lie down and take a nap.

Right after the siesta we had to clean the bathroom and empty the bedpans. The worst chore for me was to clean the basins used by the post-surgical patients. The sisters performed this duty without wincing, just as though they were simply washing a dirty dinner plate, but my stomach turned over every time I had to do it. While we were busy at these tasks, visiting hours were open—and after that, we usually had to put the bouquets of flowers left behind in vases and straighten things up in the rooms. At three, we served coffee, bread, and preserves to the patients. Then, again, the cleaning of the corridors, the washing of the blood-stained sheets from the delivery room, and the cleaning of the main ward.

There were births occurring every day. Although almost all German males were in the army, the women went on having children just the same—as though nature could perform miracles of parthenogenesis by special indult in their case! Not a day passed without some new patients being admitted, while others were discharged with their "little bundles from heaven."

Sister Maria Schumacher admitted the new patients, and she assigned them to a room and a bed. She also discharged them after the confinement, as she was head of this department. Her own office was next to the small kitchen where we prepared the patient's trays. Sister's office was a small but tastefully decorated room—with easy chairs, a sofa, a pretty table, curtains, and bookshelves. Sister had her afternoon coffee in this room, sometimes alone, sometimes in the company of other sisters in our department.

As the days passed, I got to know my fellow workers better, and I talked with them more freely during work or during our coffee breaks. My liking for Marie Kraus grew, although she made fun of my zeal for work. "Do you expect to get a diploma after you serve your term? Or are you gathering merit for a heavenly reward?" she laughed. "Or are you by any chance a candidate for the religious life?"

I took her teasing with good grace, for I had a lot of sentiment for Marie. I found her very sensible, agreeable, and, above all, good. She reminded me of my sister by her appearance. Could she, I wondered, really know why I had so much ambition and was industrious to the point of folly? No, she did not even suspect my reasons—and though I knew that she had a great deal of compassion for foreigners, I could not reveal my secret to her. To disclose my secret might be my death sentence. I could only tell her that I was grateful that here I had good food, a clean bed, and that the sisters treated me with respect and appreciation because of my punctual and conscientious performance of the duties they assigned to me. Also, perhaps here I might at last find a cure for my painfully swollen legs. This much I could confide in her.

She asked why I did not turn to Sister Maria for advice on healing my legs. Indeed, why not? I decided to do so at the first opportunity. And once, just before I left the hospital building to go to my cottage, I stopped to speak with her about it. Sister suggested that I see a doctor, but I asked if she could help me herself. Sister Maria said that she was glad that I had confidence in her and came to her for advice. "Remember," she said, "always come to me when you need help. I only wish the other girls were all like you!" She seemed relieved, for she thought that I was going to resign. She had noticed that I was doing my work with difficulty, and now that she knew the reason she appreciated my willingness and effort all the more. I was not lazy, like some others . . .

Sister took me to the bathroom in the maternity ward and gave me some powder to add to the water in which I was to bathe. Then I was to rub a salve into my legs, today and for at least several days to come.

Luxuriating in the bath, I was grateful to Sister Maria and thought of her fondly. She seemed to be older than my mother, but she reminded me of her—the same subtle and delicate features, the evenly white teeth when her lips parted in a warm and friendly smile.

I felt much better after taking daily baths. My legs were not as swollen as before, and they hurt me less. One evening, after taking my bath, I returned to my room and found Marie Kraus there, dressed and ready to go out. Though she was in a hurry, she took a few minutes to tell me how I should work—I shouldn't take it so seriously, she said. *"Du bist doch ein Dumkopf!"* she continued, and added, laughing, "Do you want to become a sister? How foolish you are! If you continue to work so hard, they will never let you go. Do you want to be decorated with a medal? Sooner, you will destroy your health. I won't be here very long. You'll see, they will throw me out soon! I wish they'd do it now, I can hardly wait. Wake up, Hanka!" Still laughing, she ran down the hall—in a rush to go to the cinema, or maybe just for a walk. Who knows?

I shrugged my shoulders, having heard her out patiently, and slowly sat down on the edge of my bed. Lena was already in her bed, resting. I noticed that she had already straightened out her side of the room; she was very neat and kept her things in meticulous order. I did not have that problem, for I had arrived here almost without any clothing. If I wanted to launder a slip, I had to go without the slip that day—or wait until it dried. I had to sleep in the same slip, because my nightgowns and pajamas were now adorning the figures of the wives of the Ukrainian police who had robbed me of nearly everything I possessed. But all this seemed insignificant to me now as long as I could save my life. Even rags would have been good enough if it meant survival.

My conversations with Lena were usually interesting, and sometimes even pleasant. She had a great deal of worldly knowledge, and she tried to be friendly. Her advice to me was, like Marie Kraus's, not to remain here longer than necessary. In fact, she urged me to try to leave before I had to register with the local police. She told me, too, quite frankly, that she did not think that she could tolerate very long being wakened from sleep by my screams at night. Again I was having nightmares! That was at the bottom of her wishing me to leave, no doubt—but I could not blame her. I understood that, of course, and handled her as gently as if she were a soft-boiled egg. Lena was of a nervous, quick temperament, and once I realized how sensitive she was, I tried not to antagonize her. It was important for me to appeal to her compassion and pity so that she would not complain to the Sister Superior about me—or to the Herr Inspektor—for I did not want to be transferred to another room, or perhaps let go.

After a few days I was summoned to the Verwaltung, the administrative office. I ran downstairs with a beating heart, in such anxiety that I did not even wait for the elevator. Why were they calling me? What did they want?

When I entered the office, the same sister who had admitted me the first day told me that tomorrow morning I would have to go with Sister Maria to the Gestapo to be registered. There, she said, I would receive a work card and a personal identification card. This news, while not unexpected, stunned me. The system of registering with the police, of course, was practiced all over Europe, and I certainly did not expect them to suspend the rules for me—but the danger lay in the fact that I was not legally there. All that day I worried about it, and at night I could not sleep. I wondered if "they" would recognize me. Wouldn't the sisters be surprised to find out who I was!

When I looked into the mirror the next morning, I saw the results of a sleepless night—I looked pale and frightened. My eyes betrayed what was going on in my heart. It seemed filled to overflowing with pain. After breakfast, Sister Maria (the "little" Maria who had brought me here from the Arbeitsamt) came over to me and, smiling, asked if I knew that we were going to the Gestapo. "Yes," I said, "I am ready."

Together we left the hospital, going down the steps that led through the flowering garden to the street. I wondered if we would return together—or would she return alone with the news that "Hanka" was a Jewess and had been recognized as such by the police? I could imagine their astonished faces when the sisters and the girls heard that! Now Lena would understand why I screamed and cried at night . . .

Sister Maria noticed my silence as we walked along and she asked how I felt. Were my legs giving me trouble again? I told her that they were much better since I had started taking the baths, as Sister Maria had advised so kindly and helpfully.

The Gestapo was not far from the hospital and our conversation ceased when we stopped in front of a large building. The GESTAPO above the doorway sent a stab of pain through my heart. I begged God to give me strength and courage, and the right answers to all the questions. Entering the building, Sister knocked on a door and a gruff voice called out, "Herein!" She went in first and I followed. In almost a whisper, as though the words did not want to come out of her throat, Sister Maria said, "Heil, Hitler!" It was not the customary salutation of the sisters, but here in a government office she had to say it.

On the wall behind the desk hung a huge picture of Hitler. It was the first thing one noticed on entering. "Heil, Hitler!" came the response, loud, brisk, and energetic, from one of the policemen. The room was very large. Several uniformed policemen sat at various desks; to me they looked like SS men. I could not tell their rank, but Germans in uniform all looked like storm troopers to me—Gestapo men, murderers. Sister Maria gave my name and said that I was a new worker at the hospital. She also mentioned the date I had arrived there and gave them my Arbeitsamt card, issued by the employment bureau. The policeman opened a big book and, muttering to himself, began writing: Hanka Buczek, born in Poland—then the year of my supposed birth. I just nodded my head affirmatively, thinking that this would be all. But now he started the interrogation: *"Ihr Vaters und Mutters Namen?"* I narrowed my eyes, as though I did not quite understand. The room seemed to move, revolving around me, and I felt my face turning red as a beet—but, I thought wryly, that makes me look more like a peasant girl. Sister Maria tried to explain that I did not understand German well, and she repeated his question for me.

I wanted this to be over quickly, so I replied, "Stefan and Olga," giving the names of Mr. and Mrs. Krupka. I did not even stop to think of the consequences—and why should I worry about a more remote future, when the next morning was uncertain?

Again, the Gestapo asked my parents' dates of birth and again Sister Maria repeated his question because I did not answer—while again I felt the blood rush to my face. I had to think quickly and take into consideration Hanka Buczek's age, as actually she was much older than I. The days and months were perhaps not so important, but I had to make the years fit—and I needed time to collect my senses to calculate my fictitious parents' birth dates. The Gestapo seemed in a hurry and with an ironical smile he said to Sister, "What? Doesn't she know her own parents' dates of birth? She must have understood my question."

I pretended to ignore this aside, and talking to myself in Polish I tried to jog my memory, as it were. Then I gave my answer to Sister Maria and she, in her gentle voice, repeated it in proper German. While this went on, I saw that the policeman was observing me closely. I did not know whether his suspicions were aroused or whether he was simply looking at me with contempt, thinking perhaps that I came from a people of very low culture, indeed, if I did not know my parents' birth dates. Then he asked what my father did for a living, and after Sister Maria explained, I replied that he was a village farmer. Then he asked me if I had any other relatives. "I have a sister," I replied, "who helps on the farm."

Then he asked if somebody in my family was Jewish—my father, my mother, my grandfather or grandmother—and I answered no. I could not know whether he believed my answers, but if he decided to verify them I knew that I was lost. But this was not yet the end. The policeman picked out a form and started to fill it out, demanding an identification photo of me. Sister Maria forestalled my reply, taking me by the hand and saying, "We'll be right back. I'll take her to have a photograph made in the studio next to the station."

On the way Sister explained to me, as if I didn't know, that the Kennkarte and the work card must have identification photos, so that in case of loss or theft nobody else could make use of these documents.

After the photograph was supplied, the policeman asked me to sign. I thought, *Now Sheva, don't sign "Sheva Weiler"* . . . My hands shook as I wrote "Hanka Buczek," my adopted name. And still I was not finished! They sent me to another desk to be fingerprinted. I tried to control myself, but my fingers did not obey my will; they shook like aspen leaves. It was a wonder that they could be printed at all, for I could not press down on the paper. Sister Maria looked at me sadly, thinking perhaps that my nervousness was due to excessive shyness. She must have thought, *Poor girl! Never saw anything outside her village. All this frightens her.*

At last the Arbeitskarte—my work card, on buff paper, with my photograph and fingerprints—was signed and stamped with the swastika and the German eagle! The sister thanked the Gestapo for me, but it was still not finished—yet. The second officer indicated that I must go to still another desk. Here, another Gestapo thrust out his hand for the document and read aloud—*"Polen!"* He opened his desk drawer. What was he looking for? A revolver to put a bullet through my head? But, to my amazement, he pulled out an alphabet of letters cut from cloth—he picked out some twenty or twenty-five large Ps and said to Sister, "Since she comes from Poland, she must sew one of these on each of her dresses, coats, whatever she has to wear. Just like the girls from Russia wear the letters OST, Polish girls must be marked with a P—without that mark she would have to pay a fine or be punished. As a Polish girl, she has no right to be on the streets after eight in the evening," he recited the rules by rote, "she has no right to go to the cinema, to a wine hall, to a restaurant or nightclub, or to any public place. If she does, she will be punished."

Sister Maria listened and nodded her head. I understood everything that he said, of course, but kept silent. From time to time the sister looked at me pityingly because my freedom would be so limited. The Gestapo added, "Because the Poles fought against Germany and resisted our armies, they must submit to the same restrictions as the Russians."

Little did he, or did Sister for that matter, realize that it meant little to me right now. The letter P was my justification, my right to a safe haven. I took the pieces of cloth and said, "Danke schön." He shouted, "Heil, Hitler!" until it echoed in the large room and I said it too. But now we knew that the interview was over and we could leave. "Heil, Hitler!" Sister repeated quietly and started toward the door, leading me after her.

In silence we left the building. No doubt Sister was also relieved that the formalities were finished. I had passed one of the most important tests of my young life. The Kennkarte that I held in my hand was my guarantee of life; it was the most valuable thing I could possess in the whole world. For no money could I have legally bought it—not even for millions—as Sheva Weiler, a Jewess. The swastika seal under my identification photo, over my false signature—what a mockery! And yet I was tortured by the thought, *Will I, at last, now have complete peace? Or will they perchance write to Rudy, to Poland, and discover that everything I have said is false?*

Suddenly breaking her silence, Sister Maria said, "Nastya and Katerina also received such cloth marks, theirs were OST, and they also have to wear them on their clothing. But in the hospital we don't insist on it. Only when they sometimes go out on Sundays they sew them on—just in case they are controlled by the police."

I said, "I'll wear mine, I am a Pole and I don't see why I should not wear the letter P. I am proud to be a Pole. It is true we fought against the Germans and lost, but we fought!" And a deep sigh escaped me.

In the evening I sewed one of the letters onto my dress. They must have thought at the Gestapo station that I came with a full wardrobe of clothes; they gave me such a supply of Ps. When Lena saw me she laughed. "They could not make me do that even if they stood on their heads," she said.

The days of seemingly endless work went on. I lived in my little cage, occupied with my own problems, and my thoughts went round and round in my head like a carousel. During my work hours, and after work, everything that I lived through thus far accompanied me constantly like a shadow. I thought about the ghetto, about my family, my escape, about the Krupka family that befriended me, and Lvov—and about the present. If I dared look forward, I thought of what the next moment, hour, or day could bring.

And yet, I was afraid to write to the Krupkas or to the Tarashkewitzes. But I felt that it was my duty to write to Dr. Jagoda and to thank him for the help he had given me, of his own free will, at the risk of his life, during my stay in the camp on Janowska Street. Should I write—should I not? Many days passed before I made up my mind about it: I finally decided that I would write to him.

I asked Sister Maria for some correspondence paper, and one evening, when Lena was out, I sat down to write. Every word brought out tears. I read the letter over several times, trying to determine whether—if anyone at the camp were to find it or open it by mistake—anything in it seemed suspicious. But I think that I composed it well, and I thought that only one who knew my whole story could possibly read into its hidden meaning.

And as I read, I wept for a long time, unable to contain my emotion. Then, feeling somewhat relieved I addressed the envelope and sealed it. The following morning I ran out to the mail box on Hohenheimerstrasse and mailed it.

As the days, weeks, months passed I became quite used to my work, even in spite of myself. I liked the sisters and they returned my affection, treating me with respect and kindness. I grew to like my roommate Lena, and Marie Kraus, and whenever the opportunity arose I also enjoyed my chats with Nastya and Katerina. They worked as I did, but in other wards, so we did not meet very frequently. As for the other girls, I kept aloof from them—especially the Germans who were staunch Hitlerites.

As for my work, I could claim that it was exceptional—and the sisters acknowledged it. They trusted me. They said openly that I was one of their best workers. Sister Maria, the head of my department, was like a mother to me; she was my mainstay and refuge. She tried to help me whenever she could and to make things easier for me.

And so, the lovely warm days of summer gave way to autumn. The flowers and leaves began to fade, to turn yellow and brown. Each day the sun's rays were weaker and shorter. But, on the other hand, it was easier to remain inside the hospital, not to long after the beauties of nature outdoors. And yet, the sad days of autumn brought to mind that somewhere, far away, someone was counting on me to help—someone dear was waiting for my return.

Each morning I looked to see whether the mail brought me a reply from Dr. Jagoda—but alas, it never came. I wondered what might have happened to my letter, or to the doctor. I did not know where to turn for advice or help. Sometimes I thought of taking Marie Kraus into my confidence, yet I hesitated to do that. By one inadvertent word I could forfeit my life . . .

Sister Maria was happy that her suggestion for treating the swelling in my legs brought such good results. They were now back to their normal size. She often asked me about my health, and tried to get me to tell her more about myself—where I came from, what my family was like, and so forth. Often she gave me cakes and fruits that were given to her by the patients; she even invited me to have coffee with her in her room.

All this, I felt, she did because she wanted to get to know me better, to be able to help me. Perhaps she could read from my face that I was experiencing a deep spiritual torment. Perhaps she wondered why my family never wrote to me, or why I had no contacts with anyone outside the hospital.

Unfortunately, I could not bring myself to tell Sister Maria the truth. Did she guess that my answers were all lies? I had long forgotten what it meant to tell the truth—yes, for almost a year; since I had left the ghetto, since I had become the counterfeit Hanka Buczek, in order to save my life I had had to resort to lies. Yet my conscience worried me that I had to lie to Sister Maria, who was so good. Would she still be good to me, if she knew the truth?

In a sense I was an enigma to everyone, including the sisters. Why didn't I go anywhere? I realized that I must at last change this situation. Deciding to take the first step, I asked Sister Maria, my superior, if she would send me to the post office to get the mail for the hospital, at least sometimes, or to expedite packages and perform similar errands. I knew that other girls were sent to the post office; why shouldn't I go occasionally? Sister willingly gave me permission, though she seemed to think that I was too delicate for the job. She said that she thought that I would not like to pull the little delivery wagon through the streets of Stuttgart, but since I had asked for this myself, she would agree gladly.

The following morning Sister Maria told me to go to the Verwaltung office to get the little wagon. I was off to fetch the mail! The wagon was somewhat clumsy to pull, until the sister in the Verwaltung office showed me how. Its wheels bounced with a loud noise off the edges of the stone steps as I turned into Hohenheimerstrasse. It was a cool morning, but pleasant, the air clean and pure. Stuttgart—a beautiful city, almost one huge garden—seemed to be enjoying normal times. One would not guess that a war was going on. The streetcars were running, making stops at regular intervals to let off or take on passengers. As I passed restaurants, I could see people sitting by the little tables, chatting agreeably. They were all dressed quite well.

Indeed, thus far Stuttgart had known no war. The houses stood intact. The German citizens who were serving in the army at the front or in occupied countries had been replaced by hundreds and thousands of foreigners, so that one did not notice a depletion in numbers of population. I had to pull my wagon through the roadway, for fear that on the sidewalk I might run into somebody or get into someone's way. It was safer all around—for I did not want to be suddenly confronted, eye-to-eye, with a person who could recognize me.

Hohenheimerstrasse descended from the hill where the hospital stood to what the Germans called the Gradaus and then to the Schlossplatz. Here in the large, tree-lined square one could see the real signs of autumn. The entire Schlossplatz seemed covered with a golden pall, and the fallen leaves formed a carpet for the feet of passersby. On the benches where a few straggling rays of sunlight lent some illusion of warmth, some people sat reading newspapers. Perhaps they, too, were looking for the words that would announce the end of the war. Most of them looked like foreigners—their features did not seem Germanic, at least not to me. Beyond the square I had to turn right in the direction of the railway depot to reach the post office. In a nearby kiosk I bought a package of writing paper, and later, in the post office, I purchased some stamps.

I picked up a few packages for the hospital, loaded them onto the wagon, and started on the way back to my "dog house." The little wagon had a mind of its own and refused to go the way I pulled it, so I tried pushing it ahead of me. Now I had a chance to look around, to get out of my shell. Tonight I would sit down and write a letter to myself. Everyone wondered why I received no mail; I had to put a stop to it. Even if they happened to notice that the letter bore a Stuttgart postal stamp on the envelope, I'd explain that it was sent from Poland to someone I knew here and she forwarded the letter to me as a favor to my family.

When I went down to Hohenheimerstrasse with an empty wagon it had seemed easy, but pulling the loaded wagon after me was quite a task. But I took my time, and after a while I stopped to rest a bit. Passersby looked at me queerly, but I learned later that they liked my wearing the letter P with brave unconcern. I started to pull the wagon again but it would not budge. Bending over, I noticed that a nail was about to fall out of one of the wheels. I started to work on it, but only succeeded in breaking the nail off completely. I removed the wheel and placed it on top of the packages, and somehow managed to pull the wagon as far as the hospital garden. Thank heaven it was not too distant! Fortunately, one of the sisters happened to see my predicament and quickly ran out to help me. Together we got the wagon up the stone stairs and into the building. As soon as we entered the office, I snatched my writing paper and took it up to my room. I did not want anyone to see it.

I could be excused for a few minutes, I knew, to go hide the paper in my room. Then I returned to my station and told Sister Maria about my experience. She was sorry that I had had trouble with the wagon, and on the first time out, but she said not to worry. The repairs would be done quickly. I thanked Sister and resumed my task of cleaning the ward. I could hardly wait for the evening to come so that I could write the letter. But that evening, as if to spite me, Lena stayed in our room and I had to postpone writing until some night when she would go out. Several days went by before Lena at last decided to visit her friends. Dressing for the occasion, she tried again to persuade me to remove the letter P from my clothing and go with her, but I said that I would wait until I received a package of clothes from home.

"Before you receive the package," she sputtered, "the Germans will have removed the best things from it!"

As soon as she left, I took out the paper. Disguising my handwriting, I began:

"Dear Hania—We thank you for your letter and are glad that you are satisfied with your job and the place where you are staying. We miss you very much. Since you left the house seems very empty. We see you everywhere we turn, but of course you are not here. Write to us oftener . . ." and so on and on. I drenched the letter with my own tears before I put it in the envelope, which I had addressed to myself—but with no return address, only an illegible scrawl on the reverse side. I sealed it and put it aside, intending to mail it the next day. I had written it just as I felt my own mother or family would have written, thinking lovingly of me so far away.

At last a letter came in the mail for me—and no one was wise to the fact that I had written it myself to myself. They did not even notice the Stuttgart postal seal. I made a point, however, of telling everyone that I had received a letter from home and now I would send them a gift. I inquired where I could buy Christmas tree ornaments—for the Krupkas, for Janko—and the next free afternoon I had I went to buy them. This time I took a streetcar, for I had a little money at my disposal, and went downtown. I found the shop and had a wonderful time picking out all sorts of glistening baubles for Janko. At that moment I really felt like Hanka Buczek, buying presents for her Ukrainian friends! It gave me great satisfaction to take the package to the post office—it was a large package, but light, and did not require much postage. I had not felt so content in a long time! It made me so happy to be able to surprise the Krupkas with a little gift.

Inside the package was a letter that I had prepared the night before. In it I wished the Krupkas Merry Christmas and Happy New Year, of course, adding to that my sincere thanks for all they had done for me. I asked them, if possible, to send me the winter clothing that I had left there, because I received nothing here in the way of clothes, and winter was close at hand. Did they know that I had lost everything in Lvov? I knew that they would understand that I had been robbed, for they knew that I had been arrested by the Ukrainian police. If they could, would they send my neighbors my greetings—to their whole family? I knew they would understand that I meant my own family. When writing the letter, I prayed it would reach them safely—and that I might receive a reply as soon as possible.

When I told the girls at the hospital that I had mailed a package to my family back home, they laughed and Marie Kraus said, "If you were smart, you'd have packed yourself inside that box and gotten out of this work!" We joked about it, good-naturedly, while enjoying our coffee break. I felt so much better now, I could laugh.

The administration of the hospital tried to make things pleasant for the girls. To my great surprise, they remembered my birthday—something, of course, I did not remember. But it was Hanka Buczek's birthday, October 10, that we celebrated in the dining room when one of the sisters from the Verwaltung announced it. Everyone, including the Herr Inspektor, expressed their good wishes to me, and the Superior handed me a present. Such a surprise, normally, would have been very delightful—but I cannot begin to describe how I felt. The tears welled up from my heart, though no one thought it strange, for they explained my emotion simply as a longing for home, and they wished me that the next year would see me celebrating my birthday with my family again.

My present consisted of a white apron, hand embroidered, and five marks. Also, Sister Maria gave me some handkerchiefs—and Marie Kraus brought various pastries and cookies that she had received from home. All this would have made me very happy, but even my birthday was a lie—it didn't belong to me, it belonged to the real Hanka. My own birthday would be November 20, that I remembered; I would never forget it, for it was also the day I left home, escaping from the ghetto, the day of parting from my mother and sister, from my loved ones. How could I ever forget?

But time passed, weeks went by and I still waited for a reply from the Krupka family, or from Dr. Jagoda—though as for the latter, I was becoming resigned to the inevitable. My letter had not been returned. Who knows what happened? And yet I waited hopefully.

The days went by slowly in an unending routine of chores that at last I grew accustomed to doing. The only task that I still could not perform without suffering a fit of nausea was washing out with my hands the blood-stained sheets after the deliveries.

Somewhere about this time Marie Kraus was discharged for neglecting her work. I heard that the Arbeitsamt transferred her to a private home. I missed her so much that I almost decided to ask for a transfer, too. *Perhaps I should have a talk with Sister Maria,* I thought—perhaps I would be happier to work in another department of the hospital? Something new; a lighter kind of work? I knew that occasionally the girls were changed to other tasks, usually after spending several months in a particular assignment, so why shouldn't I try? It was getting close to Christmas, however, and Sister Maria was very busy, but she promised to give my request her consideration after the holidays. She could not conceal her astonishment that I wanted to ask for a transfer. Why? I did not want to admit that it was because of Marie Kraus.

After the Christmas and New Year holidays, the winter made us feel its harshness—cold, icy winds, snow. More work, more dirt brought into the hospital on snow boots, mostly in the lower halls nearest the entrances.

Sometimes we had to shovel the snow from the stone steps—and we did this without warm clothing or gloves. In place of gloves that I did not have I pulled some old black stockings, discharged by one of the sisters, over my hands. It was not cold inside the hospital, but the winter gloom prevailed everywhere. Everyone was nervous and irritable. Now I felt all the more that I must change my employment. When Marie Kraus left, I lost interest in the department where we had formerly worked together. True, I was attached to Sister Maria, but I had nothing in common with the other girls. Marie Kraus had given me her new address before she left and had asked me to keep in touch. I had promised that I would visit her at the first opportunity, for I wanted to remain her friend.

Sister Maria at last arranged for Sister Superior to have me changed to the *Neustube,* the sewing room where the sisters' habits, aprons, and the hospital sheets were sewn or repaired. She thought that there I would be able to rest a while and revive from an illness I had after the holidays in different surroundings. The sewing room was located also on the third floor. Sister Maria's own sister, not a deaconess, but an older, unmarried woman—was in charge. I had seen her on previous occasions, and perhaps that was why Sister Maria had me transferred there temporarily. There were several machines in the room and a large cutting table. None of the girls worked there, only sisters well on in years.

After two weeks I was told to report to the second floor, where Sister Marta was in charge. This was a smaller ward, on the same floor as the dining room and kitchens. The main kitchen occupied a large corner room; it was considerably larger than the kitchen next to the Wochenstation, because here the dishes from the dining room were washed as well as the patients' dishes. To the left of the dining room was a six-bed ward with a large balcony, and beyond that, two smaller rooms. Two girls worked in this department: one tall, thin German girl named Mary, and another Mary who sat opposite me at meals in the dining room. I was assigned to this group. Here the work entailed the usual cleaning chores, and with the thin Mary I also had to wash the dishes when they returned from the dining room. And then there were also the patients' dishes to wash. Though Sister Marta helped us as well as she could, there was more than enough to do.

I had been working here already for more than six months, and I knew practically everyone in the hospital. I had acquired a fluent command of German—to those who did not know my past, it seemed almost miraculous. I was considered one of the best workers, and now I knew that they needed me more than I needed them. I could find other work in Stuttgart if I wanted to, and that gave me added confidence.

With the passing days, however, I felt that I had accomplished little, except for my work. My conscience troubled me, though I was beginning to think that the end of the war was no closer now than before I had arrived at the hospital. As for my lot, I was quite resigned to it. I tried not to think that I might still be in some danger of being discovered as a Jewess.

Lena went out more frequently now, leaving me to spend the long, lonely evenings in our room. This hopeless waiting dragged on. My shoes were worn thin: when I went outside to clear the snow from the walks, my feet became soaked and chilled to the marrow. My two dresses were already beyond repair. I had no stockings or underwear, and as an Ausländer I was given nothing. I hoped that I would hear from the Krupka family and perhaps I hoped so fervently that my thoughts drew a response from them, for one morning I was summoned to the Verwaltung office and was told that there was a package at the post office for me, weighing approximately ten kilograms. I took the delivery wagon and hastened to fetch it—I threw my sport coat over my ragged dress, pulled the collar up high, and ran on joyful wings! The postal notice indicated that the package was sent by the Krupkas. I told the sisters that it was from my family back home; no one asked me further questions.

I dashed down to the post office and back with the little wagon, and burst up the stairs to the first floor. When I saw Sister Maria I gave a little shout, and she told me to open the package right away—she wanted to see, too! She clapped her hands excitedly while I undid the wrappings—just one more string and the box was open!

There was something black on top. I started pulling out the contents, one by one. First, a black skirt, and then a black jacket that completed the suit. Sister watched curiously, but then, remembering that she was sterilizing some instrument on the stove, turned away. Now I pulled out a pair of black shoes, black stockings, a belt . . . Sister Maria threw a question over her shoulder, but I did not reply. I picked up the jacket again and almost instinctively put my hand into a pocket, pulling out a small sheet of note paper. It was a letter, written in Ukrainian. Unfolding it, I read:

> "Dear Hania,
>
> We received your package. Thank you. Almost all the Christmas ornaments were broken. We are sending your things and I added some of my own. You will find use for them, and also a white armband. Don't write anymore, it is very dangerous. There was a big fire at the neighbors' and everything was destroyed. We are very sorry. Take care of yourself . . . Oh, yes, our little dog Zeze was killed by a car.
>
> Many kisses,
> Mrs. Krupka

I understood that my family had been burned alive. The words blurred before my eyes. I could hardly see—and then everything went black. I began to scream and wail. No, no!

Sister Marta said, *"Was nein?"* What did I mean by that terrible "No?" But I only cried and kept swaying back and forth. The sisters and girls came running out of the kitchen to see what was the matter.

Sister Marta sent them away, but they stood in the doorway looking at me. Sister pulled up a chair for me to sit down, but I broke loose and darted out into the hallway straight to the spot where a large picture of Hitler hung on the wall. I wanted to break the glass and destroy his portrait—in my frenzied grief it seemed the only way I could revenge myself on that murderer. Sister Marta seized my uplifted hands and held on to me as tightly as she could.

"Someone will see you," she whispered, her lips close to my ear. "They will call the Gestapo and have you arrested!"

"They can arrest me—kill me—do whatever they want!"

Sister Marta was afraid that the patients would hear the commotion and that those that could would come out into the corridor. She covered my mouth with her hand and pulled me into the bathroom. There was a chair right under the medicine cabinet and she forced me to sit down. She stroked my face and kissed me, trying to calm me, asking what had happened to upset me so.

I merely told her that my mother had died. I wanted so much to tell her the whole truth, to cast from me this hateful mask of pretense. But something held me back; some unseen power, some unheard voice told me to keep silent now. I recalled my dear mother's words: "When you come through this alive, remember what they did to us. Remember, and tell the world how we were destroyed. May you never forget what happened to our nation."

Knowing her wish, how could I give myself up? Someone had to survive. Someone had to bear witness to these murders. Someone had to revenge them, yes; someone had to cry for revenge for killing so many children . . .

Meanwhile, Sister Maria made me some tea and kept talking to me as to a child. Back in the small kitchen, she finished unpacking the parcel while I just sat staring ahead with unseeing eyes. "Now, look here," Sister said, "Here is a ham and sausage at the bottom of the box. And here's a pair of nice boots—and some yarn and a crochet hook and knitting needles. You can make something for yourself."

Even thin Mary—the Nazi—stood by, trying to comfort me, telling me how useful these things would be; now I wouldn't have to freeze. But I cried and cried, and struggled with one obsessing thought: How could I wreak revenge—when would I be able to pay back the Germans, the Nazis, for their evil deeds? Sister Marta at last persuaded me to go back to my room and get some rest. Slowly, as though coming back from a funeral, I found my way back to my room. It seemed doubly gloomy to me now, and I felt that I had had enough of this place. Everything at this moment seemed unbearable. I lay down upon the bed and did not get up even when I heard the lunch bell.

I remember that Lena brought me something to eat. Everyone knew now about my parcel and the tragic news of my mother's death. Lena tried to comfort me, saying at least I had two left in my family, my father and sister! The irony of it was that I had to thank her for her consoling words and nod my head in agreement. When Lena left, I lay there, staring at the ceiling, and unable yet to realize that my mother and sister—my whole life, everything in the world to me—were no longer alive . . . I tried to imagine how they had perished, how they felt—what their thoughts were at the moment before they died . . . Did they have any idea that I was still living somewhere? Or, had I not escaped from the ghetto, would I have been able to help them in some way? Or would I be now, as they were, dead in the ruins of our home, burned alive? Did I, in any case, have the right to save my life, alone?

But, as the days and weeks passed, the worst of the pain went away. I did not lose hope in myself or in my mission to survive. I began to venture outside the hospital, sometimes without the P on my clothing, to visit Marie Kraus or Vera, a Czech girl I had met in the infirmary while ill after the holidays. These visits helped to cheer me. March 1944 was almost at an end, and slowly each day became warmer. Outdoors the snow was gradually thawing under the rays of a pale sun; there was more daylight and the nights grew shorter. Surely, each day brought us closer to the lovely springtime weather—and hope! The battlefield at the front began to recede toward the German boundary. There were rumors of expected bombings. Now the United States, England, France, and Russia were united against the Germans. One could feel the end drawing near . . .

The construction of bomb shelters in Stuttgart gained impetus. There were public shelters along the streets and in various office buildings. The hospital itself started construction on a shelter. As it was situated on a hilltop, the best place for a shelter was the slope right by the rear exit. Work on the shelter proceeded very quickly, aided by the natural contour of the terrain. To my great astonishment one morning, when I looked out of the window, I saw some ten or a dozen men, wearing what seemed like a prison uniform and guarded by German policemen, busily digging into the hillside. Slave laborers, of course! We girls took turns bringing them food.

The opening in the side of the hill grew larger day by day, but it would take time to finish a shelter for more than one hundred people; it was to serve the sisters, the workers, the patients, and newborn infants. In it there would be room for beds, or at least cots, and for operating tables to be used in case of emergency. There would be chairs, cribs and carriages for infants, instrument cases and other such equipment. The ceiling would have to be high, so that there would be enough air for so many people to breathe.

The war and the bombing raids, however, did not conveniently wait until the hospital had completely finished its shelter. One night the siren began to wail after midnight and we all jumped out of our beds in wild excitement. Everyone from everywhere ran to the main building of the hospital, where the Sister Superior and other sisters gave instructions to go to the cellar.

The cellar filled up quickly. The critically ill patients were brought there first; then we began to bring in the children. *"Die Kinder! Die Kinder!"* everyone cried. We wheeled in the patients who had just undergone surgery. We checked every room, every ward. And the sirens kept on wailing . . . It had all happened so unexpectedly! When finally we were all clustered below, the cellar grew stiflingly hot; some patients started to cough, some gasped for air. Then the lights went out, and in the darkness we could hear the sisters praying. Some sisters got down on their knees on the dirt floor, imploring God to save the hospital, to spare the city.

We were in the cellar for about an hour before the sirens gave the "All Clear!" Now we helped our charges back to their places and returned to our rooms. We went to bed, but there was not much time left to sleep—if sleep was possible. We had to be up at five. In the morning we saw in all the faces around us the signs of terror and a sleepless night. Even though it had proved to be a false alarm, we could expect a real raid anytime—and the shelter was far from finished.

Meanwhile, summer was fast approaching. The gardens were in lovely bloom, the trees gave a translucent green shade—the entire world seemed to be called to life after the rigors of winter. And yet the people thought only of hiding. Who could think of walks in the fresh air and sunshine when the air raid sirens sounded more and more frequently?

Through Vera, the Czech girl I had met in the infirmary, I had been put in touch with some Czech youths who, apart from becoming good friends, brought me into their group of resistance workers against the Nazis. They entrusted me with the carrying out of certain projects, and I willingly accepted this responsibility. Frequently I was told to put packages into a garbage receptacle that stood in a side alley running off a street near the hospital, and I always had to do this late in the evening. Later, someone would come to pick up these packages; they knew exactly when the garbage was collected, and the pickup was effected beforehand so that the packages would not accidently be thrown into the refuse wagon. I was never told what was in those packages and I did not have the courage to ask. I only heard that the men knew about the contents but would not tell the girls in the underground, for fear that if we were caught we would be more likely to give the secret away—the men obviously having more toughness and endurance under torture. I assisted them with great pleasure and satisfaction, doing it more in memory of those whom the Nazis had murdered—including my own family—than for the living. I wanted so much to do something for my dear dead, and since I could not help them directly any longer, then at least I would help those who survived, never forgetting the others.

What a great satisfaction it gave me to be involved in this conspiracy! I felt my own self-esteem grow. I knew now that I was not merely trying to survive for my own personal entity, but at the same time I was doing something against the Nazis. Though I did not know the contents of the packages, I suspected that they contained, aside from food supplies for those in hiding, some kind of weapons or ammunition, secretly being smuggled to them. I later learned that they often contained bread for some German Jews hiding in a cellar nearby.

Yet the air raid sirens broke into our lives very frequently, disrupting even my sleeping hours. The race for the cellar shelter became a daily commonplace. Meantime, the real shelter was completed and the sisters and we workers had to help transfer the cots, tables, and various instruments there, and then the shelter became like a second hospital. It was about six or seven yards wide and about one hundred yards long; there was another door that led to a second shelter for mothers and infants, and the lying-in ward. Postoperative cases were taken directly to the shelter and remained there until they could be released. The shelter was lighted with small electric lamps set in the ceiling. It was rather high, but usually rather damp; the dampness could not be helped. In all, I would say that it was a very adequate shelter—but only if we had time to reach it after the first alarm sounded. However, that was something that the Administration could not cope with—no one really knew how soon the bombs would start to fall after the first warning siren. We were well organized and always ready to help the patients and perform our tasks.

The summer of 1944 went by somehow more swiftly than any other summer. With our hospital overflowing with patients—in part because other hospitals had been destroyed—we girls had to work even in other departments. I was assigned for a few hours before noon to a ward on the main floor.

The weeks flew by, amid racing to and from the shelter to the background wailing of the air raid sirens. I had not heard from my Czech friends for quite a while, and some instinct told me that something must have happened. No letter, no phone calls—as though they had vanished from the earth's surface. Kanstatt, a small town nearby, was bombed, and the downtown section of Stuttgart had also been hit. Marie called the next day to ask about me and to find out if I had had any words from the Czechs. It was strange that they had not phoned to inquire how I was; here it was almost November, with no word from them. Their silence worried me. What could have happened? One day, I took half a day off from work to find out. Alas, I learned not only that Vera was nowhere to be found but also that Josef, a Czech fellow I had met who had so bravely immersed himself in resistance duties, had been taken by the Gestapo! I myself saw his ransacked room, and had to flee his enquiring landlord. In a daze I returned to the hospital. How could such a thing happen to such a brave man? I gave Sister Maria an encapsulated version of what had happened; she was sorry that my friends were nowhere to be found.

The next morning dawned cold and cloudy, and my mood matched the weather. When I reported for work, Sister Marta greeted me with a smile and said that she was happy that my worries were over. I looked at her dumbly, not knowing that she meant. Was the war over? She, on the other hand, did not know why I showed no reaction but stood there puzzled and silent.

"I gave them the umbrella," she said by way of an explanation that was still unintelligible to me.

"Gave that to whom?"

"I gave my umbrella to our friends," Sister said.

"My friends? Where? When? What?"

Sister was obviously mystified that I knew nothing. She said, "Last night, a man came here with a young woman. He was black and blue; bruised all over. She—she had been a patient here once. They waited for you, but could not stay longer. And as it was pouring, I gave them an umbrella."

When I finished my work downstairs, I returned to the ward and started to clean the bathroom. As I bent over the tub, I heard some voices, among them Sister Marta's.

"Hanka, here's that umbrella I was talking about." I turned around to see Sister standing in the doorway; behind her was Josef, my Czech friend. Sister had tears in her eyes. I looked at them, still finding it difficult to believe, not knowing what to say. And then the tears streamed from my eyes, too.

My friend was a pitiful sight. He had been beaten; his eyes were blackened, and bloody lumps were visible on his face. It struck me as strange that he did not extend his hand in greeting, but rather held it behind his back. When I held out my hand, he reluctantly took it and then—oh, God! I saw . . . the fingernails blackened, the fingers almost completely crushed. Sister Marta turned away and left us. I could not say a word.

But Josef broke the awkward silence. "It is by some miracle I stand in front of you."

"What actually did happen?" I asked.

"We don't have time to talk about it now. But you may be assured that they will pay for it, and soon." He looked around to make sure that no one was listening.

"But how did it happen?"

"I'll come next Sunday and we'll talk about it then. God be with you! Just be patient, and have courage. The end is not far away."

I thanked him for the visit. He stopped to say goodbye to Sister Marta, and then left. I stood still as though glued to one place. Sister observed my reactions and wagged her head in compassion.

"What a sight!" I managed to say. "God he was beaten to a pulp."

"Why did they beat him so?"

"I don't know," I replied. "You can blame it on the war, I suppose. We blame everything on the war." I looked up at the portrait of Hitler and would have killed him with a glance, if I could.

The weather continued very poor. We met in the restaurant on the corner. Vera and another friend were with us, and we spent several hours in conversation. We talked in whispers, carefully. I learned a lot; it seemed that the Nazis had found some contraband weapons, and most likely someone had informed on the group. It was not known who.

Now we counted the months to the end of the war. Because of the constant bombardments, we could not meet frequently. The air raid alarms were often sounded several times a day—not to mention during the nights. On the quiet evenings I stayed in my room and wrote in my diary.

One night I lay awake, reliving in my mind all the tragedy that I had lived through thus far. I could not sleep, though Lena in the bed across the room was snoring. Suddenly, the wails of the siren broke in on my consciousness—they seemed louder than ever before. I jumped out of bed in the dark and called out to Lena.

"I'm awake!" Lena answered, not making any attempt to rise.

"Lena, get up quickly!" I shouted. From the corridor we could hear the sisters calling out, "Get up!" There were sounds of running footsteps. I reached for my coat, and for Lena's, urging her to hurry. The sirens continued to wail as if foreseeing some great disaster.

Oddly, Lena turned her face to the wall and refused to get up. "I'm tired," she muttered. "Let all Stuttgart go up in flames; I don't care."

But we had to get out of our room; we could not disregard the alarm. So, heavy and big though she was, I tore Lena from the featherbed and began pulling on her hand. I don't know how I managed to get her out of bed, but at last she stood up and put on her coat, slippers, and stockings, but not her dress. We ran through the garden snow towards the shelter. The hospital was in darkness; I saw no one outside. We were apparently the last ones to make for the shelter. We were barely to the entrance of the shelter when we heard the explosion of the first bombs. The force threw us to the ground, and we crawled on all fours to the shelter. It was packed full, as usual. Everyone turned to look at us in astonishment, but before we could utter a word another explosion shook the whole hillside.

Now there was silence. Everyone prayed with folded hands, and God's name passed from lip to lip in trembling whispers. No one stirred, waiting in fear. The last blast had been so powerful that it must have landed very close to us. We expected the hill to collapse and fall upon us at any moment. The only sound was the crying of the infants. Fear reigned in the shelter.

The sisters began to prepare candles to light in case the electricity gave out. Though no one said it, we all thought that this time the hospital must have been hit. But we did not smell smoke, and when someone opened a door at some distance from the main entrance and looked out, there were no flames to be seen. Yet we were sure that the bomb must have fallen in the immediate vicinity of our hill. We had felt everything shake, and some of us had fallen from our chairs or cots; we were all in a state of shock. It was a lucky thing that we were not buried alive in the earth. The bombing went on longer than ever before. The bright reflection of the snow made the night luminous and provided the bombers with a precise map of the terrain they could hit right on target.

The more seriously ill patients began to faint, and the doctors stood by, giving them injections and other medication. Some wept unrestrainedly. Oh, how everyone at this moment believed in God! How they prayed for help!

It was very late when at last the bombing ceased. Finally we began to get up and straighten ourselves out. We now wondered if we had a place to return to, whether the hospital still stood intact. Everyone seemed reluctant to make the first move, to see what had happened aboveground.

Herr Inspektor and his two daughters had come to the shelter at the first sound of the air raid siren. The sisters looked at him, waiting for his first action. We observed him as he slowly and carefully—almost fearfully—walked to the exit. We waited in silence, impatient to know the truth. The faces of all were haggard, imploring, and yet hopeful of hearing some reassuring news. No one said a word. We all loved the Herr Inspektor.

It was not very long before Herr Inspektor returned. His face reflected such astonishment that we could not tell what news he brought. "God be thanked," were his first words. We sighed with relief. Then he went on, "The hospital is intact, but . . ." Tears came to his eyes.

It turned out that the residential villa, the cottage where the sisters and we lived, was completely gone. One could not even see where it had once stood; only earth and sky remained. A disbelieving murmur went around from all of those gathered in the shelter.

I started as though suddenly wakened from a nightmare. "Lena, Lena!" I cried. "Our cottage, our home is gone!"

Lena, who was usually indifferent and unemotional, put her arms around me, weeping, "Oh, Hanka, if it had not been for you, I would not be alive now. You dragged me out of bed and saved my life!" Then, her old brusqueness returning, she whispered close to my ear, "The devil take the cottage. But—my things, my fur coats!" And again she burst into loud lamenting. I tried to quiet her.

Slowly we began to emerge from the shelter. Hours of hard work awaited us. It was now about four in the morning and dreadfully cold. As we came up to the surface, everyone gasped. We looked towards the right, where the residence for sisters and girls had stood. There was not a trace of the villa. The awful realization of its destruction sent chills down our spines that were worse than the cold and wind.

We had no electricity in the hospital. The windows, despite protective taping, were shattered. The window sills and floors were covered thickly with snow and broken glass. The elevator was not running. And we, as well as our patients, were scantily dressed, clad only in what we hastily had thrown on when the alarm sounded. We could not let the patients return to their rooms—many beds were covered with broken glass—so they were told to stay in the shelter. Then we began the seemingly endless task of cleaning and reconstructing.

Temporarily, we were to share quarters with those who lived in the other villa, which fortunately had survived the bombing. After a few days they hoped to find permanent quarters for us. Lena, hearing of this, wanted to take the opportunity of asking to be sent home to Holland. She had lost everything—she did not want to lose her life, too. But her efforts were in vain; this was no time to listen to individual problems.

The next few days were quiet, giving us a chance to bring some order back to the hospital and resume our normal routine. Meanwhile, rooms were eventually found for us on a more permanent basis in a four-story house on Hohenheimerstrasse, near the hospital. Here, in this rented space, I was given a front room on the fourth floor, which I was to share with Nastya. I was even pleased with the change; Nastya was a quiet girl who seemed to be quite congenial. She seldom went out. I could talk to her in Ukrainian. She was rather simple, but of a sincere and outgoing nature.

Before we knew it, December had come, and with it the deep snows and frosty days. The Germans were suffering great losses on all fronts. We were accustomed now to the air raid sirens as though it were our daily bread. It was arranged that the sisters and girls would alternate night duty at the hospital so that, in case of a raid, there would always be some on hand to help transport the patients and babies to the shelter.

And so it happened that one night—shortly after New Year's, 1945—when Nastya was on duty at the hospital, I was alone in our room, sleeping so soundly after an exceptionally hard day that I did not hear the sirens. Suddenly, everything in the room shook. I was thrown from the bed and was jolted awake when I hit the floor. I cried aloud, for I saw a huge fire burning directly across the street. Its flames illuminated the whole room with a crimson glare. I thought that the very bricks and stones were burning. I began to shriek hysterically and run around the room. When I opened my door I saw flames lighting up the stairs, but when I ran down below to the street it was dark. The bombs exploded constantly. I saw that I could not run through the street to the hospital shelter, so I found the entrance to the cellar of the apartment building and went inside. There it was dark and icy cold. The cellar was filled with water because the pipes had burst. The water was rising higher and higher—and here I was, all alone in the entire building, shivering in my slip. I was in mortal fear. Oh, God, was this the end? I folded my hands in prayer and begged God, begged my mother—"Help, save me!"

The rushing sound of the water made me realize that if I stayed in the cellar I would drown. A few times I tried to clamber out, but each time I was thrown back by the explosions. If I perished here, no one would even know what had happened to me! At that moment I resolved that, if I survived, I must confide in someone as to who I really was. At least, let someone know what Sheva Weiler had suffered while pretending to be Hanka Buczek, as a means of self-preservation. I could hear the crackling of flames above, and through the small windows I could see flames cross the street. I heard the walls collapsing. *Oh, God—don't let me be buried alive. Don't let this building collapse about my watery grave!* I recalled the scenes of the burning ghetto.

When at last the "all clear" sounded, I could hardly believe my ears. The wait had seemed interminable. I was completely wet, frozen, and near exhaustion. Like a mouse leaving its hole, I crawled out of the cellar and groped my way to the front door. On the other side of the street the fire was raging out of control; several buildings were in ruins. I ran through the frozen garden to the hospital shelter. I could not see where I was going, moving only by instinct. I must have been almost at the entrance to the bunker when I heard a voice, like in a dream, calling out, "*Hanka, wo warst du?*" It sounded like the gynecologist's voice. The next moment I lapsed into unconsciousness.

When I came to and opened my eyes, I found myself on a cot surrounded by Lena, Nastya, several sisters, and the gynecologist. I was wrapped in a heavy blanket, and Sister Marta held her hand on my forehead. I remembered nothing of what had happened before. My first words were, "Where am I? What happened to me?"

"Hanka, Hanka," Sister Marta said, "you were lucky that you fell unconscious at the entrance to the shelter. Otherwise, who knows whether you would have lived through it, for at that moment the gynecologist found you."

I remembered nothing, absolutely nothing.

Sister Marta continued, "We had to give you an injection. He did everything he could to revive you."

The gynecologist interrupted her to ask, "Hanka, how do you feel?" Then he turned to the sisters and said, "I thought she would never regain consciousness! But now I'm sure she will be all right."

The others were coming out of the shelter, but I could not be moved. I was shaking all over; I don't know whether from cold or because of nervous shock. My forehead felt like a piece of marble and my body could not thaw out after that icy bath in the cellar. In normal times, I'm sure I would have died of it—spending a night almost naked in a cold, flooded cellar.

But these were not normal times, and it was not long before I was fully recovered. One evening I had a surprise visit from my Czech friend Josef. He knew that Hohenheimerstrasse had been bombed, and because he could not reach me by telephone he came personally to see if I was all right. He told me that now it was just a matter of weeks and days before Germany would be destroyed completely. It was dangerous to stay in Stuttgart. He asked why I did not try to leave. But how could I tell him that I would be running a greater risk if I tried to leave Germany now rather than remain in it? He did not know my true identity. Oh, how I was tempted to tell him—but I did not think that this was the time or the place. He promised to come the next Sunday, and we agreed to meet in the afternoon at the usual place. I was determined to tell him then—if only we both managed to stay alive!

To my disappointment, when I came downstairs that next Sunday, Josef was not alone—his friend was with him, in the company of a Czech girl whom I had once met before. We went for coffee to the corner restaurant, and then went out for a walk. We walked in twos and talked about a lot of things, until I managed to bring the conversation around to the subject of forged papers. Again Josef underscored the probability that Stuttgart would be severely bombed and that I should try to leave.

During our talk the other couple walked ahead a little distance, and I drew a deep breath of the fresh, wintry air. At last I said that my departure could also place me in danger of death, a death that would be worse than being killed by a bomb. We stopped still for a moment, while I told him, with a great effort at controlling my emotions, that I was a Jewess living in Germany under falsified documents. My name, date of birth, place of birth—all were untrue. He heard me out in silence, not saying a word, but I could read in his face a great astonishment—and admiration.

"You were wise in trying to save yourself," he said when I had finished. "So now you ought to keep on trying to survive."

"Yes," I agreed. "But I cannot risk being questioned about my papers. That explains why I was so worried when you mentioned leaving."

"But you took a great risk when you helped us in our work and acted as intermediary for those packages."

"Yes. I did that, however, because it gave me enormous satisfaction to be able to do something against the Germans."

Whenever we saw the other couple drawing near, we changed the subject or remained silent. Only when we moved on further away from them did I add that I had lost my entire family and now had only relatives in Palestine. I said that my mother's wish before I left the ghetto was that if I managed to survive the war, I should join my cousins and family in Palestine. "My cousin's name," I told Josef, "is Fishel Weiler—we both have the same family name. His father is my father's brother. I don't remember him too well. But I want you to know that, should I be killed in a bombing or by the Nazis, my earnest wish is for you to write him after the war, and let him know what happened to me."

"I will remember," he assured me. He did not make further comment. On my part, I felt a great relief to have someone I could trust. Tears brimmed in my eyes and I wiped them away quickly so that the other couple would not notice. Now Josef understood why I could not be induced to leave Stuttgart. His friends were tired of walking and it was getting late, so we turned back in the direction of the hospital. We did not say much after that. I was conscious of immense peace, as though I had thrown off a heavy stone from my shoulders. Josef, I suppose, was thinking of what I had told him.

I took leave of my Czech friends at the hospital gate, and went inside with a light and confident step. Now I had the feeling that there was someone helping me to carry my burden. And even if I should perish, my memory would not be lost forever. I felt sure that he would make every effort to trace my cousin in Palestine and give him a message. It was a good thing that I had this friend I could trust.

Despite all the work I had to do under pressure that cold January, I did not forget that I had not heard from Marie Kraus for a long time. Her silence was disquieting. One Sunday early in February when I had a free afternoon, I decided to go and see whether Marie's house still stood and whether her name was on the door. I took a streetcar to the Schlossplatz and from there walked the rest of the way.

Alas, when I arrived I found to my astonishment that she no longer lived at her apartment. But I was a firm believer in fate, and often felt that some special destiny was guiding my steps. On my way back from Marie's house I ran into one of those inexplicable happenings. There was a restaurant I had to pass on the way back. It was a large restaurant with a plate-glass window that filled one whole wall in the front. I knew the place well, for I also had to pass it whenever I went to the post office for mail. I paused for a moment and glanced at the people obviously enjoying themselves. I stood—and could not take a step further. At one table there were two girls—one fair-haired, the other dark. The blonde had long hair and, even while seated, looked tall; the brunette seemed tiny next to her companion. As they talked, they leaned close to one another and seemed oblivious to their surroundings. At first glance the blonde reminded me of someone, but I could not remember just who it was. She looked exactly like a Jewish girl I had known in Rohatyn—a girl who, as rumor had it, had also escaped from the ghetto several weeks before my departure. People said that two girls had escaped: Bluma Wildman and Pepa Kleinwaks—someone had helped them get to Vienna. But the dark-haired girl was certainly not Pepa; she was a complete stranger to me. And how would Bluma Wildman have gotten to Stuttgart? Maybe the girl I saw here was a German that just happened to resemble Bluma?

In the distance I saw my streetcar approaching the stop. I should run to catch it, but some instinct told me to stay here. Why shouldn't I enter the restaurant and convince myself—the girl really was the image of Bluma. I should have a closer look at her. Perhaps she would recognize me? It would not seem strange for me to enter the restaurant; I could be looking for someone, meeting a friend there. I could even sit down at the next table and order coffee. I had enough money for that. And I was no longer wearing the telltale badge with the letter P . . . no one would stop me from entering. I directed my steps towards the small table where they sat. They were so busy talking that they did not even notice me come in. The closer I came, the more certain I became that it was really Bluma. But who was the other one? Though she was dark, she did not have to be Jewish—and I resolved to be very careful so as not to betray Bluma. When

I reached their table I spoke to Bluma in Polish. "I think I know you. Do you recognize me?"

Bluma reddened and her first reaction was that of fright. The other girl was even more panic-stricken. They pushed their chairs away from the table and started to walk towards the door. Bluma said, "I never saw you before in my life. I don't know you."

I followed them and caught up with them at the door. At that moment the other girl ran away and disappeared in the crowds on the street. But I stopped Bluma, and carefully avoiding mention of her name or mine because I did not know who might overhear, I said, "We don't know each other very well, but we come from the same town."

Then Bluma took a close look at me and I thought for a moment that she would faint. Her eyes filled with tears. "Oh, God," she whispered, "you are Sheva Weiler!"

"Yes. I am called Hanka now. Hanka Buczek. What is your name here?"

"Marysia. The other girl is also one of us," she replied. We went out into the street and walked quite a distance before Bluma started calling, "Zosia, Zosia!" She was thrilled by our meeting.

Zosia was standing on the corner, pale and frightened. She must have thought that someone had come to denounce her friend to the Nazis. Now she came closer, her eyes questioning.

"Zosia," Bluma assured her, "this is one of us, from Rohatyn."

Now I could observe the girl at closer range. She was delicate, short and frail of build, and young—about the same age as Bluma and I. She asked nervously who I was. She was dreadfully upset by this meeting, and all the more so because the streets were full of passersby. We turned into a side street that was not as crowded. Bluma Wildman wanted to know what happened to her family, her parents—but all I could tell her was that I had left in November 1942 and later heard that our ghetto had been liquidated in June 1943. I also mentioned that I had had a letter from the Krupka family from which I learned that my mother and sister no longer existed.

"And what about my folks?" she asked nervously.

"Who knows?" I replied. I called her attention to my black suit—Mrs. Krupka had sent it to me as a sign of mourning.

"Do you know who else is here?" Bluma asked, and without waiting added, "Pepa Kleinwaks."

"I knew that you two left Rohatyn together," I said. Bluma expressed amazement that their departure was known to the rest of us in Rohatyn. It was supposed to have been a deep secret! But she should have known that in the ghetto there were no secrets.

As we stood on the street corner, we talked about our experiences and agreed that we would not really be safe until the war was over, until the day of our liberation. Bluma told me that she was working in Möhringen in a bakery; Pepa Kleinwaks—who went under the name of Steffy—worked in a bakery beyond Stuttgart. Zosia, her friend, was working in a private home at Vaingen near Stuttgart. Before we parted, we exchanged addresses.

This meeting was unbelievably strange. We promised to see each other again and to remain in touch. I also gave them my telephone number at the hospital. As I left, I kept turning back and waving to them again and again. As soon as I returned to the hospital and entered the ward Sister Marta knew from my expression that something extraordinary had happened. I told her that on the way back from Marie's house, after not having found her there, I had run into a girl from my home village.

"You see," Sister said, "and you thought you were the only one who was caught! There were others that were enrolled for work here."

I waited eagerly for the day when "Marysia" (Bluma) would come to visit me. I was also anxious to get in touch with Steffy (Pepa Kleinwaks), and I decided to call on Pepa myself. On the first afternoon I was free, although I was exhausted after the almost daily and nightly alarms, I asked Sister for permission to go to see Steffy. Sister explained which streetcar I should take and said that it would take me about an hour to reach that suburb; she also advised me not to take chances, because one never knew when a bombing raid might take place.

It was a lovely afternoon. The sun's rays had cleared the streets of snow. I felt like a bird loosed from a cage. It seemed such a wonderful thing to be able to go out, breathe in the fresh air, obtain some new experiences. And what could give me a greater thrill than to meet another

Jewish girl from Rohatyn! I imagined how happy Pepa would be to see me. What a surprise meeting!

Eventually, after changing streetcars and enduring an air raid warning, I arrived at the street where Pepa worked and lived. Altogether I was nearly one-and-a-half hours on the way by trolley, and I still had to walk some distance.

In this area one could see the awful effects of bombardment. The entire street was filled with rubble, brick, and stones, and there were some laborers working on clearing the road. There was not a single house that had not been damaged more or less seriously. From stone to stone and from brick to brick I hopped. At last I saw a lone house that had not been bombed. There was a sign—BAKERY; I knew that I had found my goal.

A tiny bell tinkled as I opened the door. It was a small bakery store; a few customers were at the counter making their purchases. I looked around and saw Pepa Kleinwaks at the cash register—the same Pepa I had known back home. As she finished counting out the change for the customer, I heard her familiar, pleasant voice saying, *"Danke schön!"* When she raised her eyes she saw me immediately.

She merely waved to me, however, and motioned for me to sit down and wait. She went on serving the customers as though nothing had happened. Finally she came over and sat down next to me. She looked well but seemed terribly nervous and frightened. She asked how I had arrived, and I told her by streetcar.

"No," she said, speaking to me in German, "I meant how did you get to Stuttgart?" It seemed to me that Pepa did not want the German women to know that we knew each other well.

I answered her also in German, in a low voice. "I got here the same as you did, Steffy. They caught me, as they caught you and all the rest." I realized that we had to be careful because Steffy's boss stood within hearing distance.

"Steffy" was amazed that I had run into Bluma Wildman—"Marysia." Now we started talking in Polish. She told me in a whisper that she seldom saw Bluma, because she feared that if one of them were caught it might also incriminate the other. It was safer not to meet—even in a group it was possible to draw attention to oneself.

Where we were talking, several customers entered. Steffy had to help out behind the counter, and soon it became no longer prudent to continue our conversation. I said goodbye to Pepa and told her that if she ever wanted to get in touch with me, she had my address in the letter I had sent her. With that I went away.

I was still in a state of shock. I could not believe that our meeting had actually taken place. Now I had the long trip back ahead of me; I prayed to God to let me return safely to the hospital, without air raid alarms or bombardment.

It was dark already when I returned to my ward. As soon as Sister Marta saw me, she exclaimed, *"Hanka, du hast Besuch gehabt!"* Someone, it seems, had been to see me while I had been gone. Expressing surprise, I asked who it was.

"Oh, some tall blonde who called herself Marysia. I told her that you went to see a friend from your village, and she seemed to know who that was. She waited for a while, but went away. She said she came especially to see you."

Well, that was hard luck! Here Bluma Wildman came especially to see me—all the way from Möhringen—and did not find me in! I recalled that I had mentioned to her that my Wednesday afternoons were free . . .

That night I could not sleep. I kept thinking about the incident—it was almost unbelievable. Three Jewish girls from the same city, so close together here—it could certainly arouse grave suspicions.

Two days later, I received a postcard from Pepa, asking me to wait for her Sunday. She wrote that she would come to the hospital. That Sunday when I came out of my ward before dinner, carrying a tray in my hands, I noticed a familiar figure going up the stairs. Sure enough, it was Pepa. I asked her to come into the kitchen attached to the ward and told her to take off her coat and sit down.

We had a very pleasant talk, remembering old times in Rohatyn and describing to each other our experiences after leaving Poland. I told her about my Czech friends, and how they were opposed to Hitler. Pepa asked me if they would take the names of her uncles and aunts in America in case anything happened to her.

It was a great comfort to know that there were three of us from Rohatyn here, close to each other. Now with the coming of spring the air seemed fragrant not only with the early scent of awakening life but also with the scent of war's swift end. Even though the news from the front was censored and consisted mainly of lies, we knew that things were going very badly for the Germans. And if the Germans were no longer talking of victory, we knew that defeat was certain. My unexpected contact with these girls from Rohatyn was like a balm for my wounds—like the best medicine for a sick soul.

The days rushed by and I had hardly a moment for myself, but whatever free time I had I spent with my Czech friends at the restaurant rendezvous or with Steffy or Marysia. My antagonism toward Hitler increased even more; once, in chapel, when Sister Superior prayed for his victory and long life, I walked out, almost getting myself into quite a bit of trouble. One Sunday when Marysia came by, we went together to the restaurant and I introduced her to the Czech group. We thought that we could almost smell the end of the war in the spring air.

In April 1945, the radio brought us news that stunned me. I was standing in the kitchen, washing dishes, when I overheard one of the sisters tell another that President Roosevelt had died. The name of Roosevelt echoed in every corner. I knew he was the president of the United States but did not know much else about him—yet the news of his death shocked me deeply. Tears started to course down my cheeks and I was shaking. When my free hour came, I ran out to the nearest newsstand and bought a paper—a German paper, of course. The street was swarming with people. A boy stood on the corner, selling papers and shouting, "Extra! The American president is dead!" The Germans snatched at the papers with gleeful smiles, as though this news gave them a ray of hope. I could see it in their faces as I returned to the hospital: They seemed certain that with the death of President Roosevelt the United States had lost the war.

When I came into my room, I threw myself on the bed and cried. I did not care if the others whose rooms were on that floor heard me. I sobbed loudly, for I too feared that all was lost. The front page of the paper, in giving the news of Roosevelt's death, made it look like a victory for Hitler.

One night the sirens called us to the bunker. This time the bombardment seemed to last longer than ever. We huddled there in fear and waited, some talking in whispers, some praying, but in general a tense quiet reigned underground. I found myself near Lena, and in the dim light we exchanged questioning glances. We heard not only bombs but also what sounded like house-to-house shooting. With the echo of each shot people looked at each other, puzzled and afraid.

That was a very long night—it began early, and seemed to have more hours in it than any other night we knew. This waiting set our nerves on edge. From time to time someone would unpack a bag of provisions and pass around some biscuits or candy. Most of the patients, as well as the sisters, usually had with them something to eat in the air raid shelter—just in case. And we always kept containers of water handy. Thank God, until now these bags and fire pails had stood unused and unnecessary. This time the food supplies were distributed freely, as if we sensed that there would be no further need to come down to this shelter again. After midnight we all tried to catch some sleep, but new salvos of fire and new explosions of heavy bombs gave us no rest.

Oh, God, I thought, *if this is really the end, let us stay alive. Don't let us be killed right before the end!*

10

At Last—The Liberation!

NOW IT WAS ONLY A MATTER OF HOURS, not days. It must have been near dawn, but it was always dark in our bunker. The entrance door was closed and no one had the courage to look out. Suddenly, we heard a knocking on the door of our shelter and the sound of heavy steps—military steps. Such a sound had often brought fear to my heart. The door flew open and we saw the figures of four soldiers in French helmets and uniforms, armed with guns.

"Where is the doctor?" one asked in halting German. "We have wounded who need care."

I could hardly believe it! These were not Gestapo whom I hated and dreaded. These were my liberators. We had been expecting them for a long time, I and many others like me, waiting for them to deliver us from bondage. But I could not believe my own eyes, could not move from my spot.

Lena called out, "Hanka!" but could say no more. And the quiet Nastya took hold of my hands and suddenly burst out sobbing like a child.

The sisters started to leave the shelter, to go to tend the wounded. I felt I would have liked to run to these soldiers and kiss them, to thank them for this surprise, but I felt unable to move. We heard the French soldiers giving some orders, and a sister who understood French repeated that we were to move out of the bunker; that all was quiet; Stuttgart was in their hands. That day was April 30, 1945—the day of my liberation, a day I shall never forget. It seemed that all the anguish I had lived through, all the accumulated suffering, descended upon me and weighed me down.

I must have been dazed and in shock. I realized that I was free, that the dream I had lived for all those years had come true, but I also realized that I no longer had a home to return to, no one was waiting for me . . . After a while I got up and started walking in silence.

The Herr Inspektor stood by the exit and told everyone to take care in getting out of the shelter. When I passed him, he said, *"Guten Morgen, Frăulein Hanka."*

"Good morning, Herr Inspektor," I replied. And now tears started running down my face as I took my first steps in freedom.

It was already daylight. We could smell smoke everywhere, and we could see fires in the distance. We all quickly went to our stations. In the operating room several wounded soldiers were already waiting. Not much was said by anyone.

There was little talk at our meals, but I could read the pain in people's faces at the loss of the war. One could easily tell the Germans from the others now, simply by looking at them—the foreigners were smiling. Nastya and Katya were already planning to leave as soon as it was possible. I also said something about leaving, but I did not as yet disclose my identity—and the fact that I had no home left. Experienced as I was in dealing with treachery and deceit, it seemed to me wiser to wait a little longer. Things might change at the front—one could never be too sure.

The following morning, when I reported at my station, the picture of Hitler was gone from the wall, and only a square of lighter paint and a nail indicated the spot where it had hung. I wondered how Pepa and Bluma had reacted to the occupation of Stuttgart by the French. I wanted very much to see them and to share my joy with them, but for the time being there was no communication and I had to wait. In the hospital things were restored as quickly as possible to a normal routine.

After several days, "Marysia" came to see me. I greeted her very warmly, and simultaneously we said—as though the thought were uppermost in our minds—"What are we going to do now?"

Marysia told me that she had already seen her friend Zosia and that they were only waiting for me to decide where to go. She also said that she had as yet not disclosed her identity; I remarked that it was wise to wait. Bluma went on to tell me that the people she was staying with still talked as if the ultimate victory would be Germany's, that things would not remain as they were now.

"It is no longer important what the Germans believe," I replied, "but it is better for us to be careful. My mother said that in a war, the front can change."

"Have you heard from Steffy?" she asked.

"Not a word. Who knows what might have happened to her?" We decided to go together to visit her if she did not get in touch with either of us by the following Sunday. (We learned later that she had vanished, found a cousin in the French army, and left Stuttgart with him.)

A couple of weeks had gone by since the end of the war on May 12, 1945. The Germans had to get used to one fact: that they had lost, completely and irrevocably. I felt that now I must disclose my true identity. But where, and with whom should I begin? The moment of the great revelation, the one moment I had dreamed about always, came rather suddenly, and because of a very trivial incident. It happened that one morning Sister Marta joked with me, saying her usual, *"Hanka Buczek, putz weg gibt's Dreck"*—when something within me revolted. I felt that I could not go on like this anymore, that it was time that they knew who I was. I said aloud, with tears in my eyes, "Sister Marta, I am not Hanka Buczek—my name, my real name, is Sheva Weiler and I am Jewish. My time for hiding is over and I don't have to go on acting a lie any longer."

Sister Marta's face reddened with embarrassment, and tears rolled down her cheeks. She exclaimed fervently, *"Du mein lieber Gott, Hanka!"* She took my hands in hers, laughing and crying, and made me sit beside her. She said, "I always said that you were a very intelligent girl, but now I must admit that you were smarter than I thought." After a moment she continued, "But how could you have lived like this? I would have died of fright." She shook her head in wonder.

"The fight for survival is stronger than any fear," I replied.

Now I resolved to go directly to the Verwaltung and tell the Sister Superior and the Herr Inspektor. Sister Superior's reaction was as though what I was revealing to her was perfectly normal; the Inspektor was stunned, and could hardly believe what he heard. *"Unmöglich, unmöglich,"* he said. "Can it be possible? I can now imagine, Fräulein Hanka, what you must have gone through!" He had tears in his eyes and was visibly moved. Oddly enough, I remained calm. Only then the Herr Inspektor said, "But thank God you have somehow managed to survive and you were fortunate enough to come here. You will admit, I think, you were not treated too badly at the hospital? And if you have no other place to go, no home to return to, this hospital can still be your home for the future." When he repeated, almost wistfully, "You had a good home with us, and good care," then I said—truly—that I had been treated on par with the German workers and that they had not made me feel that I was a foreigner. He added, "You were a good worker and the sisters were very pleased with you and love you."

"Thank you, Herr Inspektor," I said, "but at the first opportunity, when I can find a place to go, I would like to say farewell to my pail, mop, and broom."

A faint smile crossed his lips, and he said, "They helped save your life. Don't hate these humble tools on that account. We would be happy to have you stay at the hospital and I say this on behalf of the entire staff."

"No, thank you. I would like to leave here as soon as I can and go to Palestine, where I have some cousins. All my family at home has been killed."

"Well, wherever you decide to settle," he said, "may God bless and help you. However, do us a favor and stay here until we find someone to take your place. Everybody is leaving, and it is so difficult to find replacements."

I agreed to that and went back to my work station. I felt a great relief, having thrown off this heavy stone that had weighed upon me for nearly two years at the hospital.

One day, Marysia told me that her friend Zosia had heard of a committee, organized by an American Army captain of Jewish background, named the Eskin Committee. All of us who had lived through the war were supposed to report to this committee. There we would receive food packages and clothing and we would be helped to get in touch with our relatives. If we had any family abroad, the committee would give our names to the newspapers in the United States, or South America, Canada, Palestine, France, and so on. Could we have asked for more?

At last the day came when I met Marysia and Zosia at Schlossplatz and took a streetcar to Eskin House. We reached the building where the committee was located and went up a short flight of stairs.

When we knocked on their door, someone called out in English, "Come in!"

Entering, we saw a GI sitting behind a desk. The soldier took our names and asked if we had any relatives abroad with whom we would like to communicate. The committee would help us locate them. He also registered us for rations of food and clothing. He said that as soon as more of us would apply, they planned to open a camp for survivors.

Marysia gave the name of her sister, who was in Buenos Aires; Zosia gave the address of her uncle in the United States, as well as someone in Palestine. I mentioned my cousin Fishel Weiler in Palestine, and when the soldier asked if I had someone in America, I said no. I recalled that two of my friends from Rohatyn had emigrated with their parents before the war, but no relatives of mine lived in the United States.

"But if you have friends, they might want to get in touch with you, or learn from you news of what happened in your town," he said, and he took my name to report to the newspapers in America. Before we left, he told us that on Saturday we would gather for prayers. If we knew of more people like ourselves who had survived, he added, we should tell them to come and register with the committee.

We turned to go home, feeling ecstatically happy. At last there was someone who cared about us. Now we were able to meet with our own people. It was a day of hope, of joy!

The early summer days passed slowly. Eskin House became a place we often visited, for prayer meetings and in the vain hope that mail might arrive for us. When Josef left for Czechoslovakia, Marysia and I took his room in Vaingen—and I said my final (rather sad) goodbyes to the hospital. We continued to go to Eskin House; one day, beyond our wildest hopes, Marysia received a letter from her sister in Argentina!

In our daily trips there, we began to see people who had been released from the concentration camps. Several young girls arrived about that time, who looked like boys with their shorn hair; we knew they were girls only because they wore dresses. They were emaciated, their eyes circles with shadows, deep-sunken; it was fearful to look at them.

I went back day after day to the Eskin House. Maybe, after all, someone would write to me! I lived in hope. And one day, to my great amazement, I saw my name: Sheva Weiler! It was the first letter that I received after the war. I did not cry at once, but my hands shook when I reached to take the letter. Who had sent it to me? It was not from my sister, nor from my mother, nor anyone in my family, but from a stranger. The sender was Max Altman, Florida, America.

Though I was glad to receive the letter, I wondered who this Max Altman was—then, in a flash, it came to me. Back in the ghetto I had been a close friend of his daughter Klara. Now, reading her father's letter, I began to cry. He had noticed my name in the newspaper in a list of survivors. Like everyone else who had a family in Europe, Mr. Altman kept scanning the papers, and he remembered me from Rohatyn. He wanted to know what had happened to his family and if he could help me in any way. His letter was precious to me, almost as if it had come from a blood relative of mine, for I deeply appreciated hearing from this good man who, after all, was a stranger—and yet wrote to me so feelingly. I took the letter back to Vaingen and let Marysia read it.

"Oh, God!" she exclaimed. "It's from Klara Altman's father."

Bluma and I talked about that letter for a long time, wondering how I could break the news to Mr. Altman about his family that I knew he had lost in Rohatyn. Although he might be expecting it, how could I tell him that his whole family had perished? Nevertheless, I wrote him soon, thanking him warmly for getting in touch with me, and—to spare his feelings—merely telling him how and when I had left Rohatyn, and that at the time my family as well as his were still alive. I mentioned that his daughter Klara and I had been close friends, and if I should hear from her I would write again.

Each day when I went to Eskin House I saw the same eager, lonely faces bent over the "magic table" in expectation of hearing from somebody. And how happy I was when I too found more letters as time went on—a few letters from people in the United States who had emigrated from Rohatyn before the war. Letters filled with compassion, offering encouragement and help—even affidavits for coming to the United States. One of these letters was from Dr. Isaac Lewenter, who in Rohatyn had been our family doctor. He had left with his wife in July 1939 to visit the World's Fair in New York. His letter was very sad, because he knew already from Pepa Kleinwaks that he had lost his only son and the whole family. (Now we knew that Pepa was already in the United States!) All those letters were sad, for everyone had lost somebody among his relatives in Poland, but they filled my loneliness and poured a balm on my hurts when I read them.

It seemed to me that it was a waste of time to be sitting here in Germany, just waiting—not knowing for what. I was still under the cloud of my war experiences and the loss of my family. I still could not accept the idea that with the end of the war I must begin a new life and must forget whatever happened in the past. Those who had perished did not want to be forgotten. My mother's last words to me had been: "Do not forget what happened to us and tell the world what they did to us."

Whenever I stopped at the hospital for a visit, Sister Marta was happy to see me—no matter how busy she happened to be. I usually brought something for her, to prove that I had not forgotten her kindness. On one such occasion, Sister Marta ran to greet me with the news that there was a letter waiting for me. I snatched the envelope with trembling hands, my heart beating wildly. My eyes sought, first of all, the sender's address—no, it was not from home—but from Mrs. Krupka. While on the one hand I was disappointed because it was not from home, I was nevertheless glad to hear from the Krupkas. What surprised me was that the postmark was German. I opened it nervously and began to read. She wrote that the whole family had escaped in February 1944, from Brody to Vienna. The Krupka family, as well as many other Ukrainians, had fled before the Soviet Army. Now they were living in München. She did not mention anything about my family, not about Rohatyn, only adding at the end that Mr. Krupka's sister Olga and her mother had remained in Poland.

When I returned home, I found no one there, so I sat down and penned a letter to the Krupka family, telling them that I would be there to see them very soon. I mailed the letter right away and waited for the return of Marysia. She had recently gotten married to an American soldier and was very happy. When she returned and heard the news, she liked the idea of visiting the Krupkas and decided to go with me. Her husband, who had returned with her, said that he would talk to the mayor, and perhaps he would give us the use of his automobile and chauffeur. And so it was that two days later Marysia and I went to München. The weather was bad, and it took us several hours to get there because of the snow and ice. I was eager to see my friends. Having spent six months with them under extreme conditions, I felt a strong bond of gratitude. They had nursed me through a siege of typhus, they had sheltered me at the risk of their own lives—even risking the life of their only child—how could I ever forget that!

We eventually came to the place where the Krupkas lived. At the entrance sat a woman with unmistakably Slavic features, and I asked her in Ukrainian if she knew where the Krupka family lived. She immediately pointed out the direction of their house and mentioned the number of their apartment. We went into the building and along a seemingly endless corridor, our German chauffeur following us in sullen silence. At last, I found the number of their door. My heart almost jumped out of its ribcage in excitement as I knocked.

A well-known voice answered, and when the door opened—there stood Mrs. Krupka. "Hania, Hania!" she exclaimed, "Oh, God."

We fell into each other's arms. Yes, it was Mrs. Krupka—but somehow she had changed. At Brody, as I remembered her in their lovely apartment, she had always smelled of good perfume, wore fancy clothes, kept her hair neatly combed, and her complexion well-tended—all this was gone! But she was still the same good-hearted person. We stood a long while in a warm embrace, crying for joy at our reunion.

I found that my arrival had preceded my letter and was therefore a complete surprise. Bluma and the German chauffeur stood by without a word, but when at last I recovered my composure somewhat, I introduced Bluma, for although she came from Rohatyn, Mrs. Krupka did not recall ever meeting her. Mr. Krupka and their son Janko were not at home, so she quickly threw on a coat and went to fetch the boy, who was with neighbors. Mr. Krupka was expected back soon.

Waiting for them, I looked around the room and mentally compared it with the apartment they had had in Brody. This room was dark, furnished with cheap old pieces. While it was, of course, a temporary refuge, it was a change as from a palace to a storeroom.

Shortly, Mrs. Krupka returned with Janko. I could hardly recognize him; he had grown, he looked very thin and pale and his clothes were quite shabby. He had difficulty remembering me. Now bashful and shy, he was about six years old. His mother wanted to give us something to eat, but we thanked her. Instead we plied her with questions, still talking in Ukrainian.

Only now did I learn all the news in detail. On June 6, 1943, our Rohatyn ghetto had been completely liquidated. Then the Germans gathered all the inhabitants and shot them; those who tried to take shelter in cellars or caves were exterminated with grenades. The Germans set fire to the ghetto and the Jews perished to the very last soul. It was rumored that a few managed to escape just hours before the liquidation went into effect; they hid in the woods or in neighboring villages but later were killed by the Ukrainians.

Mrs. Krupka insisted on making something hot to drink and started preparing sandwiches. Meanwhile, her husband came home and recognized me immediately. After our greetings were over, I introduced Bluma to him, but he also could not recall meeting her or her family in Rohatyn. We sat, talking on and on, making up for lost time.

Eventually, we had to leave. We thanked the Krupkas and promised to write and come for another visit when the weather became milder. I thanked them again for everything, saying that had it not been for them, I would not have been there alive that day. "I will never forget you as long as I live," I declared. "Your names are written in the book."

They looked at each other, not understanding my words. Amid tears and embraces we took our leave of them. When the auto started, I turned back to wave. For a long time Bluma and I did not exchange a word. We were reliving the entire visit in our thoughts.

Now I could write to Mrs. Krupka as often as I liked, and we soon had a lively exchange of correspondence. In each letter she told me something new about themselves and other Ukrainian people who visited them. At the same time, I kept receiving letters from Dr. Lewenter in the United States, in which he seriously discussed bringing me to America. He said that he was getting the affidavit of support ready, and he urged me to send him the information he needed. Bluma joked about it: "You may go to America even before I do!" To lose no time I arranged to take English lessons from a German woman who lived in our neighborhood; sometimes I paid her with money, sometimes with food. I bought Polish-English and German-English dictionaries and tried to learn words of daily usage.

I tried to keep busy to make the days go faster. Whenever I wrote to Dr. Lewenter in America I always put in a few words in English to show that I was earnest about learning the language.

Soon the festival of Purim came up, and they decided to hold a ball in the residence camp nearby. When we entered the dining room on the appointed evening, I could hardly believe the change. The hall was decorated in many colors. Everyone received a paper hat and corsages. A pianist and accordionist made up the "orchestra." A buffet was stacked with sandwiches and drinks. Later there would be coffee and cake.

Almost everyone knew everyone else, as most of the guests were from the camp. Some danced, some sat and talked. I sat at a small table with my friends, chatting. It was already past ten o'clock, but people kept coming in. Suddenly I saw two young men enter. One of them was tall, handsome—a striking fellow. They sat down at a table with two girls who had arrived with them and started looking around. No one seemed to know them; they must have come from some other camp, it was whispered. I noticed that the handsome one kept looking at me intently, and when the music started again he resolutely got up and came in our direction.

Before I realized what had happened, he was standing before me, asking me to dance. I did not know how to dance well, but he was an excellent partner and I let him lead me lightly through the steps of a waltz. I was very slim then, and in his wide arms I thought I'd flutter like a feather in the breeze. He complimented me on dancing so well, and I gratefully looked up into his large, fascinatingly blue eyes. He said that his name was Israel Lederman. He politely asked in which camp I had spent the war. I told him briefly about my experiences. Did I have anyone of my family left? No, I had lost my mother and my sister, all I had . . . Then in turn I plied him with similar questions, and learned that he too was all alone in the world. Then I asked him where he had spent the war, realizing as I spoke that I had touched a raw nerve. He had been in almost every concentration camp, it seemed, pushed from one to another—Auschwitz, Kaufering, and Dachau. He had lost a wife, a child, three brothers, and his parents. He showed me a metal ID with his number: 96447. He had been under the Germans since 1939, as a native of Lodz. Six years might not seem like a long time, but to him it was an eternity.

Between dances we rested, chatting with my other friends at the table. He spotted several persons who he knew in the camp and exchanged greetings with them. After a while the two blonde girls left, but he remained with us until the end of the ball—until it was almost dawn. And then he took me home.

A few days after the Purim ball, I wrote to Mrs. Krupka and, of course, told her about the new friend I had met. The girls at the camp, too, teased me about him the next time I was there. They wanted to know if it was serious! How could it be, I said in mock indignation; I dance with someone one evening, and they want to make a match between us! But their intuition must have been right, for that was not the last time I was to see Israel Lederman. He came again in a few days and spent several hours with Bluma and I. He was a sociable person and made friends easily. After that, he was a frequent guest, and we felt as though we had known him a very long time.

One day I received a notice from the American Joint Distribution Committee to come to their office, for they had received an authorization from the American Consulate to have me registered. I told Lederman about this, and on the appointed date we went there together. When my name was called, I entered a room where an American woman in military uniform sat behind a desk. This was Miss Levine. Looking through some papers, she said that my affidavit had not arrived, but that in any case I was on the list and would be able to go to the United States. Meanwhile, the Joint Distribution Committee would give me an affidavit and most probably I would be able to leave by the first transport. This was good news—more than I had expected. She began to fire questions at me as she filled out a form: Did I have anyone in the family who would be going with me? Perhaps my mother? No. My father, then? No. A sister, brother? No. A distant relative? No, absolutely no one.

She shook her head and looked at me. "All alone?"

"Yes," I replied.

Miss Levine was very officious and energetic, almost brusque. I sensed her dislike for lengthy conversations, and so I replied to her in monosyllables. She thought a bit, and asked, "Do you have a boyfriend?"

"What do you mean, a boyfriend?" I did not understand.

"A friend," she said impatiently.

It was my turn to think. Then I asked if I could be excused for a moment, and when she nodded, I opened the door to the waiting room and called Israel in.

"Here I have a friend," I told her. "He also has no one in the world, no relatives. He's all alone, so I will take him with me if I can."

But when Miss Levine saw Israel, she said, "I know him. He was in the Biediegheim sanatorium. He was sick, and cannot go to the United States. We send only healthy people, understandably. Anyway, what do you mean you'll take him? Do you intend to pack him into your suitcase? You can only take a husband with you. I thought you might be engaged."

When my friend heard this, he spoke up promptly. "Well, how long does it take to get married? We'll be married."

Miss Levine looked sharply at him and me. "How long have you known each other?" she asked.

"Altogether, five days," we said.

She shook her head. "There must be an announcement three days prior to the marriage," she said. "But first, I must look through his papers at the sanatorium to see if he is qualified to go. Frankly, I don't think we can let him go to the United States."

"They released me after eight months," Israel interrupted. "I look well and nothing bothers me. What has been is past."

We had quite a hard time with Miss Levine. She said that she still would have to talk to the doctor at the sanatorium. X-rays might be necessary. Anyway, she would let us know. "And if you want to get married, that's your business." For the time being, she was not going to put my name on the list, for in case we got married she would have to change the name to that of my husband and that would prolong the formalities and delay my departure; we would have to leave on the second transport.

We thanked her and left. Outside on the street, Israel said, "I think we convinced her. When she sees my papers, she will know that I am cured and in good health and she will have to let us go." As we walked back to the car stop, we talked about the illness he had received from his stay in the camps.

I suddenly had the idea that we should go to "my" hospital and have him X-rayed there. We did, but the sister in the Roentgen room told me that she did not like the look of the X-rays she had made—in particular the left side of Lederman's lungs—and told me that I would have to go to a specialist. She gave me the X-rays and the name of the best lung specialist she knew and told me to tell the specialist that Sister Gertrube had sent me.

Later that afternoon, Israel and I were able to get an appointment with the specialist. He looked the X-rays over solemnly, as we waited impatiently. Finally, the doctor said, "I'm sorry, but the man whose X-rays these are is very seriously ill. He must have a high temperature, and I'm sorry to say I don't think he will live more than a few days. Maybe three at most. He is dying, isn't he?" Apparently the doctor was under the impression that we had brought him the X-rays of a bedridden man. "I'm very sorry," he continued, handing us the X-rays, "in his condition there is no help." When the doctor asked, "Who is it?" Israel replied, "My brother."

We thanked him and went out. Going down the hill to the trolley stop, I still could not speak but looked at Israel. He was pale and tears glistened in his eyes; he was trembling with the effort to hide his emotions. "Don't believe him!" I exclaimed fervently. "The doctor mentioned a high fever; he spoke of a dying man. You look fine and healthy."

Israel could not say a word. In a few days we were to be married, and—here was a catastrophe! But I did not let him lose hope. "Don't worry. Tomorrow we'll have our marriage license and we'll get married. Then we will register and wait for our chance to go to America."

"And suppose they won't let me go?" he said.

"If they don't let you go, we shall wait as long as you need to be completely cured. Even months, if necessary. I won't go without you. And if they still won't let you go to America, then we will go to Palestine. I have cousins there—they will help us. All right." I paused for a moment and went on, "And if we go to America, I am sure people there will help us, too. I have friends there who, as soon as the war was over, volunteered to send me packages and kept on writing to me. And there's that doctor who is to send me an affidavit—no doubt he would be able to direct you to a good sanatorium, if necessary, or to a lung specialist. They realize we've gone through so much during the war, I have no doubt everyone will want to help. And if there is anything wrong with your health, you will be cured in America. But I still don't believe that you are so seriously ill. Why, you yourself don't feel sick."

When Israel came next to visit me, he seemed to be in a brighter humor. He had confided in the friend who shared his apartment, and the man had also said that it was impossible he was so ill and had told him to destroy the X-ray and never think about it again. His friend assured him that he looked the picture of health and that the doctor must have been mistaken.

Hearing Israel talk this way made me very glad. He needed such encouragement. And now, as he had brought with him all the necessary papers, we went to arrange for the marriage ceremony.

April 30, 1946, was our wedding day. Even my dear mother could not have dreamt of a bigger reception—but the marriage ceremony was without parents on either side, without guests or music, only the necessary witnesses. My witnesses were Bluma and her own new husband, Willy.

After our marriage we had two homes—I kept my room at Bluma's house, and my husband still had the apartment in Bietigheim where his friend lived; it was a large, comfortable apartment, with maid service. Without losing time, I wrote to my cousins in Palestine about my marriage. I also informed Dr. Lewenter in the United States—who was arranging for the affidavit of support—to have him change the name on the document, and told him that if I went to America it would be with my husband. After a while I began receiving replies from everyone, all expressing surprise—because I had not hinted at getting married before this; not even a hint that I was engaged. The next step was for us to return to the Joint Office and register as man and wife; thus it would no longer be Sheva Weiler, but Sheva Lederman, who would go to America.

This time Miss Levine said nothing about my husband's illness, nor his having been in the sanatorium. On the contrary, she was very affable and wished us happiness in our married life. And, as a matter of fact, she had been the catalyst that had brought on our unexpected marriage by her questions at my first interview. She told us now that the first transport to the United States would leave in May, but we would not be able to go then; most likely we would leave with the second transport, and we should start making preparations.

We left the office feeling quite satisfied with everything. It also comforted us to believe that Miss Levine must have obtained information concerning Israel's health, and she must have been convinced that he was cured and well enough to leave for America. It still puzzled us, however, that a specialist in respiratory diseases could have made such a wrong diagnosis. This would remain an unsolved mystery for us. We said no more about it and decided it was best to forget the whole incident.

We lived in hope of leaving Germany soon, and we seemed to have a myriad of things to do meanwhile. I informed the Krupkas that most likely we would go to the United States and gave them an address where they would be able to communicate with us in New York, as they also had plans to go to America. They promised to come to Stuttgart to see us before we left, and we eagerly waited for their visit. I introduced my husband to Sister Marta, and she could only marvel at how everything had happened so quickly.

At last we were advised that our departure was set for June 17 from Bremerhaven on the steamship *Marine Perch*. A few days before sailing we were to go to Bremerhaven. We wound up our preparations, packed the last things, and started saying our goodbyes, writing letters to friends at a distance whom we could not contact personally.

We became so impatient and tense the last days before departure that we could hardly remain at home. Almost every day we went somewhere. We said goodbye to the sisters at the hospital—starting, of course, with the Superior, then Sister Marta and the others. I thanked Sister Marta especially for all her kindness to me, and she expressed her sorrow that she would never see me again. I shed a few tears at bidding the sisters farewell, but most of all when it came to Sister Marta.

In Bremerhaven, upon our arrival, there was a crowd of people gathered into a large hall in a barracks-like building. There were rows of double bunk beds; the women were to sleep in the lower berths, the men in the upper. In this hall there were about thirty people, and there were several such halls. That one night seemed like an eon; our impatience grew along with our discomfort. In such a crowd there was bound to be some coughing, snoring, and some groups of friends who found the day too short for celebrating and continued their loud conversations well into the night. But we could take it with a smile, remembering that tomorrow we would be on our way.

And so, on June 17, 1946, we formed into lines and started to board the ship. It was a warm and beautiful day, the sky and the water the same shade of blue—a bright omen for our trip. Five years previously—also on a beautiful summer day, but under a pall of black war clouds—five years previously the Germans had entered Rohatyn. Five years of fear, wandering, living under strain—years of loneliness; sometimes hoping, sometimes resigned. Five years that I had lost out of my life—out of what should have been my happy youthful years.

As I set foot on the deck of the ship, together with my husband who had lost no less and suffered as much as I—as had everyone here—I thought; *Now we shall see what the future will bring.* We were happy that we were going to a free country. I was leaving behind all my past, save that which I had recorded on paper—my chronicle, my documents with the name of Hanka Buczek; these I guarded and took with me with the intention of completing the story.

And lost in our thoughts, we heard the engines start up. At that moment, I recalled my home and my dear ones. Will anyone ever commemorate them with a stone monument? I did not even know where my loved ones rested. But, in my heart, I promised them that I would put up a memorial stone for them in a cemetery when I arrived in the United States.

Almost everyone stood on the deck, watching the activity on the shore. And when the ship started to move away from the pier—and the last farewells were said—tears fell into the sea, perhaps to be carried out by the tide into the vastness and depths of the great unknown that our beloved families had not been lucky enough to reach. Everything was like a dream. It was so difficult to believe that it was actually true. I don't think that I was alone in having such thoughts, for when I looked around I could see the same sentiments reflected in the faces of those near me. "Yes, now we are going to America!" I could hear the whisper going around from lips to lips, accompanied by sighs.

Our sea voyage passed slowly. Finally, in one thrilling moment, we saw the famed Statue of Liberty. All of us stood once again on the deck, with tears in our eyes, all looking in the direction of the statue. Freedom was greeting us. And while looking at this symbol of approaching freedom, the thought in my mind was, *why couldn't it have happened a few years sooner? Why couldn't the Marine Perch have come for us and taken us away to a haven of peace before all the terrible things happened?* This was a wonderful moment for us, yes—only it came a few years too late . . . Those who had perished were with us only in memories.

I stole a sidelong glance at my husband. He was also sobbing, and many others around us could not restrain their tears. Whoever has not lived through a hell such as ours will probably never understand the depth of our feeling at this solemn moment.

As we neared the pier, we could see the automobiles on the streets in the area. The passengers began to make nervous preparations to disembark, looking anxiously to see if their relatives were waiting for them on the pier—almost afraid of their own emotions at the first sight of a brother, sister, or some other close relative. Israel and I did not speak, following the others step by step in a long file toward the gangplank. Perhaps someone among those friends who had written us might be waiting, perhaps not. The main thing was that we were at last at our goal.

We could see many people on the pier, waving excitedly from a distance, crying. Those who had already landed were embracing their kin. We could hear their exclamations of joy mingled with loud sobs. Now it was our turn. At the foot of the gangplank sat a representative of the Joint Distribution Committee and HIAS. They asked each one of us whether we had any family here, and whether we had a place to stay. Everything was wonderfully well organized. The Joint Committee and HIAS extended their services with praiseworthy efficiency.

When asked whether we had family in the States, my husband answered promptly and truthfully, "No." So we were sent to another table where we were issued paper slips and—what a surprise!—the address of a hotel where we were to be taken by taxi. As I turned toward the exit, I saw Dr. Lewenter running toward me. He looked hot and was perspiring; that June 24 was one of the hottest days on record, as I learned later. I started to run towards him, embraced him, and burst into loud weeping. The doctor also had to choke back his tears. His first words to me were: "Thank God, you are here at last! The ship was late by four hours and I've been waiting for you. Where is your husband?"

My husband was still attending to some formalities, but as soon as he turned around I caught hold of his hand and introduced him to the doctor. Dr. Lewenter said, "Now don't worry about anything. You will be taken care of. The main thing is that you survived." He wanted to take us to his home, but my husband said that as long as we were given lodging in a hotel thanks to the Joint Distribution Committee, and a taxi would take us there, it would be better to avail ourselves of this. The doctor looked at the address on the slip of paper and said, "Aha, the Barclay Hotel near Broadway—that isn't far. Go then in good health, and when you have rested a bit I will come by."

We got into the taxi. On the way to the hotel we did not say much, for we were very hot—perhaps all the more so because of the excitement of our being there. The change was too great; there were too many new impressions crowding in on our minds. We arrived at the Barclay, registered, and were taken to our room. The few words of English that I had learned in Germany suddenly became very useful. At least I could make myself understood at the hotel. Our room was large and faced the street. We were delighted that it also had a balcony. We sat in our room until it was time to have dinner. We had received a meal coupon from the Joint Distribution Committee, which we could use in a nearby restaurant.

After dinner, we walked along Broadway, looking at the window displays until we were tired enough to return to the hotel. After seven days of travel—and almost seven wakeful nights—we needed a rest badly.

A little later, after his office hours, Dr. Lewenter came to see us. He came alone because his wife had gone out of town for a few days. We sat and talked. What else could we talk about, if not about our families and the people who did not exist anymore, and about Rohatyn—the town that had become one mass grave filled with Jewish victims! And when I mentioned that the only thing that remained for me to do was to erect a stone memorial in a cemetery here in the United States, Dr. Lewenter said that such a group memorial was being planned already; that the Rohatyners were going to put up a monument in Mount Hebron Cemetery in Flushing, Long Island, and that I should give the names of my loved ones. Sobbing, I gave them to the Doctor: Gitel and Rose Weiler. Also, I took the liberty of including the names of Bluma's parents—for this, later, she was very thankful. (This monument was erected in a short time in the cemetery and was unveiled in the presence of the survivors of the families it commemorated, or the families which were in the United States during the war.)

It was already late and the room was stiflingly hot. After Dr. Lewenter left, my husband and I prepared to go to bed. We were still under strain of all the happenings of that day, and sleep was long in coming to us. I don't know how long I had been sleeping, but when I woke up past midnight I noticed my husband was not at my side. I raised myself up on one elbow, looked around the room, but not seeing him anywhere I got up and went out on the balcony. There he was, sitting in a chair, looking out at the big city. When he heard my steps he seemed to arouse himself from a dream, and he said, "It is too wonderful and too beautiful—it is a pity to sleep. What a beautiful sight out there—the lights, the humming streets, skyscrapers, automobiles—so much life here! The world is so beautiful and free—and all this was forbidden us. We lost so many years of life without reason. All the things that the thousands and millions died without ever knowing . . . They never lived to experience this freedom. The world is so large, there are so many nations—there's room enough for everyone on this big globe to live in peace and amity. Yet for us there was no place. For us Jews there was only death."

I stood there and listened, watching the tears roll down my husband's face. My tears joined his, and the whole suffering and past stood before my eyes. I recalled my last farewell to my loved ones . . . Even though my husband's and my thoughts traveled back to different towns in Poland, our thoughts were essentially the same. And the echo of my mother's words I could hear clearly; my mother's last words to me: "Sheva, do not forget. If you ever survive, do not forget what happened to us and to our people."

Will anyone ever be able to forget? Never, Mamma, never!